Exponential Living

Exponential Living

STOP SPENDING 100% OF YOUR TIME ON 10% OF WHO YOU ARE

Sheri Riley

NEW AMERICAN LIBRARY
NEW YORK

NEW AMERICAN LIBRARY
Published by Berkley
An imprint of Penguin Random House LLC
375 Hudson Street, New York, New York 10014

Copyright © 2017 by Sheri Riley
Foreword copyright © 2017 by Usher Raymond IV
Penguin Random House supports copyright. Copyright fuels creativity, encourages diverse voices,
promotes free speech, and creates a vibrant culture. Thank you for buying an authorized
edition of this book and for complying with copyright laws by not reproducing, scanning, or
distributing any part of it in any form without permission. You are supporting writers and
allowing Penguin Random House to continue to publish books for every reader.

New American Library and the NAL colophon are registered trademarks
of Penguin Random House LLC.

Library of Congress Cataloging-in-Publication Data

Names: Riley, Sheri, author.
Title: Exponential living: stop spending 100% of your time on 10%
of who you are/Sheri Riley; foreword by Usher.
Description: First Edition. | New York: NAL, 2017.
Identifiers: LCCN 2016026862 (print) | LCCN 2016042537 (ebook) |
ISBN 9781101989029 (hardback) | ISBN 9781101989036 (ebook)
Subjects: LCSH: Self-actualization (Psychology) | Happiness. | Success. |
BISAC: SELF-HELP/Motivational & Inspirational. | SELF-HELP/Personal
Growth/Happiness. | SELF-HELP/Personal Growth/Success.
Classification: LCC BF637.S4 R5735 2017 (print) | LCC BF637.S4 (ebook) | DDC 158.1—dc23
LC record available at https://lccn.loc.gov/2016026862

First Edition: February 2017

Printed in the United States of America
1   3   5   7   9   10   8   6   4   2

Jacket design by Emily Osborne
Book design by Kristin del Rosario
Book starburst straight lines by Tidarat Tiemjal

Dominique,

you are my sunshine and the overflow of my prayers.

ACKNOWLEDGMENTS

You desire truth in the inward parts. And in the
hidden part you will make me to know wisdom.

{ —PSALM 51:6 }

Every word in my book is inspired by the Father, Son, and Holy Spirit.
Thank You for Your faithfulness.

Mama, Daddy, and Cora, love is too weak to describe how much I
adore you. Because of you, I am. Thank you, Daddy, for your wisdom.
Thank you, Mama, for your pure love. Thank you, Cora, for your unconditional support. You are my threefold chord that will never be broken.

Jovan, Dynasty, and Dominique, it's all in vain if my book touches
the hearts of the world and not the three hearts that matter the most.
Jovan, I am the greatest fan of your life. Your love covers me and lifts
me. Forever and one day. Dynasty, may God continue to unveil the
greatness He put in you. You have a gift that can heal and touch hearts
around the world. Dominique, you're the only person to hear my
heart beat, and it beats for you. Your love saved my life. Psalm 37:4.

T*T and Grandfather, you are truly a blessing, and my family would not have made it without your unconditional support and assistance. Love you much!!

Marcus, Donovan, Eden, DeMarcus, and Mekhi, I love you.

My biological sister is in heaven, so God sent me so many women who are truly my sisters. I love each of you DEARLY. . . .

My Spec, Sadiqa Reynolds, our friendship and sisterhood is one of my greatest treasures. Tashion Macon, I am forever grateful that God chose you to lead me to Him and then bonded our hearts. My love for you goes beyond words. Monica Green, we've traveled the world together and created a lifetime of laughs and great times. It's so appropriate that you purchased the first book. Gladys Parks and Latoscia Mason, your friendship means the world to me, and I love how you love my mama. Shanti Das, thank you for opening your heart and home to me in the darkest season of my life. We still have more work to do together. CMB! Patti Webster, for twenty years I called you my Angel. Now you are sitting at the right hand of God, truly covering me from above. I MISS YOU MORE THAN WORDS CAN EXPRESS. Rashan Ali, thank you for not taking no for an answer and trusting me with your life and dreams. You are the midwife for *Exponential Living*. Jacquie Lee, my Five Boo!! You are one of my greatest inspirations. We will have your Cabin in the Sky!! To my prayer warriors, Antoinette "Toni" Miles, Camay Davis, and Natalie Roseboro. This book would not have happened without your prayers. When I couldn't pray for myself or put two sentences together and this journey was too much for me to handle, you prayed me over the finish line. Melanie Few, no matter when, no matter where, you are always there!! My SanDs, Sheila Wilson, we are forever bonded in love, Delta, and sisterhood.

To my cousins, who are like siblings, I love you. To my aunts, uncles, and family. I love you.

Jeanie Tye, thank you for being a woman who lived by faith and strength.

LaShon Allen-Spearman, you are truly the rock that holds me down. You are my GLUE.

Tracy Prather, thank you for the Tracy Nicole original for my book cover. Marie Thomas, thank you for photographing me and my family for years. Lisa Pope, you did your thang with my hair, makeup and styling. Thank you. Bridge Boutique, thank you for the beautiful clothes. Thank you, Cantoni, for allowing me to take my photos with your amazing furniture. Halthea Hill-Latty and Captured in Time Productions—I appreciate you so much. You are an amazing video producer and director.

Glenda Hatchett, thank you for telling me in 1996, "You need to write a book." Raoul Davis, thank you for being my guide through this whole process. I know I am the longest book you've ever worked, but remember what I told you. . . .

Nicole Ari Parker, you were the first person I shared my purpose and vision with, and you immediately said, "I GOT YOU," pulled out paper, and wrote my plan. You are truly a jewel, and I love you and your amazing heart.

Grace Raymond, thank you for your continued support. Usher Raymond IV, our journey is the heart and anchor of *Exponential Living*. Heart and soul.

Denise Marcil and Anne Marie O'Farrell, thank you for believing in me from that awful first draft of my book proposal to a bestseller. Andy Wolfendon, thank you for your excellence and expertise. Denise Silvestro, thank you for saying, "I want that book," and then getting it done.

I so appreciate your insight, time, expertise, creativity, wisdom, and for ALWAYS being there. Thank you, Michael "Blue" Williams, Charlie and Stephanie Wetzel, Sonia Murray, Imara Canady, Christian Ruffin,

ACKNOWLEDGMENTS

James Andrews, Monaica and Andrew Ledell, Gerald Washington, Aaron Schleicher, Blossom Martindale, Monica Coleman, Erika Kennedy, Dorinda Walker, Dawn-Marie Gray, Teddy Reid, Kimra Major-Morris, Danielle Hester, Tanisha Sykes, Aliya Crawford, and Kiera Lytle.

To all of the powerful high achievers who took time to share their journey, from the bottom of my heart . . . thank you: Aiyisha Obefemi, Chaka Zulu, Jeff Dixon, Chris "Ludacris" Bridges, Boris Kodjoe, Bert Weiss, Tom Hughes, Karen Mason, Tracy Mourning, Will Packer, Shayla Cowan, Junior Bridgeman, Lisa Cambridge-Mitchell, Lisa Tanker, James Lopez, Mark Cole, Kimberly Whetsell, Dolvett Quince, Alan Bracken, Joy Pervis, Ceasar Mitchell, Deanna Hamilton, Denise Hendricks, Derek Anderson, Paul Martinelli, Peerless Price, Jini Thornton, and Kidada Muhammad.

Darrell Griffith, thank you for being my first client, still a client twenty-plus years later, and for sharing your journey in *Exponential Living*.

Tanya Forrest-Hall, thank you for trusting me with your heart and teaching me that love NEVER dies.

I am forever grateful for all of my clients. Thank you for trusting me with your journeys. It's my purpose and my pleasure to serve you.

Claire Zion, Tom Colgan, Jeane-Marie Hudson, Craig Burke, Allison Janice, Jin Yu, Heather Conner, Caitlin Valenziano, Diana Franco, and the entire team at Penguin Random House: You guys ROCK!!!

John Maxwell, the John Maxwell team, faculty, and mentors, thank you for everything. Each of you has truly been a blessing in my life and business. And a special thanks to Karen Lombardo, Dexter Godfrey, Mel Holden, Chris Robinson, Nathan Eckel, Michael Harbour, Mfon Ekpo, Tracy Washington, Taunya Lowe, Natalie Fikes, Beverly Kaye Thorne, Barbara Littles, and Tracy Worley,

There are so many others who have impacted my journey, and I am forever grateful.

CONTENTS

FOREWORD

by Usher Raymond IV

In 1993, I was a fifteen-year-old kid working on my first album. My mom and I had moved to Atlanta a few years earlier, and I had caught the eye—or rather the ear—of a talent scout from LaFace Records. The label ended up signing me to my first recording deal.

So there I was, a couple of years into my contract and still not sure what the future held for me. Though I felt fortunate to be with La-Face, I didn't feel I had the full support and commitment of everyone at the label. I think the team was still trying to figure out what to do with me. Because of my particular voice and style, they felt I could appeal to an older audience, but chronologically I was boy-band ma-terial. A kid with acne and a fresh crop of hormones. I had recorded a whole album, but now my voice was changing. Everyone at the label was trying to figure out who I was as an artist.

Me? I was just trying to figure out who I *was*.

I didn't have anyone I could talk to. I mean *really* talk to. My mom and I were close, but because she was my manager too, there were things I couldn't even talk to her about. I had no peers. I felt lost and adrift.

That's when Sheri Riley came aboard. She was assigned to be my marketing person, but I immediately sensed something unusual about her. Her humanity. She was interested in me not just as a marketing project but as a whole person. She asked me questions and *really listened* to my answers, with no hidden agendas.

Sheri soon became my friend and life consultant. Sometimes she was like a mother to me, sometimes like a big sister, sometimes like a coach. But she always had my back, and I always trusted her implicitly. Whenever I was confused or frustrated or just plain lost, Sheri was my go-to person. Going to her office felt like therapy to me.

Sheri not only helped launch me as an artist; she also helped me develop myself as a person. She believed in *me* at a time when my mom was the only other person in the world who did, and she fought for me every chance she got.

A few years after I joined LaFace, Sheri decided it was time to move on. Even though she was at the top of her game professionally, she felt there were other things she needed to do in her life. This, I would later learn, was typical of Sheri. She makes decisions that are right for her *whole life*, not just for her career.

I was disappointed to see her leave LaFace, but also excited. See, I figured I could hire her to work for me full-time. But when I mentioned that possibility to her, Sheri said something that felt like a slap in the face at the time. She told me she would *never* work with me.

"Why not?" I asked, confused and a bit hurt.

"Because," she said, "I always want to be a friend and support to you, someone you can talk to anytime about anything. And I can't do that if we're tied together professionally and financially."

Sheri believed I was going to become a superstar, but she was willing to pass up her opportunity to be part of that ride in order to remain my friend and confidante. That tells you everything you need to know about Sheri Riley.

Sheri was as good as her word. She remained my friend, my life consultant. I called her day and night to share things I didn't feel free to share with anyone else, and at crucial moments, she helped me avoid making some of the bad choices many other young artists have made.

I remember when I was about twenty or twenty-one, I was the opening act for Janet Jackson. This was when Janet was at the peak of her career, so it was a huge breakthrough opportunity for me. The first concert of the tour was in Washington, DC, and Sheri flew in to see it. After the show, she came backstage to my dressing room, and we started talking as we always did. After a while, she said, "Hey, this is your breakout moment. Why are you here talking to me?"

"Because you are the one person in this world, besides my mom, who truly loves and knows me," I told her. "I want to savor this moment because of all the hard work you and I have done to get me here."

One thing I had already learned as a performer and recording artist is that you can have the whole world screaming your name, while no one knows you at all.

Sheri understands that world, the lonely world of the high achiever. She has seen it from the inside. She knows how easy it is for artists and athletes and other intensely career-focused individuals to "spend 100 percent of their time on 10 percent of who they are," to the point where they become unknown even to themselves.

It did not surprise me, then, when Sheri told me some years ago that she was transitioning into a full-time career as a life strategist—and now as an author. I feel this is the work she was born to do. What makes Sheri such a unique voice in a crowded field of "helpers" is that she has lived all of the principles she speaks and writes about. She doesn't get her wisdom from books or experts or current trends. She gets it by challenging herself to live life more fully and by helping others do the same. Though she began by counseling people in the sports and entertainment fields, she later realized that her principles are equally powerful for *anyone* who is focused on achieving "outer success" at the expense of their "inner success."

After all, who among us doesn't need to learn to live more wholly and truthfully?

When I read the manuscript of this book, it felt "real" to me. I immediately identified with many of the principles and examples. I loved what the book said about presence and service and the power we all have to choose our own happiness. It made me want to deepen my commitment to live *for* and *from* my whole self.

But still, it's my nature to be provocative. So when I sat down with Sheri to discuss the book, I challenged her on a few of her ideas. "One of your principles is 'Pursue Peace and a Positive Mind,'" I said. "Isn't that a bit delusional? Isn't that just saying everything's okay when it isn't?"

"No, it's the opposite of that," Sheri calmly replied. "It's about recognizing that your life may be falling apart, but that you can remain peaceful in the midst of all that. How? By seeing possibilities. Look at that banana," she said, pointing at a piece of fruit in a nearby bowl. "It's starting to turn brown. If I were to say, 'My, how fresh and yellow that banana is,' *that* would be delusional. But a positive mind says, 'I may not want to *eat* that banana, but I can use it in a smoothie.' Having a positive mind is about seeing the possibilities from wherever you stand right now." Somehow that simple example made me see positive-mindedness with a fresh set of eyes.

I threw down another challenge. "Sheri," I said, "I want you to coach me now. I mean right here, right now. Tell me: Why is it that I'm constantly working to achieve success, but I don't feel successful?"

Sheri immediately responded, "How do you define *success?*"

Oh. Right. That. I realized that I had never actually defined *success* for myself. Maybe that was my problem. I took a stab at defining it right then. "*Success*, to me, is freedom," I said. "Freedom to do what I want to do."

"You don't have freedom now?" she queried.

"Not really. I have money, I have access—to people, places, and things—but I don't feel free."

"Why is freedom success for you?" asked Sheri.

"Because I want to be able to do the things *I* want to do," I explained.

"Why is that important to you?"

"Because I always feel torn between doing what's expected of me and doing what I truly want."

"And how does that make you feel?" she prodded.

"Conflicted. Uneasy. Frustrated."

"So you want to be at peace in your work and in your life?"

"Yes. Absolutely."

"*Peace,*" said Sheri, nodding. "That's what we all want. That's what it always comes down to. Peace."

I thought about what she said. "That's true," I responded. "When I think about freedom, it's all about peace."

"Then why don't you just pursue peace?"

I paused for a moment and admitted, "Because I don't know how."

"Exactly," she said with a smile. "That's what the nine principles in this book are all about. They *give* you the *how*. Practice these principles, and you'll find peace in every area of your life. You'll stop striving frantically to *make* your life happen and start *allowing* it to unfold, fully and naturally. That's what Exponential Living is."

Amen to that.

I wish I could give you the gift of spending an hour or two, live, with Sheri Riley, the coach, the person, the life strategist. I can't do that, but I can give you the next best thing. This book. Sheri Riley lives in every word on every page. I highly recommend that you open up your heart and mind and let her in.

She'll change your life.

—USHER RAYMOND IV

Introduction

Are you an achievement-driven person, as I've always been? Are you forever *doing*, from morning till midnight? If so, you're probably good at making "to-do" lists. You probably have to-do lists to get you through every day of the week, every hour of the day. In fact, I'm willing to bet you have a "master" to-do list that you've been working on since about fourth grade. You know the one I'm talking about. It's the list of goals and achievements you think you need to accomplish in order to live a happy, successful, and satisfying life.

Your lifelong to-do list probably has lots of goals on it. Like mine did. You've probably checked off many of them already. Was your goal a college/graduate degree?—check. Is an important-sounding job title more your style?—check. Did you always plan to be a super mom or dad with two point five kids and a white picket fence?—check.

House? Cars? Travel?

Check, check, check.

And even if you haven't checked all of your goals off the list yet, you probably have a plan for doing so. All those pretty little checks. Then why aren't you happy? Truly, deeply happy? Why isn't your heart aglow with a feeling of peace and the contentment of a life well lived? Why do you sometimes wake up in the middle of the night with a sick feeling in your chest, asking yourself, "Is this all there is? What am I missing?"

How could you possibly feel so empty when your life is so full?

Well . . . that's the problem with living by lists. They're jam-packed with achievements we *think* will make us happy or *we're told* will make us happy. Many of us even convince ourselves we're *actually* happy each time we check off a new accomplishment on our list. Perhaps we even feel some genuine joy—for fifteen minutes or so. If not, we just tell ourselves, "That's only because there are still more goals on the list I need to achieve! When I finally achieve Goals Twenty-two and Twenty-three, *then* I'll be happy, once and for all." So we keep plugging away. Week after week. Month after month. Year after year.

It never occurs to us that the to-do list itself is the problem. When we live purely for the sake of achievements, life is all about an imaginary future. We convince ourselves that personal satisfaction—and peace of mind—is something that will come later, after we reach our major goals. Until then, family, friends, service to the community, and meaningful interests will just have to wait. We assuage our guilt about family by telling ourselves our hard work is for *them*. "When I get to income level x, I can provide for my family even better. I can catch up on quality time once that is settled."

For many of us, "looking good" becomes the CEO of our lives. We invest so much in our title and income and image that soon we begin to jettison from our lives anything that falls outside our battle for career achievement.

Meanwhile, we're missing life along the way. We've tossed aside the passions and pursuits that make us who we are, and put our relationships on "secondary" status. We are stressed and anxious and driven. So even in those times we actually make available for our families, we are still not present. We're fighting an internal struggle of "I *want* to be present. I *want* to enjoy this moment with my children, family, friends." But in the back of our mind we're thinking, "Oh my God, I'm not working toward x. I'm not applying myself to y. I didn't finish z." We are ruled entirely by our to-do lists instead of by the people and passions that make life worth living.

"Balance" Isn't the Answer

Often it takes a crisis to make us reevaluate our focused and driven mind-set. A relationship crumbles. A child starts acting out. We develop a health issue. We burn out. Then perhaps we seek out some counseling or start reading a few self-help books. We do just enough self-examination to realize that our lives are out of whack. And so we strive to achieve more balance.

"Work-life balance," that's the career mantra of the new millennium. Sounds good, right? This idea of creating more balance between our work lives and our personal lives? The problem for us goal-focused types is that the desire for balance quickly gets translated into a new set of goals that we add to our to-do list! Now, instead of just having to-do lists for work, we have them for our health, for our family lives, for our spiritual lives, for our community and social responsibilities, and so on. We join a gym, we go on a diet, we add blocks of "family time" to our weekly schedule, and we volunteer for a church group. And in doing these things we may, in fact, make some improvements to our lives. But overall, we end up feeling even more stressed, even more thinly stretched, than we did before. Sound familiar?

This is not a book about work-life balance. Balance is an illusion anyway, and you don't need more tools to help you juggle your priorities. Odds are, you're already such a great juggler, you qualify for a job with Barnum & Bailey.

What you need is a new way of seeing and being.

A New Way

This is a book about pursuing *peace*, not balancing your life. Peace, I want you to know, is the key to everything. When you choose peace as your priority every day, you gain access to an inner compass that directs you on how to invest your time and attention in every living moment. Instead of constantly worrying about what you are *doing*, you begin to focus on, and be empowered by, *who you are being*. And everything else falls into place.

When you do the inner work I'm going to suggest in this book, you may decide to throw away your to-do list entirely. Your life will find its own rhythm, harmony, and direction. You will accomplish more in less time. You will actually begin to feel the glow of true happiness and fulfillment, perhaps for the first time in your life. That's Exponential Living.

The dictionary definition of the word *exponential* includes many meanings, from "becoming more and more rapid" and "rising or expanding at a steady and rapid rate" to "a positive constant raised to a power" and "explosive growth." When you commit to Exponential

Living, you experience rapid and explosive transformation in both your personal and professional lives. Exponential Living empowers you to integrate your deeply felt personal desires into your life without sacrificing career achievement.

That doesn't mean you'll stop having goals and stop striving to achieve them. Not at all. I still have goals and I still love to excel at the highest level. But I also love volunteering at my daughter's school, hanging with my mom and watching *Blue Bloods* with her on Friday nights, dating my husband, and listening to my teenage daughter giggle about the funny things that happened to her at school. I love to exercise, travel, pray, and have dinner with friends.

Exponential Living means no longer trying to gain 100 percent of your fulfillment from only 10 percent of your life.

What to Expect from This Book

Exponential Living is a mind-set, not a destination. And there are nine powerful principles that will help you live in that mind-set. The 9 Principles of Exponential Living are the heart and soul of this book—and most of its bulk as well. After the first two short chapters, which will help prepare you for the adventure to follow, each of the remaining chapters delves into one principle apiece. The 9 Principles of Exponential Living, in order, are:

1. Live in Your P.O.W.E.R.
2. Healthy Living Is More Than Just a Diet
3. Pursue Peace and a Positive Mind
4. Have a Servant's Heart and a Giving Spirit
5. Stop Working, Start Maximizing

6. Happy Is a Choice, Joy Is a Lifestyle
7. Build Lasting Confidence
8. The Courage to Be Faithful
9. Exponential Living

All of the nine "principle" chapters follow a similar three-part structure. Each one starts with (1) an exploration of the principle, along with examples, stories, and illustrations from my life and work. I then offer (2) exercises, developed from my coaching work, to help you incorporate the principle into your life. These are found in the section of each chapter called "Vision, Action, Results." Then, finally, *every* chapter in the book concludes with (3) an "Exponential Conversation." Here's where ideas from the book come to life through actual conversations with people who are living examples of Exponential Living. Many of these are names you'll recognize from the worlds of entertainment, sports, and business. The Exponential Conversations have been edited for length and (slightly) for readability, but they are the actual words of my friends, clients, colleagues, and peers. I didn't provide any of my Exponential Conversation participants information prior to our interview. They weren't given any details on my book or my Principles of Exponential Living. And in each one, their journey speaks directly to the essence of the Exponential Conversation. In some cases the content of the conversations may not map exactly to the chapter content. That's the nature of real conversations. Taken together, though, all of the Exponential Conversations serve as a fitting counterpoint to the chapter material and a dynamic illustration of Exponential Living in practice.

This book is not about theory or academic research; it reflects my own experiences and those of other high achievers from various walks of life. It's difficult to inspire others to accomplish what you haven't done yourself, so I want you to know that I have lived every word printed in these pages, in order that you may experience your own Exponential Living.

One thing I do want to mention up front is that I am a woman of faith, so I will often refer to God and spiritual truths that have guided me on my journey to Exponential Living. I don't do this to force my faith on you. People of all faiths, believers and nonbelievers, can gain the peace, clarity, courage, and power that come from the 9 Principles of Exponential Living.

Who Should Read This Book

Exponential Living is for doers, influencers, and achievers who know how to get things done but have trouble living with their accomplishments in peace and joy. It is not only for those who have attained financial or professional success; it is for anyone who is anywhere on the achievement-driven path of life. Many high achievers focus on financial and career goals. Others of us are "at home" achievers, dedicating ourselves to raising well-educated, productive children and/or making our mark in civic, social, or community circles. Some of us seek to achieve creatively or spiritually or academically. What we all have in common is the belief that when we achieve our goals, we will gain freedom, security, status, and control, and that these things will help us achieve our ultimate goal: *peace.*

But we have our steps in reverse order. It is peace we should be pursuing *first.* The courageous pursuit of peace allows us to begin living fully today, not at some hoped-for point in the future.

Exponential Living is about making peace the CEO of our lives. Learning to live in peace *today* is what empowers us to live 100 percent of who we are. With peace comes gratitude, which marks the end of a mind-set driven by lack, scarcity, and fear. With peace comes the courage to say, "I am enough!" When we stop comparing ourselves to others, our true greatness begins to shine. We gain access to our pure and unlimited power, which opens doors of possibility like never before. Stress begins to dissipate. Self-love begins to blossom. Fear of rejection/failure loses its grip on us. As a result, we experience fulfillment, perhaps for the first time in our lives. When our true power is driving the bus, the cascade of positive transformations is limitless.

So how do we *get* to such a place? That's the whole point of this book.

This adventure is going to require your courage. It is going to ask you to shine the light of honesty on your whole life, the comfortable places and the not-so-comfortable ones. And it's going to ask you to be truthful to what you see there. Are you ready to take the next step toward living more fully and truthfully?

Then let's go.

What Is Exponential Living?

Many people worry so much about managing their career but rarely spend half that much energy managing their lives. I want to make my life, not just my job, the best it can be.

—REESE WITHERSPOON,
OSCAR-WINNING ACTRESS

Exponential Living, that's what this book is all about. So, what does the term mean exactly? Before we explore that, I'd like to share this "testimonial" from a friend and colleague of mine. It was during a conversation I had with her, back in 2001, when I first spoke the words "Stop spending 100 percent of your time on 10 percent of who you are." Ever since that moment, the driving force in my work has been to create the "how" to do exactly that. Kiera's story beautifully captures what this book is about, and whom it's written for.

Throughout my twenties, I held positions that many would consider dream jobs. I started my career working for one of the most respected and successful record labels in history, during a time when the music industry was creative, vibrant, and exciting. I got invitations and tickets to the city's most exclusive events. I had a network that allowed me to walk into any club, party, or VIP section in my city and several others. I worked daily with multiplatinum music acts. By my mid-twenties, the pages of my passport were so heavily stamped that I had to order a new one, and I had enough Delta SkyMiles to keep me in first class and allow me to vacation for free. By outward appearances, my life was exciting and fun, and my professional trajectory was beyond promising.

But beneath the surface something was off.

I felt unfulfilled and out of balance . . . and I didn't know why. It didn't make sense to me that I was feeling such restlessness in a life that, by every tangible measure, was enviable. That frustration became a constant distraction, and I had to address it. After a lot of prayer, I found myself bringing it up in a conversation with Sheri Riley. Sheri, who was then, and still remains, a mentor and a professional, personal, and spiritual resource for me, was patient and thoughtful as I tried to express a discomfort that I hadn't yet learned to articulate. When I had finished fumbling through my little soliloquy, she asked me this simple question:

"Why are you trying to derive all of your satisfaction and fulfillment from something that is only a fraction of your life and of who you are? Why are you spending 100 percent of your time on 10 percent of who you are?"

And just like that, clarity began to emerge. I began to see how narrow my view of life had become. I wasn't comfortable in my life, because I didn't have *a life! All I had was a career. And even there, I wasn't guiding the trajectory; I was following it. I knew I was searching for something, but my job was the only place I had even thought to look for it!*

In college, beyond being a student, I had been an athlete, an RA (resident assistant), an intern, a fitness instructor, an alto in the glee club, a volunteer, a model, and a fixture on the social scene. My life was full, and I was content. At some point, as I transitioned into "adulthood" and full-time professional life, I had sacrificed that fullness on the altar of my profession. I had unknowingly made work the center of my life instead of relegating it to its proper position: my method of earning a living. I had no hobbies, no personal pursuits, and my only social life (such as it was) was rooted in my work.

After that conversation with Sheri, I took a fresh look at my life, stripped it down, and rebuilt it in a way that embraced all that I already was, while giving me room to discover more about myself. I found ways to indulge my love of family, the outdoors, sports, and the arts. I joined a choir and a softball team. I took a voice-over workshop. I accepted invitations to do things I had never done before. I skipped "industry" events to spend time with family and friends. I went on new adventures with new people in new cities. I found lots of new things that I was good at and lots of good things to be new at. And the more I opened myself to life, the more life opened up for me. And something else interesting happened: either that sense of emptiness disappeared, or I was too busy enjoying my life to notice it. My money is on the former.

—KIERA LYTLE, MARKETING DIRECTOR, REACH MEDIA

Thank you, Kiera.

My Story

So who am I, Sheri Riley, and how did *I* arrive at Exponential Living?

In the current chapter of my life, I'm an international empowerment speaker, personal development coach, and life strategist. My passionate purpose is to help other people uncover the truth of their own lives so they are empowered to pursue peace and to be happier, more fulfilled, more productive, and more creative. I have helped many powerful, influential, and outwardly "successful" people do just that. I've worked with A-list recording artists and actors, business-people, entrepreneurs, corporate executives, and professional athletes. I've also worked with high achievers you've never heard of. Before this particular purpose unfolded in my life, I had a successful strategic consulting firm, and before that, I was an executive in the recording industry.

From the time I was about fifteen years old (and probably even younger), all I wanted to do was work in the entertainment industry, specifically at a record label. That was the number one goal for me. I lived in Richmond, Kentucky, a small town of about twenty-five thousand people (at the time), and, growing up, I told everyone I was going to work at a record label and live in Atlanta. This sounded about as realistic as saying I was going to build hotels on Mars. You see, at the time, there *was* no music industry in Atlanta. Antonio "LA" Reid and Kenny "Babyface" Edmonds, who started the most successful record label in Atlanta, were still launching their recording career with the R&B group the Deele. Other key Atlanta-based industry players like Dallas Austin and Jermaine Dupri hadn't even reached their teens yet.

Through hard work, persistence, prayer, sacrifice, and belief, though, I became the senior director of marketing at LaFace Records. And, yes, it was in Atlanta. Getting there was a worthy goal and a great adventure all its own. During my time at LaFace, I developed some exciting new approaches to marketing and helped introduce the world to some of the most influential multiplatinum artists of the nineties, including TLC, Toni Braxton, and Usher. I built strategic partnerships with NBC, the NBA, Boys & Girls Clubs of America, and Sega, and helped sell over thirty million albums worldwide.

My time at LaFace Records was absolutely amazing. I experienced everything I had dreamed about and more. I worked with some of the most important artists in music history. I launched a promising career and established lifelong friendships and business partnerships.

I was also miserable. I didn't have a life beyond my career.

After three years at LaFace, a couple of things happened that set me on the path to Exponential Living. The first was resigning from my position. The second was passing up a business opportunity that could potentially have earned me millions.

My resignation came as a shock to many, but I couldn't go on living as I had. Though I was a "power broker" in the industry, my hair was falling out and I came home every night to an empty apartment—I was single then—where I drank wine and watched movies by myself. The emptiness and absence of fulfillment were killing me. I knew I had to have the courage to give up the career track I was on in order to have both the career *and* the full life that I desired.

And so I did.

I remember going to Kmart to pick something up in the middle of the day after I stopped working at the record label. I was blown away because the store was full. It was a huge "aha" for me to realize that not everyone runs out to stores in the middle of the night—because that's the only time window you have to grab your bare essentials; some people actually go shopping during the day. I saw mothers laughing and playing with their kids in the store and thought, "Wow, there's more to life than just working." I had actually forgotten that! Suddenly, all I wanted to do was sit in my yard and put my hands in the dirt and plant flowers. So I did that. For a while. I spent some time just *being*. I spent time with my family and was actually present, not just in their presence.

Then I began to put together a plan for the business I had been contemplating for some time. As much as working at a record label had been my dream, being an entrepreneur was also a dream. And I had never intended to eliminate my A plan of being a wife and a mother. I was hoping this new move would allow me to create a life for myself that included a family *and* a career. My business was called GLUE and it specialized in consulting, public relations, celebrity procurement, partnership brokering, and event management. In the seventeen years I ran that company, GLUE secured more than five hundred celebrities, athletes, and dignitaries for personal appearances, performances, and/or corporate partnerships, and partnered with international brands and individuals like Converse, CVS Health, BET Networks, the Ludacris Foundation, Jermaine Dupri, BMW, Porsche, Turner Network Television (TNT), NBA Entertainment, T-Mobile, and the Atlanta Hawks, to name a few.

But before all of that success, one of the very first decisions I made was *not* to work with Usher, and that changed everything for me.

Let's go back to my first day at LaFace: July 31, 1994. That was the day before the legendary Outkast "Southernplayalistic Cookout," which was organized to celebrate Outkast's first gold album, *Southernplayalisticadillacmuzik*. That event, to this day, was one of the most amazing ever hosted in the music industry. One of the emerging artists who performed there was a fifteen-year-old named Usher Raymond IV.

The record label had spent substantial money recording him, but his voice was changing, and though he had powerful charisma, the label wasn't clear on how to market or position him. When I arrived on the scene, he would come to my office, and we would talk for hours. During these talks, I didn't see an artist to be marketed; I saw a teenager who was someone's son, a kid who was committed to living his dream. I identified with him because of that. After all, I was only a couple of years removed from when I couldn't get any record executives to talk to me either. But the reason I was sitting there talking to him was that I had stayed true to my dream. And so I was committed to helping him do the same.

When I first began the marketing that was instrumental in the launch of Usher's career, TLC, Toni Braxton, and Outkast were platinum and multiplatinum artists at LaFace. Our label was breaking artists who were changing the landscape of the music industry, but we were still a very small company. We were a lean, committed team but there were only so many hours in the day. Usher was an emerging artist, and the primary focus of the team was on the more established artists. During our marketing meetings, we would mainly discuss the priority artists—those with records in the market that were selling at the time. And even though Usher was on the agenda, when it came time to discuss his project, everyone was mainly focused on their immediate priorities. They listened respectfully, and then went to their offices, caught their flights, or went to more meetings, and got on with their more pressing and immediate concerns. It wasn't personal; Usher just wasn't a priority at that time.

This was actually a good thing for both Usher and me, because it gave us the freedom to create marketing ideas, plans, and partnerships that established the foundation for launching his career. Everyone knew Usher was an exceptional talent and one hit record away from being a superstar, but there was no real marketing focus on him yet. And so Usher, his mom, Jonetta, and I were able to be as creative as we wanted. I was able to successfully fight for the things that Usher and his mom wanted to do and I was able to create alliances with companies that gave him many platforms to showcase his talent and massive charisma.

During this time, Usher and I formed a bond that had nothing to do with the music business. Our dreams bonded us. Our underdog status bonded us. From day one (as I've told him for many years), I was more concerned about Usher the man than about Usher the brand.

When I resigned from LaFace to start GLUE, Usher was excited because I could now focus more of my professional time on his career. It was hard to tell him that I could not and would not ever work with him. And all these years later, we have never worked together. Why? you might ask.

Because it was clear to me that he needed my friendship more than my marketing expertise. From my point of view as an entrepreneur, this decision made no sense. It has, in fact, cost me hundreds of thousands, if not millions, of dollars. But I knew the money would have minimized my ability to be the friend, support, and "big sister" that he needed, especially during his transition from teenager to young man. During these critical years, his career took off and everyone in his circle worked with him or for him, except me. But when he needed to just be Usher Raymond IV, he had me. And we could speak with no agenda and no motive other than the simple fact that I loved him and wanted the best for him.

By resigning from LaFace and refusing to work with Usher, I gave up a high-six-figure career, a powerful client, and influence—three things that form the bedrock of success in the entertainment industry. I gave them all up to honor my true self. When I did this, I didn't have all of the answers; I was operating on faith and principle alone. But, to my surprise, I discovered that I felt a tremendous sense of power, such as I had never felt before. It was inner power, not outer power. It was the power of being true to *who I am*, not just what I do. I came to realize that with all the money, access, and influence I'd had in my music industry career, I had not been living in my power. I had been living in someone else's power—drawing the meaning and focus of my life from external forces, like the opinions of others and societal expectations—and that power could be removed at any time. I saw this happen over and over again to many of my peers. They lost their jobs, lost their way, and lost their minds. And I saw clearly that it could happen to me too if I didn't make a change.

Conversely, when you live in your power—*your* truth, *your* peace, *your* wholeness, *your* integrity—you live in a place that is invulnerable to assault from the outside.

"Having It All"

It was at that time in my life that I had a revelation. That is, it's impossible to enjoy a fulfilling life by living only a portion of who you are. We must strive to express our full selves, every day, in order to be happy. We must have love, beauty, fun, joy, laughter, meaning, and purpose in our lives all the time, not just once in a while. That includes truthful relationships, enriching physical surroundings, good nourishment, meaningful spiritual practice, charitable service, passionate pursuits and interests, and empowering courage. All woven together organically and blending into one another like a tapestry, not balanced against one another like pieces in a Jenga puzzle, ready to collapse the moment a little extra stress is added or some support taken away.

And so I began committing myself to the daily application of this truth, sharing these truths with others and slowly developing the transformational principles of Exponential Living contained in this book. If you live these 9 Principles, I believe you truly can "have it all"—not in a "balancing act" way, but in a "woven tapestry" way.

Many of us try to "have it all" by living sequentially—focusing *only* on our career for a decade or two, *then* on our relationships, then on our true passions, and then maybe, if there's any time left over, on a little charity or service work. But happiness doesn't work that way. *All* of who we are must be honored and given voice today. Right here, right now.

Nowadays my personal goals for my life are bigger than ever, but I don't *chase* those goals anymore. Rather, I hold them deep in my heart as intentions, work towards them each day in excellence, and let the details unfold according to God's will and my obedience to that truth. The moment I put my goals in proper perspective and started living the fullness of who I am right now, my life transformed. Not only did I begin to truly savor my life for the first time, but I also began to experience more success!

We may not be able to have literally everything we want, but we *can* experience overall fulfillment in every area of our lives. Many of us high achievers don't really believe this. That's why goals are so important to us. We secretly fear that without whipping ourselves toward our goals like racehorses, we will *become* nothing and *achieve* nothing. We have no faith that there is a power and glory that lies within each of us that naturally allows us to grow into our own fullness, without distress and strain, if only we let it.

That's what Exponential Living is all about. It's about discovering the brilliance of that power within you—peace—and letting it illuminate your whole life. Today, tomorrow, and into the future. The light of your true being doesn't need to-do lists; it just needs to shine out and show you the way.

So, What *Is* Exponential Living?

Exponential Living is pursuing peace, choosing clarity, and living courageously. The 9 Principles outlined in this book are the steps we can take toward that future.

Exponential Living is not something to understand intellectually; it is something to be lived—a lifestyle. It's not about achieving more, though it will help you do just that. It's not about discipline and time management, though it will increase your productivity because inner peace amplifies our clarity and this empowers us with the courage to not only simplify our lives but to also take on bigger challenges. It's about discovering who you really are outside of your career identity, and releasing the power of your true self into the world. It's about living a life rooted in peace, not frantic urgency.

Exponential Living is not a mental or emotional state. It's the power of knowing your truth, being true to yourself, having confidence that your life is perfectly on track, and living in peace and joy. It is living a life of honest self-evaluation and service to yourself and others, a life that is full, complete, and in sync with its own parts. You *can* have it all. You are not meant to use 10 percent of your skills for 100 percent of your daily existence, or to rely on 10 percent of who you are to provide 100 percent of your fulfillment.

Exponential Living is not about finding a new comfort zone. It's actually the opposite. It's about continually stretching to live beyond your comfort zone. It's about having the courage to demand more from yourself and your life. President Barack Obama once said, "Hope is that thing inside us that insists . . . that something better awaits us if we have the courage to reach for it." The most powerful words in this quote are "if we have the courage to reach for it," for they remind us that change is only possible if we choose it.

Exponential Living takes courage. When I was learning and developing these 9 Principles, by working through the changes in my own life, it was far from easy. But in doing so I discovered my own truth, which I'll share with you as the book unfolds. This realization of my truth—that my definition of success extends beyond career achievement and is anchored in the daily pursuit of peace—has profoundly affected the way I live and work and has actually helped my career, not hindered it. For example, now that I know who I am, I no longer give my value away. As a result, I earn more income than I did when I was striving for pay! I'm more discerning about whom I work with, and I make sure my business relationships benefit me in the same way I seek to benefit others! The stress and conflict I'd always thought were an essential part of life have melted away. I am confident you will have similar results if you approach this book with seriousness of intent.

I am so honored and excited that you have decided to take this adventure with me.

EXPONENTIAL CONVERSATION

For the first Exponential Conversation of the book, I am thrilled to bring you my chat with three of the most influential figures in modern music: Chris "Ludacris" Bridges and his managers, Chaka Zulu and Jeff Dixon. Chris, as you know, has been a chart-topping music artist since 2000, as well as an actor, philanthropist, and successful businessman. Jeff and Chaka (who are brothers) have been managing Chris for the better part of twenty years, an eternity in the music business.

I met Chaka back when he was the music director at a local radio station in Atlanta where Chris worked as an intern. Chris eventually convinced Chaka to manage him. I have collaborated with these three men many times through my company GLUE, and have always been impressed by the way they show up in excellence. They are three men of character and enormous integrity.

The reason I chose them for the book's first Exponential Conversation is that they are the personifications of Exponential Living in a general, overall sense. These men do the courageous work on *themselves* first—as men, as husbands, as fathers, as friends—and carry that inner work forward into their careers and into the world. This is the opposite of the way most people in entertainment work, where it's typical to focus on the career product first and the self later, *if* there's any time and energy left over. As diversified businesspeople, these men believe they must be diversified human beings first. That means living in their 100 percent, not their 10 percent.

Their talk touches on many ideas that will come up throughout the book.

SHERI RILEY: Our conversation is not centered around your career success, but on who you are as men, how you communicate, how you've been able to sustain your integrity. That's the essence of

Exponential Living. What did you see, Chris, that has allowed you to stay loyal to Jeff and Chaka all these years?

CHRIS "LUDACRIS" BRIDGES: For me it's simple. Honesty is key—and communication. We never really step on each other's toes. I let them do their job and they allow me to do mine. I think most relationships go sour because one person's not honest with the other. I think it's as simple as that. We continue to stay honest with one another. I really just feel like it's as simple as that.

SHERI RILEY: When have you had a moment where you had to make a decision that benefited your family but it may not have been beneficial for you in your career? Or it may not have advanced the business the way you want it to?

CHAKA ZULU: That's every day for me.

CHRIS "LUDACRIS" BRIDGES: I have been dealing with that the last year.

SHERI RILEY: Walk me through how you've been doing that.

CHRIS "LUDACRIS" BRIDGES: It's like Kobe Bryant being arguably one of the best basketball players in the game. As things started changing for him, like his body, all he did was change his game up to be able to shoot and maneuver and have a strategy to continue to score baskets. After all those years. That's literally what we all have been doing. Especially over the past three or four years, because I've been growing my family.

With that being said, it's all about working smarter and not necessarily harder. We work hard, but when we can work strategically smarter from one place—like home, for example—as opposed to having to continue to travel everywhere, we can be just as progressive and just as efficient. That's something I know I've been dealing with, and same thing with them, because we all have family members, we all have kids, we all have individuals that we're taking care of.

SHERI RILEY: How do you define success?

CHRIS "LUDACRIS" BRIDGES: In so many different ways. I think success is definitely about having a strong team around you and being grounded and continuing to stay humble; continuing to educate yourself and progress as individuals and as men; remembering the saying that "it's the journey, not necessarily the destination." Success to me is going along that journey and having so many different challenges in life but never quitting on any of your dreams no matter what. Because you're going to have certain times where you feel like giving up. But as long as you press through, that's what success is to me. Never giving up and continuing to fight through, that's how I define success.

JEFF DIXON: I think as you get older you start to understand knowledge and wisdom. So now, at my age, success is completion, completing things, dreams and aspirations, but also my family—raising kids and putting them through school. Knowing that you're going to pass on the legacy, that's how I define success. Being able to give people some knowledge. Giving back, that's success. We have lofty goals, all of us; we are really ambitious. But you start getting to that point where you're happy to be breathing, to have your health. I'm at that age now where I'm getting calls: "So-and-so just passed away." I've still got the hunger, but as far as success, it's just being able to complete tasks, making other people better.

SHERI RILEY: What does peace mean to you guys?

CHRIS "LUDACRIS" BRIDGES: Peace is making sure your entire family is taken care of, first and foremost. That's when I have peace. And health. Health is number one. Being healthy and making sure that you have a lot more fight in you. You have to eat the right things; you have to exercise in order to plan out your next ten to twenty years and make sure that you're at a space where you know you can continue to work on the same level, or an even better level than you've been working on. That's what peace is to me.

JEFF DIXON: Peace to me, like he said, is making sure my family and people I care about—I've given them all I could.

CHAKA ZULU: For me peace would be probably two words, freedom and fearlessness. They're connected to what Chris and Jeff are saying; it's just when you have the things they're talking about, you have a freedom and a fearlessness about how you approach things. So when you've got your family situated, you've got certain things lined up—it creates a fearlessness because you know you've done what you've done, and that creates a freedom. Now you can either do more or do less; you're free enough to accept what it is or change what it is. It's a two-sided coin, freedom and fearlessness, for me, but it's connected and rooted in what they're saying.

SHERI RILEY: The essence of Exponential Living is "peace is our power and peace is the new success." What's the one thing that you know makes you uniquely powerful?

CHRIS "LUDACRIS" BRIDGES: That's easy for me. It's continuing to top anything that I've ever done, and continuing to surprise people. What I mean is, we may have arguably conquered one realm of entertainment, so it's just trying to continue to conquer other areas. So dreaming big to the point where the phrase "If your dreams aren't scaring you, they're not big enough" is your guide. I continue to dream and that's what keeps me at peace, because I know I will never be complacent. I'm at peace knowing that I continue to dream bigger and bigger. That's it for me. Just continue to dream big.

CHAKA ZULU: Exponential Living is me being able to call my brother Jeff and my brother Chris and say, "Hey, this is what's going on," or "Hey, this is my idea." He's the dreamer, I'm the visionary, and he's the executor. That's peace—knowing that Chris is going to communicate what he wants to do, and the belief that his success is my success, or my success is his success and vice versa. All of that is exponential—multiplying and growing, the way we become conduits running for and through each other.

JEFF DIXON: One thing about us: we always want to learn, and that's why you, Sheri, are a great part of us. I read your Exponential Living e-mails. What's made us great is that we want to keep learning. We're humble. We want to learn, and we still feel like we haven't accomplished a lot. But being together and then finding people that can take us to that next level, whether it be spiritually, mentally, financially, that's what it's about.

I AM JEFF DIXON AND I AM EXPONENTIAL LIVING.

I AM CHAKA ZULU AND I AM EXPONENTIAL LIVING.

*I AM CHRIS "LUDACRIS" BRIDGES
AND I AM EXPONENTIAL LIVING.*

Key Takeaways

» Sustained success is about learning to work smarter, not harder.
» Success is not all about you shining like a star; it includes being humble and grounded and having a strong team around you.
» Peace is connected to taking care of yourself and your family.
» Peace is a choice. Freedom and fearlessness flow from that choice.

Your 10 Percent and Your 100 Percent

If success is not on your own terms, if it looks good to the world but does not feel good in your soul, it is not success at all.

—ANNA QUINDLEN,
JOURNALIST, COLUMNIST, AND AUTHOR

Midway through my career I realized the only thing I was doing was working, and I honestly wasn't enjoying that anymore. What had happened? I had sacrificed so much to have my dream job and now the dream had become a nightmare. I still wanted a career; I just didn't like the way mine was robbing me of my life.

That's because we are not designed to live a life that relies on only 10 percent of who we are to produce 100 percent of our fulfillment. We are designed to live a life that flows from 100 percent of who we are. Moving toward that "100 percent life" is what Exponential Living is all about.

One of my coaching clients, Deanna Hamilton, is a brilliant businesswoman who has been both a CFO and an entrepreneur. She has been the president of the largest chapter of a national business organization and has a database filled with the personal cell phone numbers of corporate CEOs, celebrities, and professional athletes, all of whom respect her opinion, want to do business with her, and/or enjoy time in her presence.

So why did she feel she needed to change? On top of her career, she was a beautiful woman in her mid-forties—Deanna was the picture-perfect image of a successful woman.

But she didn't feel complete inside. It's not that she was unhappy; she was enjoying many aspects of her life. It was just that there was something missing within her that she knew no outer achievement could restore—not the accolades, not the career achievements, and not the success of yet another organization. Not even the love of a good man. Something she could not define was gnawing at her gut, creating an unfillable hole inside of her.

For years, she had ignored the hints and nudges she felt inside of herself by taking on more work and more responsibility, but the tension within her was growing and causing her happy, energetic spirit to be eclipsed by depression, doubt, and anxiety.

Deanna had spent most of her life, up to that point, developing only 10 percent of who she was, and this imbalance was causing a huge rift between her professional self and her personal self. Deanna's story is one I've seen often with high achievers and others who are living only 10-percent lives.

When I began working with Deanna, one of the first questions I asked her was the simplest and deepest question we can ask another human being: Who are you?

Deanna shifted uncomfortably in her chair and gave me the "stock" answer—in other words, she rattled off her job description.

I smiled and asked the question again.

She repeated the answer, phrased in a slightly different way, throwing in a few details about her charity work and family activities.

"You are telling me what you *do*. Why is what you *do* so much more important to you than who you are?" I asked.

"That's not true," she responded. "I'm very concerned with who I am. That's why I do what I do—so I can enjoy who I am. My work is a part of me. I love what I do."

"I totally understand that, but again, I'm asking you, why is what you do so much more important to you than who you are?"

"What do you mean?" she said, getting just a bit testy. "I just answered that question."

"No, you shared with me why you love your career and enjoy your work, but that wasn't the question. What I'm asking is, 'Who are you?'"

"Well, I don't know the answer to that question," she said, her body language strongly suggesting that we move on to something more important.

"'I don't know' is not an acceptable answer." I smiled.

Deanna looked at me long and hard. Then she sighed and began to dig down beneath the easy answers. Her journey to Exponential Living began.

Why This Chapter

Before *you* can begin *your* journey to Exponential Living, you must be willing to explore who you are when you're not playing whatever roles you've taught the world to expect you to play—CEO, husband, mom, teacher, lawyer, neighbor, athlete, daughter, actor, executive, friend. Until you do that kind of exploration, your role(s) will continue to define you in every situation, and you will remain forever trapped in your 10 percent. That's why understanding the difference between your 10 percent and your 100 percent is crucial before diving into the 9 Principles of Exponential Living.

The Personal Self Vs. the Roles You Play

Have you felt that disconnect between your personal self (who you are) and the roles you play in life (what you do)? Of course you have. We all develop a set of roles that we play in the world—actor, doctor, lawyer, athlete, CEO, student, mom, dad, PTO member, community organizer. For many of us, our professional or work role is the biggest role we play in life—and that goes for full-time parents, students, clergy, and volunteers too. Some of us learn how to turn that professional self on when we are in work mode, and then turn it off when the workday ends. But the problem for high achievers is that the workday hardly ever ends. We're in work mode most of the time—during our long days at the office, when we're on our smartphones in the car, when we're writing e-mails at home, even when we're walking around town, projecting a chosen image for all to see. This is true for those of us who identify with a role such as "parent" as well. From doing housework to running errands to cooking dinner to helping with the homework, the role begins to dominate our behavior from morning till night. And so the personal self begins to get less and less "airtime," and begins to feel like a stranger to us.

Who we truly are—our personal self—is usually quite different from the roles we play, and is vast dimensions larger. We sometimes hear celebrities, such as Beyoncé, describe this phenomenon. Beyoncé even gave her stage persona its own name: Sasha Fierce. Why? Because her personal self is more than the "star" everyone gushes over. This is true of many of us. The confidence, strategic thinking, and deal-making skills we may attribute to our "work" personality may not be key aspects of our personal self when we're out of the spotlight. As for me, for example, when it comes to work, I am a relationship builder. I am outgoing and personable, and love to engage with people. But my personal self often loves to sit quietly alone or in a crowded room without talking to anyone, just enjoying the community of people. I am an introvert (my personal self) who has learned to live as an extrovert (the roles I play). The goal of Exponential Living is to make sure your 100-percent personal self is not overshadowed by your 10-percent professional self. Because when that happens, you begin to live as a two-dimensional version of yourself, which you manage to convince yourself is "you." Meanwhile, the unexpressed parts of you clamor for attention below the surface, which can lead to self-defeating behavior, resentment, and depression.

Personal First

The truth is, personal development fuels career growth. Many high achievers disregard this truth, as I did for many years—I was only concerned with developing skills I could directly apply to my job performance or to further my career. But it's worth noting that with all her success—from singing for US presidents and touring the globe to becoming known as one of the top music artists in the world—even Beyoncé has said, "My goal was trusting myself and my growth." A personal goal, not a professional one, is what fueled her. Practitioners of Exponential Living are always working on personal goals first, professional goals second.

If you want to experience Exponential Living, personal growth is not an optional aspect of the process. Nor does it just *happen* as a function of age or job advancement. Achieving the next promotion or multimillion-dollar deal does not come with personal-growth injections. Personal growth is an intentional daily process just like growing your business or career is. If you run a business, then you know you must carefully tend to its growth and development, or it will suffer. In a similar way, your relationship with *yourself* needs constant tending and upgrading.

As influencers and high achievers, we have skills and talents that often elevate us to levels of achievement that our character can't sustain. We find ourselves leapfrogging ahead of the pack because of our advanced ability, but we haven't yet developed the wisdom, self-knowledge, and leadership skills to handle such success. And so we end up sabotaging ourselves. This is a situation we commonly see with young superstar athletes and performers whose career achievements can come faster than their personal maturity. They spend the majority of their days developing their skills, knowledge, and expertise for their professional craft but little to no time is focused on their decision-making ability, discernment of the character of people in

EDDIE GEORGE

Eddie George, who is a Heisman Trophy winner, played nine years in the NFL, was selected to play in several Pro Bowls, and made one Super Bowl appearance. During a broadcast of the 2015 Heisman Trophy award ceremony, he was asked who he was at the time he walked away from football, and he shared his truth.

"The reason I played the game was to fulfill a dream my father never had the chance to fill, and that was to be a professional football player, to win a Heisman Trophy, and to play college football. Really that was my dream, but it was more his dream than anything else. Then, at thirty-one, when I retired, I was left with nothing. So I had to go on a journey to find out who I was, what I was passionate about, and pursue it, like no other. To do what it takes to be honest, to be in that moment, takes a great deal of courage."

their lives, or who they are becoming in the midst of their career success.

That's why personal development is so critical. We must be intentional about building our character, which happens through a steady process of making clear, intentional choices, pursuing inner peace, and living courageously. That all starts with knowing ourselves truly and deeply. When we spend 100 percent of our time on 10 percent of who we are, there's no way we can develop a "pool" of good character to draw from when we face challenges and dilemmas.

I have heard my mentor, John Maxwell, the world's leading expert on leadership, say that when he started his career, leaders didn't think they needed to learn leadership skills. Leaders just told people what to do and expected their employees and followers to follow orders without question. Now learning actual skills is a global requirement of leaders.

Many highly successful people, however, still don't believe they need personal development, no matter how much importance they place on honing their professional leadership skills. High achievers believe if they keep pressing toward their professional and career goals, their personal lives will eventually take care of themselves. But it doesn't work that way. This is why we need to change the paradigm and make peace and personal development an expected "requirement" of people in all career fields.

When I met Dolvett Quince, who has since achieved fame as an actor, author, wellness coach, and trainer on NBC's *The Biggest Loser*, he owned a successful personal training facility in an upscale area of Atlanta. He had great connections and professional relationships, as well as the resources, network, and skills to elevate his brand to an international level. He had big dreams of transitioning from a successful Atlanta-based trainer to one with high-profile clientele and media recognition. Dolvett was so focused on where he was going that he lost sight of the person who was trying to get there. He was on a path where his talents and skills would take him to levels of success that his character could not sustain. As he uncovered during our work together and shared with me, his professional achievements had blown up his ego, which was preventing him from seeing his true self and blocking him from higher levels of success.

My priority in working with Dolvett was to help him gain deeper clarity and perspective on himself and take greater ownership of his actions. In our private coaching sessions, I asked him questions that allowed him to see those areas where his ego was limiting both his personal and professional growth. "I learned that I had a lot more to learn," Dolvett shares. "I thought I was in a position of power. I owned my own private personal training gym. I had taught over twenty trainers how to properly train. I had grown my business and was a strong salesman. [But by taking an honest look at myself] I was humbled in a lot of ways. . . ."

Gradually, we were able to strengthen his awareness of who he *really* was and who he really wanted to be—namely, a person of principle and character—which allowed him to gain clarity in his direction for both his career and personal life. By objectively comparing the self he wanted to be with his present words and behaviors, he began to see the places in his life that were out of alignment. He saw areas where he needed to mature, behaviors he needed to eliminate, and actions he needed to take. Taking ownership of his personal growth allowed him to make better decisions and to bridge the disconnect between his professional ego and who he really was and desired to be.

This intentional transformation allowed Dolvett to maximize

several career opportunities, including becoming a bestselling author, a featured trainer on NBC's *The Biggest Loser*, a cast member on *Stars Earn Stripes*, a spokesperson in national commercials and for international brands, and a guest star on BET's *Real Husbands of Hollywood*. Developing his personal self has allowed him to connect with his team on *The Biggest Loser* in a way that transcends weight loss and expands into a fuller appreciation for who they are as human beings. This, in turn, inspires his teams to perform better for him, elevating his career goals as a natural result.

Personal comes first; everything else comes second.

You Either Change or You Don't

One thing that drives me to do the work I do now is thinking about the friends and associates I have lost because their talents took them to levels of success that their levels of personal development couldn't sustain. A dear friend of mine worked very hard in his professional life as a gifted and internationally recognized singer, songwriter, and producer. But he struggled when it came to managing his personal life. He once told me early in my career that, as a woman, I couldn't have it all—that I couldn't be happily married, have children, and reach the highest levels of success in the entertainment industry. I know he felt he was giving me this advice for my best interest, as a way of looking out for me. I know that's the story he chose to believe for himself—that a person can't have it all. But the truth was, in the depth of his heart, he *wanted* it all: the family, the career, and most importantly, the peace. But he died before he could make the shift. He died, in a way, *because* he was trying to live 100 percent through his 10-percent self.

When someone dies, the true tragedy is not their death, but the death of the untapped potential and unrealized dreams that die with them. Ever since my friend's death, and the loss of several other dear friends and associates, I've been inspired to tell the world that you *can* experience Exponential Living. You *can* have a healthy relationship with yourself, a loving family, a successful career, and passionate hobbies—all grounded in joy and peace. In other words, you *can* live in your 100 percent, not just your 10 percent. Not only *can* you, but you MUST, before it's too late.

It's not easy, and it takes courage, but it is simple and it's an essential journey.

Most of us high achievers manage to continue to live 10-percent lives until—if we're lucky—we hit some kind of wall, or receive some kind of ultimatum, and life gives us a huge opportunity to change. Usually that means we hit one of four "pain points."

The Four Pain Points

In my work I have observed four types of life challenges that often occur for those who have attained career/professional success.

1. "Now What?" I'm exactly where I want to be in my life, goalwise, but I know there's more. I want to do other things. I don't want to leave my job/company, but there are other things I want to do in my life *in addition* to my current career, family commitments, or role in my company. I've always wanted to start a foundation, travel, pursue a spiritual path, and/or do other important and meaningful things, but how? I've allowed myself to become boxed in and defined by my professional role. How do I expand the box? How do I create more margin in my life?

2. "Is This It?" I'm living my "dream," and I am miserable. My career is exactly what I thought I wanted, but my life is awful. I work harder and harder because I keep telling myself that more money, bigger contracts, higher positions, more [fill in the blank—cars, homes, jewelry, women/men, awards, parties] will fill the void. The world sees me as successful but I am so unhappy I need to "medicate" myself with work, bad behavior, drugs, gambling, affairs, shopping, collecting, etc.

3. "What's Next?" I've reached my goals, but I've always known these were only some of the things I wanted to do. I feel complete with what I've done in the past, what I've accomplished, and want to move on. The time has come for a major career change, a life change, and/or a shift into doing what I love to do. But I don't really know where or how to start. I feel like I'm standing on a giant blank sheet of paper, waiting for a new story to appear. In a December 2015 article by basketball great Shane Battier, published in the digital magazine The Measure, he describes just such a pain point as he approached the end of his sports career: "What's next? Is there a more frustrating thing a lifelong overachiever can ask himself? My path for the last twenty-five years was clearly defined. Make a shot, stop your opponent. Rinse. Repeat. It was a simple formula I followed from my driveway at 2220 Yorkshire all the way to the NBA Finals. . . . Thanks to scoreboards, records, media, fans, coaches, I always knew where I stood. . . . At any given moment, I could look at a score or at the standings and know if I was winning, losing, helping, hurting. There was always a metric." Now, suddenly, all his old metrics were gone, as they are for all who reach this pain point.

4. "How Do I Live?" I have been on a dedicated path of success and have achieved many of my goals, but now a major planned or unplanned

life change is happening. I am having my first child; my last child just left for college; I just lost my job after fifteen years; my longtime marriage has ended; I was recently diagnosed with a serious health condition and need a new lifestyle. Change has been thrust upon me. I must adapt and grow, but I have no idea how.

Though each of these pain points feels confusing and unpleasant, it is actually a gift. Yes, a gift. It represents an opportunity, an opening, a chance to reevaluate and break through to your 100 percent. If you are at one of these pain points, you are one of the lucky ones. Some people, like my friend who died, have the curtain drawn down on them before they have the opportunity to change. Others go on in dull misery, day after day, year after year, never quite reaching an acute enough level of pain and discomfort to feel forced to change.

The fact that you recognize that you are at a pain point means you know your "old way" is no longer working for you. You have a chance to take a step toward Exponential Living.

Permission

The process of growth from 10-percent living to 100-percent living begins with *permission*. We must give ourselves permission to think, act, and question differently. We must grant ourselves license to explore our other 90 percent and to make room for it in our day-to-day choice making.

We live, for better or worse, in a culture that rewards outer achievement but does not reward introspection or the deep questioning of human life. That is one of the main reasons high achievers are able to continue living 10-percent lives, year after year. Their achievements bring them approval, envy, fame, admiration, acceptance, and/or financial rewards from society. Consequently, there is little incentive for them to question their life approach; in fact, there is a strong *dis-incentive* to do so (until they hit a pain point).

I've worked with lots of amazingly successful people. I can't tell you how many of them when asked the simple question "Who are you?" or "Why are you here on this planet?" get a blank look or a mildly annoyed expression on their faces. They either 1) have never thought to ask such questions, 2) believe such questions are side issues— something to think about after they reach all of their goals, or 3) fear that embarking on such an introspective exercise will shatter the carefully constructed persona that has been essential to the achievements they have reached so far.

Even when they hit one of the pain points above, many high achievers are confused or reluctant to ask essential questions such as the following:

» What is my true purpose?
» What do I really want from life?
» What do I wish to leave behind as my legacy?
» What do I value?
» What does integrity mean to me? Is it important?
» What is my essential nature as a human being?
» What is my relationship with God?
» Who do I care about?
» Am I living in a way that reflects my highest purpose?
» What does peace mean to me? Is it important?
» What is my "why"?

Asking such questions seems like a philosophical luxury to busy, action-oriented people, far less critical than beating quarterly profit goals or winning Sunday's game. And so we need to give ourselves *permission* to ask such questions and to receive and hear the answers. No one else can or will do this for us; we must give *ourselves* permission. And we must ask the questions now, not later. We must discover the 90 percent of our iceberg that is hidden below the surface. When we do this, the answers we get change our entire approach to life. They don't necessarily change *what* we do for a living, but they provide a blueprint for our personal fulfillment in a way that no list of goals can ever do.

When we hit one of the four pain points, we need to recognize it as the opening that it is. But here's a crucial point: *We don't have to wait till we hit a pain point in order to make a change.* We can give ourselves permission now. Permission to start making room for our hidden 90 percent. When we do this, we can start living more joyfully and peacefully right now, and can even avoid the pain points altogether.

I recently spoke to Tom Hughes, who is vice president of communications for Compass One Healthcare. Earlier in his career, Tom worked in high-level PR and communications positions for the Atlanta Hawks, the Atlanta Thrashers, and Philips Arena, as well as Turner Broadcasting. The Hawks/Thrashers/Philips job, in particular, represented the kind of high-profile position that many people dream of. It included travel and media interaction and face-to-face dealings with top pro athletes. It also included long workweeks and many evening hours. For a time, it was an exciting professional challenge for Tom. After a while, though, he knew that moving on "was a move that I needed to make personally and professionally." Tom, you see, had other priorities that needed to be given time and attention. "I was married and had a young family. Inevitably, something would happen at home when I was on the road. Our house was burglarized. One of my children had trouble at school, or a litany of challenges was thrown in along the way. . . . I think the number one thing [that troubled me] was missing out on things, events, and happenings with my family." Tom went on to say, "I've always known what motivates me, which is making my family proud . . . providing for them and trying to give them as good a life as I can provide." So he began looking for new career possibilities. Though the professional sports team job "was a chance for me to take a big step forward with my career . . . every step that I take . . . starts and ends with family."

Because Tom asked important questions of himself and clarified his values, he was able to resign from his job at the professional sports team and secure an equal position at another company, without waiting for a major crisis to erupt in his family or marriage. In making the change, he had to give up some of the perks of his profession. "In sports and entertainment," Tom says, "they're very sexy, enviable positions from a lot of people's perspectives. [When you leave], you give up people taking your phone calls and reading your e-mails and things that happened very quickly in the past. You have to work a little harder to maintain relationships. The biggest thing is giving up that sense of [being known]." Many high achievers have a hard time giving up such perks, because these are the very perks that symbolize success in their minds.

Recently, for example, I spoke at the Global Women's Summit, and afterward one of my sorority sisters—I affectionately call them my "Sorors"—who had a three-year-old and an eighteen-month-old shared with me her greatest fear. She had a vision of receiving an award from *Essence* magazine and everyone in the room is giving her a standing ovation *except* her kids and husband. She was afraid of being "seduced" by the glory aspects of her career, at the expense of the things she cared most about. It's a legitimate fear. The applause *is* seductive. And we don't always get applause for standing up for our values.

But in return for standing up for his, Tom gained things like the time and freedom to coach his kids' sports teams, something he couldn't have done before. Had Tom put his true values on the back burner, as many high achievers do, his family situation probably would have turned into a pain point eventually, but by giving himself permission to honor his own values sooner, rather than later, he was able to make a better choice for his life. Not only is he happier but so are those who love and depend on him. That's Exponential Living.

Who Are You?—Paint the Picture of Your 10 Percent and Your 100 Percent

I encourage you to make that kind of proactive choice in your own life. And it all starts with asking the same question I asked Deanna at the start of the chapter. It is the primary question I'll be asking you to think about throughout the course of this book, and, as with Deanna, "I don't know" is not an acceptable answer.

That question, of course, is: Who are you?

Who are you?

Yes, you are the CEO, the vice president, the owner, the consultant, the parent, the employee, the contractor, the politician, the husband, the wife, the athlete, the publicist, the actor, the singer . . . but these are only titles, not who you are. Remember, I am not asking, "What do you do?" I am asking, "Who are you?" What matters to you? What moves you? What does life mean to you? What are you here to learn and express? What are your values?

We'll be coming back to this question, in various ways, throughout the book, but for now I'd just like you to do a short thought exercise.

I'd like you to pause, close your eyes for a moment, and try to mentally "paint the picture" of your 10-percent life and your 100-percent life. I want you to begin to appreciate the difference between the two.

Paint the Picture of Your 10 Percent

What do you excel at in your professional life? (Remember, if you're a full-time parent, that's your profession.) What do you get paid to do? What have you always been good at? What personal traits do you strive to project on the job? How do you like others to describe you? What's your professional comfort zone? What do others expect from you? What do you do in order not to let others down? How does it feel to live in your professional persona? What rewards do you get from being your 10-percent self? What do you like about your 10-percent self? What do you dislike? Are you stimulated and challenged at a deep level by your work?

Paint the Picture of Your 100 Percent

What aspects of yourself do you need to "shut off" in order to play your professional role? What things or people do you care about, but are not consistently including in your life? What are some interests that used to be important to you, but that you no longer pursue? Why? How's your spiritual life? What relationships are important to you? Does your daily behavior reflect how important these relationships are? Where do you want your life to be heading? What are the main things you want your life to include? Are you deeply satisfied? Why not? What are your passions? What brings you joy? Laughter? Awe? What emotions are not currently being expressed in your life? What are your deepest values? What causes would you like to champion? How do you want to be remembered?

Hold those "pictures" in your mind as the backdrop for the journey ahead.

The 9 Principles of Exponential Living

Now we're ready to dive into the core of the book, the 9 Principles of Exponential Living. Each of the following chapters focuses on one of these life-changing Principles, along with exercises that will help you incorporate that Principle into your life. Take these Principles to heart and you *will* experience Exponential Living. It's taken me over ten years to develop, live, teach, and refine these Principles, and they have transformed my life and the lives of many influencers, celebrities, athletes, corporate executives, entrepreneurs, parents, and other high achievers. The 9 Principles stand independently of one another and yet they are deeply interrelated, as you'll see. In the order presented, they create a rhythm and momentum that build powerfully and have an inner logic, so I encourage you to approach them in order the first time unless you are strongly moved to do otherwise. After your initial read, you can work on them any way you choose. And you can come back to any one of them and work on it alone, anytime you want.

The Principles are like instruments in an orchestra. Each one can be played and mastered individually and enjoyed for its own unique beauty. However, when they are all played together, they create something larger than the sum of the parts. It's called Exponential Living.

The Principles are not meant to be merely read, but to be acted upon and used as a road map to transformation and a guide for pursuing peace, choosing clarity, and living courageously. I challenge you to use them that way.

Peace and courage be with you.

EXPONENTIAL CONVERSATION

Jini D. Thornton is my guest for this chapter's Exponential Conversation. I love talking to Jini; she is someone who truly "gets it." Jini is a CPA who founded and owns Envision Business Management Group (EBMG), a financial services company that represents some of the music industry's hottest entertainers, such as Chris "Luda-cris" Bridges, CeeLo Green, Jeezy, August Alsina, Raury, and Rock City. You can hear Jini regularly on the nationally syndicated *Willie Moore Jr. Show*, *The Rickey Smiley Morning Show*, and *The Ed Lover Show*. She has been featured and quoted in articles in the *Wall Street Journal*, *Atlanta Business Chronicle*, *Upscale* magazine, and *Rolling Out* magazine. When Jini talks, people listen!

I've chosen her for this chapter because she is an amazing living example of someone who has gone from 10-percent living—highly successful but "missing something"—to Exponential Living. I think you'll see that immediately as you start to read her words. . . .

SHERI RILEY: When you and I first started working together I was doing a mastermind group [a group of like-minded individuals who focus on a topic, a book, or a goal, with the understanding that the sum of the group thinking is more impactful than the individual thinking] and you participated. What was going on with you that led you to that group?

JINI THORNTON: I had been getting a nudge, that push, for a few years, but I had chosen to ignore it. So my life was feeling very one-dimensional. I was working really hard. I was thinking I was doing a very good job of my personal life. I'm married, I have two children, and that was it—my youngest son was getting ready to graduate from high school, and my life was beginning to change. I had a major shift coming, and I was trying to pre-pare for that shift.

SHERI RILEY: Describe that nudge.

JINI THORNTON: It's kind of like this gnawing feeling, and it just got to the point where I couldn't ignore it anymore. I had been ignoring it for a while. I would just put my head down and get busier. Working harder, focusing more on my kids, instead of paying attention to what was trying to get my attention. You just get these little signs. Things that used to bring you pleasure begin to annoy you. You begin to question your routine. You begin to question how you're spending your time. I think a lot of it had to do with my age. I was coming to the point where I was over forty. I was thinking about the fact that I've lived probably close to half of my life; is this where I want to be? Does this represent who I am and what's important to me? I finally gave myself permission to listen.

SHERI RILEY: Okay, so help us understand. You've got the multimillion-dollar company, CEO, you have the marriage of over twenty years, you have two sons—young men who are doing great. So your life represents what everyone says we're working toward. How could you not feel great about that?

JINI THORNTON: I think other people's perspective of the picture clouded me. People are always saying to you, "Oh my gosh, you're so fortunate. You're so lucky. How have you accomplished this?" People are constantly patting you on the back and you're just like "Something just still isn't right. Something is still missing."

SHERI RILEY: And many people don't heed that gnawing.

JINI THORNTON: Oh, absolutely. I ran from it for a long time.

SHERI RILEY: What gave you the courage to heed it?

JINI THORNTON: I made a decision that when my youngest son, Cameron, graduated from high school I was going to begin to look at my life differently. I picked that date. I could have picked a date before that, but for some reason that made sense to me and gave me a timeline. It's funny: When you're a mother, you think you will be so happy when your kids graduate. You've succeeded! It actually was a letdown for me. I had a vision of how wonderful my life was going to be after my children graduated and they were happy and healthy and successful in college. But I hadn't done the work to prepare for it.

SHERI RILEY: The external accomplishment was there; the internal was missing.

JINI THORNTON: Definitely. And now my kids were gone, so the only thing I had left was work. That's all I had left. My life was literally that one- or two-dimensional. I had nothing else that brought me joy. I had nothing else that I was interested in. I didn't have any other passion.

SHERI RILEY: So your 10 percent—you would describe it as what?

JINI THORNTON: Oh, it was work. There's no question about that. It was work.

SHERI RILEY: What got you to that place where your 10 percent became your 100 percent?

JINI THORNTON: I come from a family of entrepreneurs. We work hard. In our family there was a lot of accolades for working hard and accomplishing. So I think I just got in the rhythm of what was normal for my family. You went to school, you worked hard, you accomplished. . . . So me being an entrepreneur, it was kind of my path. I had seen it my whole life. So we grind and we work hard, and that's the reality of my family. You didn't sleep late; you always had to be about doing something. And who gets criticized for working hard?

SHERI RILEY: Right. It's celebrated in our culture.

JINI THORNTON: Absolutely. So the harder I worked, the more I did, the more I was patted on the back. What's interesting is, although I was working hard that whole time, I was very intentional as it related to my family and children. I will never forget it when I was pregnant with my first son: my mother-in-law said, "I raised my own children." So I always knew I needed to raise my own kids. I had always had this saying that if my children grew up and spent money on therapy, it wasn't going to be because of me. I was very intentional about how I designed my life around my children's activities. Not just events I had to be at, but really being engaged in their lives, knowing all their friends, being active in school. I put those big rocks in first. Then I would do my work around that, and that's all I made room for.

SHERI RILEY: You have the children, you have the marriage, you have the business; sounds like the only thing missing was Jini.

JINI THORNTON: Oh, there was nothing else there.

SHERI RILEY: How did you not know that there was something missing?

JINI THORNTON: I think I *kind* of knew it, but I kept telling myself I was too busy, that there wasn't time, that there wasn't a way. Now, having some wisdom, I can see that I just never gave myself permission. I never gave myself credit that I could figure it out. I figured everything else out—why couldn't I figure this out? . . . There are some additional trappings in the entertainment industry. It can consume your entire life. You can work all day and have thirty-two things to do at night, seven days a week. I think as a woman, I felt that I had a lot to prove. I just went about working and literally did not pay attention to or really acknowledge anything else.

SHERI RILEY: I had the mastermind group. What made you go, "Okay, I'm going to start here"?

JINI THORNTON: Well, I was already familiar with the mastermind process, so that was relatable to me. I immediately connected with that. From a scheduling perspective everything lined up so I could say, "I can commit to this, and this is a good first step." I knew I needed to just take a step. I was okay with the fact that I didn't have the full solution, but I just wanted to begin taking some steps forward.

SHERI RILEY: How did you feel when you started to take those steps?

JINI THORNTON: You begin to see your everyday life very differently. Not necessarily in a negative way, but there's something I call "mass consciousness," where you are just in the flow of everyday life like everyone else—get up, go to work, go to bed, start over again. I began to question my participation in this mass consciousness. And I knew better than to do that because I grew up in a house where my mother was extremely nontraditional. She created the life that she wanted. She adopted two kids; she never married and didn't want to be married. She rode motorcycles. So I knew that that was possible, but I think having children so young and then immediately starting my company, I lost sight of the fact that I had control to create exactly the life that I wanted. I started to realize, "The world isn't putting me in a box. I've put myself in a box. I've put these boundaries on me." I started questioning, instead of just doing. I started asking myself the "why."

SHERI RILEY: So your life wasn't in a box.

JINI THORNTON: I put myself there. Nobody put me there. I was 100 percent responsible. I made those choices that gave me that very narrow life.

SHERI RILEY: What was your journey to open up to this 90 percent that was missing?

JINI THORNTON: I had to begin to look at, what am I willing to let go? And why did I have such an attachment to certain things? I began to think, "What if I didn't do this anymore? What would that mean for me?" Clearly I was identifying myself with work. So if I didn't do it anymore, if I had a completely different profession, moved out of the country, what would that mean for me?

SHERI RILEY: So in this process of evaluation what did you have to reject? And what did you have to redefine?

JINI THORNTON: I had to reject the value that I was placing on work. Because work wasn't just what I *did*. It was *who I was* as well. So I had to begin to separate those things. Although this is my company, it's not who I am, and it's not my baby either.

SHERI RILEY: Tell me a moment that you started making that separation.

JINI THORNTON: I had always felt life would be incomplete if I didn't have the opportunity to work with my clients. How could they go on if I wasn't present? I began to say, "If I got hit by a bus today, that wouldn't be true." At the end of the day, is this all I want my life to represent? I began questioning those things. I have this saying in my conference room: "Real change requires real change."

SHERI RILEY: Was it painful going through this process?

JINI THORNTON: I think part of it initially was, but then it just became part of the flow of life. Instead of labeling everything good/bad or right/wrong, I just started looking at things. Questioning things.

SHERI RILEY: Why do you think so many people in your position are afraid to do that?

JINI THORNTON: Because it means that everything they've been doing all this time is wrong, bad.

SHERI RILEY: The labeling.

JINI THORNTON: Yep, labeling versus saying, "It was just part of my experience, and now I'm just ready to do something different." I equate [growth] with college. I loved college. I loved every second I was in college, but my senior year, it was time to go. I loved high school, but it was time to go. The thing about high school and college is, it's very defined when it's time to move on. We don't have those definitions when we become adults. Once you enter the workplace, you have to set the timelines and the parameters yourself.

SHERI RILEY: Many people don't do that. What is your "why"? And has that shifted?

JINI THORNTON: Although I'm still doing the same type of work, my intention is different now. I've created more space for my personal life now, and it's allowed me to be more creative now since I've gotten out of that rut of "push, go, deliver, more business, more clients, make sure they're happy, make sure they're good." I've really started to think about what I want my legacy to be. What contribution do I want to make? I think that's part of the shift that I've had to do. I was focused on significance and now I'm focused on contribution.

SHERI RILEY: Many of us think that peace will destroy our edge, when the reality is, peace *enhances* our edge. It increases our productivity. How has your faith played a role in this journey to your 100 percent?

JINI THORNTON: I think that was probably the biggest thing I was missing. I didn't have a connection with a place and a community. Also, I had, again, kind of just put my head down and had not acknowledged that part of myself. So I became very intentional and decided, "I need to belong somewhere. I need people to know who I am. I need a sense of community. I need to go somewhere I get filled." When I made that decision it just began to unfold for me, so I've made a commitment to my spirituality. It's been huge.

SHERI RILEY: How do you define peace?

JINI THORNTON: I have this sign across from my desk: "Peace does not mean to be in a place where there is no noise, trouble, or hard work. It means to be in the midst of those things and still be calm in your heart." And that's what I've been working on. Initially I didn't want anything unsettled in my life. I didn't want trouble. I didn't want to work hard anymore. Then I had to come to terms with the fact that that's not real. So I had to learn to change, because a lot of those things I cannot control. I can only control me.

SHERI RILEY: And how did you change?

JINI THORNTON: Knowing that I could have peace in the midst of turmoil, in the midst of significant challenges, personal and professional. Peace is a choice. It is very intentional. It's a practice too, so I'm not saying that I never get flustered or frustrated, but I have learned that I can choose . . . how I show up. So that's been big for me.

SHERI RILEY: Describe your new normal, not from someone looking in, but from you looking out.

JINI THORNTON: Professionally, I've given myself permission to be creative, I think, for the first time. To do what I really want to do. Not what people expect of me based on my education and my experience. The closer you get to fifty, time matters. I want to be very intentional about how I spend my time. I think my life is multidimensional now. I have given myself permission to have more of a social life than I've had. I've given myself permission to have adventure and spontaneity. I've allowed myself to get engaged in my community differently. I've allowed myself to get engaged with church differently. I've shifted the priority of my time. It's made me a better parent. It's definitely made me a better spouse and partner because I'm not just suffering in my own life anymore. It's made me more whole and complete, and I think it's made me a better role model and example for my family too. I see how they're getting engaged differently. This has probably been the most open I've ever been. Also, high achievers—we can be so hard on ourselves. I think I've definitely given myself more grace. I've learned to just enjoy the journey more. I'm working hard, but it's different now.

I AM JINI THORNTON AND I AM EXPONENTIAL LIVING.

Key Takeaways

- » Pay attention to that "gnawing" feeling in your gut; it means more of your 100 percent wants to be known and expressed.
- » Other people's perspectives of you can cloud your truth.
- » Peace is not freedom from trouble and stress; it is the ability to be calm *in the midst* of trouble and stress.
- » Giving time to your 100-percent self can create more time in your life.
- » If you want to experience Exponential Living, *you* need to decide when it's time to "move on" to a new phase of life. No one else can do this for you.

Live in Your P.O.W.E.R.

No matter how much money you have, you can't pay
for personal clarity.

—SHERI RILEY

In 2013, my sorority, Delta Sigma Theta Sorority, Inc., celebrated one
hundred years of scholarship, sisterhood, and service. During our
centennial celebration, my longtime friend and sorority sister (who is
very special to me and affectionately known as my "spesh") Sadiqa
Reynolds and I were having dinner.

"Girl, you were amazing on your panel," she said to me. "You
have such a commanding and humble presence. Everyone gravitated
to you, and you shared such powerful insight on every question."

She was pointing out my strengths because she knew about the
devastation I had been enduring since the previous year. While transitioning from a successful business—GLUE, the company I started
after leaving LaFace Records—in order to pursue my purpose of
being a full-time speaker, life strategist, and author, I had "hit bottom." I was broke, homeless—not living-on-the-street homeless, but

living in my girlfriend's bedroom and a hotel—and, worst of all, broken emotionally. Dispirited, dejected, and deep in a financial hole.

She continued. "People from all walks of life hold you in such high esteem, and you are so gracious. Why don't you reach out to people? Why don't you tell them the kind of year you've had?" I didn't have an answer. Being the lawyer she was born to be, she kept digging. "Do you believe you are in this situation because of the choices that you have made?" she finally asked.

That word, "choices," hit me like a blow to the head and a punch to the gut. In the weeks to follow, it kept echoing over and over and over in my mind, like a bell going off.

I began to think intensely about the choices I had made in my life. How had I gone from business prominence to a position that felt like failure? Had I chosen poorly? Should I have continued working at LaFace? Should I have stayed single instead of getting married? Instead of walking away from business deals that represented great money but didn't feel aligned with who I am, should I have taken the money?

Those questions, constantly echoing in the back of my mind, forced me to get solid in my answers and in my choices.

During those tough weeks of self-appraisal, I came to realize that I've always taken ownership of choices that bring leanness or lack to my life—deciding not to work with Usher, for example, because I believed he needed my friendship more than my professional involvement—but I didn't take ownership of choices that bring me positive value and forward movement. I will allow one negative situation to weigh heavily on me, crushing me beneath it, and ignore the ninety-nine great situations that should be buoying my strength and lightening my load. I will take ownership of a financial setback, for example, but I won't take ownership of what I've done to create a strong family. Instead of appreciating all of the amazing opportunities that I maximize, I focus on the one or two opportunities that don't go the way I want them to.

I realized that by living only in the places where there was lack or hardship and by focusing so intently on disappointments and hurts—convincing myself that homing in on these failures would make me stronger, tougher, or more prepared next time I was in the same situation—I was choosing not to live in my power. By power I mean the positive, inborn strength and essence of who I am as a human being. I was, in fact, spending the vast majority of my time living in an extremely disempowered state. I was dwelling in absence, lack, and unfulfillment, instead of joy, presence, and satisfaction.

The truth was that there were many good—even great—things

GOD, WHAT AM I DOING WRONG?

One of my clients was struggling in her life and shared with me that she was waking up at four a.m. every day, praying feverishly for answers, but not getting any. "God, what am I doing wrong?" "What do I need to do differently?" "What do I need to change?" Every thought, every question was framed as a negative. I suggested to her the possibility that God is not attuned to that kind of question. Maybe the silence she was getting as a response was telling her that she wasn't doing anything wrong. Maybe she needed to develop a whole new mind-set, one that was 100 percent centered around what she was doing right. Maybe she needed to dwell in her strength and power instead. The next time we met, she told me she'd made a major breakthrough. She said that she woke up every morning, no matter how early, and took the opportunity to thank Him for the experiences during this time. In the end, once she changed her perspective, she realized this is an exciting time and she is learning. Now she can take those learnings and teach others that sometimes it's okay to "just be"!

all around me but I was only noticing the absences. I was defining myself by the places where things were missing in my life, counting the failures and setting aside the successes.

This realization that I was owning only my negative situations spurred me to make the choice to be fierce in everything I do, to take ownership of ME and what I bring to the table. Some of my choices, I realized, have been extremely empowering, successful ones. For example, I committed to being in the entertainment industry at the highest level, and I accomplished that goal against tremendous odds. I committed to having a loving, caring marriage, and productive, God-loving children, and that is my truth today. I committed to securing a publishing deal with a major publisher, and you are reading the manifestation of that. I committed to being a successful entrepreneur with a slate of top clients, and I've had a thriving business for almost twenty years.

There were also choices I made that may not have made sense to anyone—including myself at times—but were critical to my life journey and my growth as an empowerment speaker, life strategist, and author. Resigning from LaFace, for example, and walking away from hundreds of thousands of dollars brought more good things into my life than music industry success could have ever given me. Turning down opportunities that would have brought me tons of money but ran against my sense of personal integrity has allowed me to become a person that I deeply respect, and to build the foundation for Exponential Living.

Taking ownership of all of my choices, no matter the result, and living in them created a remarkable shift in my life. I began to live in my power—and in all the good situations my power had brought to me—instead of living in the negative places where my power was not presently manifest.

It's All About Choice

In my work with high achievers (including myself, as I am my first client!), I have discovered a surprising thing: Many of us don't own the choices we make. We make choices that give our true power away and we don't even know we're doing it. We pursue money, titles, degrees, access to influential people, and other outer goals in order to wrap ourselves in a package that says to the world we're successful. But inside we don't feel good enough. We don't feel powerful. We don't feel worthy of our success. It is, in fact, our lack of confidence that becomes the drive that pushes us onward. We keep telling ourselves that if we score one more victory, one more achievement, we'll feel powerful and fulfilled. We'll finally have proven ourselves.

But, of course, the one person who never believes that "proof" is YOU. You may feel full for a moment, a day, or a week, but then the emptiness settles back in, no matter what goals you achieve. That's because you don't really live in your power, in the positive essence of who you are. So even as you rack up trophies and victories and acquire all the outer symbols of success—money, possessions, prestige, promotions—those accomplishments land in the bottomless pit of your insecurity. Your life feels stressed and stretched and empty.

True power has nothing to do with the goals you achieve. True power comes from who you really, authentically are. This is the basic truth that eludes many high achievers and keeps them locked in an endless struggle for results and recognition.

High achievers (and many others as well) have trouble making the choice to live in the power of who they are. It is easier for them to get distracted by what they do, especially when they're really good at doing that thing.

But choosing to live in our true power is the most important thing any of us can do. That is the reason "Live in Your Power" is the first principle of Exponential Living. You must make this choice in order to live fully the other eight.

I repeat: Everything flows from your choice to live in your power.

True (Inner) Power

Many high achievers spend a lifetime chasing *symbols* of power and *trappings* of power, but all the real power we could possibly want or hope for already resides within us. Every person who walks this good green earth has access to an astonishing source of power that is, quite literally, limitless. It is as close to us as our next breath; all we need to do is recognize it and turn on the tap.

You can choose to have authentic power run your life. The way to do that is simply to base your actions and decisions on who you really are, not on who you are trying to tell the world you are.

For many years, I had tremendous outer success but I didn't feel any peace, and I definitely didn't feel powerful. I felt trapped, with a ceiling on my growth, and I was never present in the moment. I was constantly stressed, anxious, and overwhelmed by what I could have done differently or what I needed to do in the future to achieve the next . . . *something*. I rarely celebrated the achievements of today, because I needed to stay focused on the goal for tomorrow. I was worse than a gerbil running on a wheel—at least he knows when to get off! I kept running on *my* wheel, thinking that the deep-rooted misery I felt would go away with the next goal met, accomplishment achieved, client secured, or financial goal reached. Even as I continued to achieve these markers, none of them brought me peace or helped me feel grounded in power.

This power—which we all possess as our birthright—is inner power. It is the core essence of what God created you and me to be. When you choose to live a life of inner power, you no longer need to worry about what other people are doing; you need only worry about being true to yourself.

Inner power is impossible to fully describe in words, but it has the following characteristics.

INNER (TRUE) POWER IS:

Peaceful. It is quiet, still, and confident. It is, in fact, peace itself.

Cooperative. It does not thrive on conflict. It doesn't require winners and losers. Everyone can win.

Vertical. It flows from the deep roots of your being. It doesn't get its power from scoring "victories" in the physical world.

Inherent. It comes from who you are, not what you do.

Limitless. Its source is eternal and infinite. You can tap into it anytime, no matter how badly things are going or how defeated you feel, and it will always feed you energy.

Supportive. It aids you in doing what God designed you to do: fulfilling your true purpose.

Secure. It can't be taken away or diminished by others.

Connected. Its source is divine. It connects us all to one another and to the world itself. Pursuing true power brings us all closer together, not farther apart.

Loving. It's motivated by love, not fear.

EXTERNAL (FALSE) POWER IS:

Ego-driven. It arises from a desire to look good to the world.

Adversarial. It's all about one person or one group winning at the expense of others.

Horizontal. It comes from scoring conquests, victories, and achievements in the physical world.

Extrinsic. It flows from what you do, not who you are.

Limited. It must be constantly regenerated. It never lasts or satisfies for long.

Self-consumed. You're limited in everything you do and can't see beyond yourself.

Insecure. There is always a fear of losing it or having it taken away by others.

Separate. It is individualistic and cut off from others.

Fearful. Motivated by fear, not love.

Success and Significance

When high achievers make the choice to live in their authentic power, a paradigm shift occurs, allowing them to accept that they can have both success and *significance*. We stop caring so much about how we *appear* to others in our world—our communities, our families, our work teams—and begin to care about how we *contribute* to our world. We start wanting to use our energies in ways that matter. It's not that we want to stop being successful; it's that we want our success to serve something greater than our ego or our fears.

Earlier I talked about the four realities that high achievers eventually come up against, which I call "Pain Points." Some of us face only one or two of these in our lifetimes; some face all four:

What's next?—I've achieved my goals. I love what I do, but I know there's more that I want to do. How do I create more bandwidth and margin in my life?

Now what?—I've reached my goal and I'm ready to move on to something else. I have more than one dream.

Is this it?—I have the life I've dreamed about and worked so hard to achieve, but I'm unfulfilled.

How do I live?—I was "succeeding," but now a major life change has been forced on me—having a baby, losing a spouse, divorce, empty nest, facing a health crisis, losing a job.

All of these challenges can be seen as a call to shift from a success-only mind-set to a mind-set that includes significance, which I think of as a broadened definition of success. Many high achievers struggle when they hit one of these pain points. They fear abandoning the security of what has worked for them so far and adopting the faith it takes to move into uncharted waters. Shane Battier, in the article I quoted earlier, says, "[A]s I got closer to the end and started to think about the unexplored wilderness of my postbasketball life, I felt something completely new. It was anxiety, fear, the pressure of expectations."

Be ready: obstacles may arise in the face of change.

Most of these obstacles are generated by the ego. Why? Because the ego is that part of you that is completely dependent on external power—whether it be praise or money or titles—and it doesn't like giving up control. For many high achievers, the ego has been running the show since childhood. External success feeds the ego and makes it stronger and stronger. And so *of course* the ego doesn't want to give up its position of power. *Of course* it's going to fight to maintain its dominance over us. It wants to live in outer success, not inner satisfaction.

My Shift from Success-Only to Significance

When I was shifting my career focus away from marketing, my ego kicked up big-time. After all, I had built a solid brand for myself. I was highly respected and had influence. My company had been providing me a substantial income and a comfortable lifestyle. I liked all the goodies I had earned. My ego did not appreciate this pull I was feeling to make a move toward significance that might appear to be a step backward.

What was that pull? Well, since I was seven years old, I had known I was going to be a public speaker. As a child, naturally, I didn't know what that profession was called or even that it was a profession, but I knew I was a talker. Lord, could I talk. I commanded attention from a very young age and was never afraid of being in front of a group. But when I reached adulthood, I set this gift aside to pursue other things.

As I grew into my forties, though, the call toward speaking began to reannounce itself more and more loudly. I knew my season had come to transition full-time to public speaking. I knew not only that this path was my purpose, but also that I was doggone good at it and had a powerful message for the world. But I really struggled. Every fear, doubt, and insecurity I've ever had flooded my mind, heart, spirit, and soul. I felt a powerful resistance that wanted to keep me locked in my current success rather than allowing me to broaden my definition of success to include serving and significance.

When we are in this struggle for Exponential Living, our ego will try every trick it knows to sidetrack us and hinder our journey. *I'm too old. I make too much money to do something else. My spouse won't support me. My friends/colleagues will think I've lost my mind. The time, effort, money, and sacrifice I put into this transition will be wasted.*

The ego will attack us where we are most vulnerable. I have talked with many high achievers who have experienced this internal struggle. When they were faced with transition, their ego fought them like crazy. Many of them gave up the fight and stayed locked in their ego-driven success state. Many of those who pressed through to the other side, though, have opened the door to Exponential Living.

The way to make it through to the other side is by taking ownership of your true power, the power of peace. This means releasing yourself from your ego, your pride, and your need for validation. This means getting comfortable with what may appear to be backward movement in order to understand that you are actually at a slingshot moment in your life.

The way you can do this is by following the P.O.W.E.R. steps I'm going to share with you right now.

P.O.W.E.R.

In my work with clients over the years, I have identified five essential steps that we can all use to claim our true power and stay grounded in it. These five steps can be used when making any decision or when trying to put any new change into action in your life. The five steps are:

P **Perspective**—Adopt a point of view that empowers you.

O **Ownership**—Own what is important to you.

W **Wisdom**—Identify your one or two next best steps.

E **Engagement**—Commit to the implementation of those steps.

R **Reward**—Stay consistently engaged with the process in order to experience the positive outcomes.

When we commit to the process of living in our power—through the P.O.W.E.R. steps—our purpose and our motivation align and we can freely transition from ego-only success to Exponential Living. We can move to a place where we're more concerned about how we serve the world than how we serve ourselves. Interestingly enough, when we do that, our career success often takes a leap forward as well.

Let's take a little closer look at the five P.O.W.E.R. steps.

Perspective

> Many people die after living a long life with their dreams never fulfilled because they don't have a vision to guide them through the process. Vision is born in the soul of a person who is consumed with the tension between what is and what could be.
>
> —PASTOR ANDY STANLEY

If you want to make a change in your life or respond effectively to a challenge, the way you look at the situation—your perspective—is critical. Do you see the situation as a roadblock, a piece of bad luck, a crushing blow? If so, you will not be able to resolve it. You have already declared it too big for you to handle. On the other hand, if you see the situation as an opportunity, a blessing, or a chance to elevate your game, you are halfway to a positive resolution.

When you come to a crossroads, ask: What do I see? What is my vision? Everyone reading these words has a dream. The difference between dreamers and those who achieve their dream is vision. Vision (as I define it) is how you see yourself getting to that dream, how you see yourself accomplishing it.

I've had the good fortune to work with Steve Harvey, both as a speaker at his Act Like a Success Conference and as an instructor for his Radical Success Institute. Steve has shared the story that at one time he was twenty million dollars in tax debt. Can you imagine that—twenty million dollars? But he had vision. He had a bold perspective. He saw the power within himself to transform his situation. He felt God was directing him to create a media empire that would help empower people, while also generating enough income to pay off his tax debt. And that's exactly what he did.

A very sad contrast to Steve Harvey's success story is the fashion designer L'Wren Scott. Reportedly, she had six million dollars in tax debt. That concealed debt, paired with other unknowable tragic circumstances, led the seemingly successful Scott to take her own life. So you have one person who was twenty million dollars in tax debt and saw his way past the problem. You have another person, six million dollars in tax debt, who couldn't see to the other side of it. Two different perspectives on similar situations, two very different outcomes. You may not be in danger of taking your actual life, but what other things are you "committing suicide" to or giving up on in your life? Relationships? Potential conversations with your children? Special moments with your spouse? Business opportunities? All because of a limiting perspective.

My Shift in Perspective

I can testify to the power that perspective can have. A few years ago I spent a week in Guatemala with John Maxwell, along with the heads of his companies and 150 John Maxwell Team members. We taught leadership principles to over twenty thousand Guatemalans in the seven streams of influence (government, business, academics, faith, military, public service, and sports).

This was my first mission work and it was life changing for me. When the trip was over, one of my fellow team members asked me how my vision had elevated and expanded after the trip. As I thought about her question, I realized my vision has always been strong. It's like a hot-air balloon I'm constantly filling. But in Guatemala I came to recognize the sandbags that were holding me down. I realized I was holding on to ideas, mind-sets, fears, doubts, insecurities, and relationships that were like weights holding down my vision, just the way sandbags hold down a hot-air balloon.

What were these sandbags? Well, things like the massive to-do list that kept me trapped in busy action, the overabundance of time I spent looking outside myself for power that was already inside of me, and my habit of defining success as a number in my bank account. Another sandbag—hard to admit—was my company, GLUE. This one was my baby, so it was tough to release. I loved my company and

I loved how we served in the world. I loved the clients we worked with. I loved my team. But GLUE was holding me down from the power of Exponential Living.

Seeing these impediments as sandbags was a crucial step for me. It gave me perspective. It allowed me to discover what the real problem was and empowered me to take action. It gave me the clarity to become very intentional with my time and to refocus my vision.

And so, after seventeen years, I closed my company and began shedding my "sandbags." And now that those weights have been released, my vision has materialized and I have shifted into the rhythm and flow of my true purpose with renewed perspective.

Ownership

> You either walk inside your story and own it or you stand outside your story and hustle for your worthiness.
>
> —BRENÉ BROWN

Ownership is the next crucial step. Ownership means laying claim to what's true and authentic to you and focusing on that. It means recognizing that your power doesn't come from how you posture or position yourself in relationships or from the "wins" you score in the world; your power comes from your ownership of your own truth in every situation.

Psalms 110:2 says, "Rule in the midst of your enemies." This doesn't mean being a dictator or a jerk—quite the opposite. It means taking control of your life in a positive and empowering way and living in the true power that is within you. This power doesn't come from your job title or your position; it comes from *you*. Anytime you are feeling disempowered, you need to realize that the cause of this is not a negative bank account, conflicts with your spouse, problematic coworkers, an unfair boss, or disrespectful clients; the cause is the lack of power you have allowed to exist in your own mind, heart, and soul. In order to pursue the path of Exponential Living, you must learn to take ownership of that power.

Being Offended Means Not Owning Your Power

A good friend of mine had worked at a company for nearly two decades. Promises had been made to her about advancement, but there had been some managerial changes at the company, and those promises had not been delivered on. In fact, she went from being a direct report to her VP (which allowed her to be one step away from the CEO) to having another person, with less experience and tenure, positioned between her and her VP. She felt these changes had been made out of spite, and that she'd been given a demotion instead of the promised promotion. As a result, her work, and her relationships at work, began to suffer. This was causing her anguish, frustration, and borderline depression. She was filtering her entire work experience through lenses tinged with negativity and colored by the perceived slights and the offenses that had built up over time.

I encouraged her to stop wasting energy being offended and remember that she was a skilled, knowledgeable, and highly competent manager who was vital to the running of the company. She needed to take ownership of those truths about her. She took my advice to heart and had a hard conversation with her CEO, where she was able to speak her truth. This allowed her to release the energy of offense and reclaim her power. She's now more at peace, and her work relationships have vastly improved. "Just yesterday," she reports, "someone on my team said I am an inspiration because she's watched me handle the challenges and witnessed my transformation." Her actual job situation didn't change—she didn't receive the promotion—but she became much more impactful in her position and happier in her life.

Ownership Equals Focus

> If your calendar is full, you are ineffective.
>
> —TIM SANDERS

> It's not the daily increase but daily decrease. Hack away at the unessential.
>
> —BRUCE LEE

Many high achievers have lives that are "out of focus." They're busy, yes, and they're achieving goals, yes, but those goals represent only a small portion of what they deeply and truthfully care about.

Many people live their entire lives, cradle to grave, in such an out-of-focus way. They fail to own the things that are vital to them.

What are your true, authentic desires? I'm not asking what you think you should be doing or what can make you money, but rather: What is truly authentic to you? What matters to you? Family? Artistic expression? Spiritual growth? Community organizing? How much focus do you put on those things?

When I'm doing talks and workshops, I'll often ask the group to make private lists of their top five values. Then I'll ask them to estimate how much time they actually spend every day focusing on those things. Without fail, I see faces in the audience looking awed, upset, and/or appalled as they realize how little time they devote to the things they value and that mean the most to them.

LIVE IN YOUR P.O.W.E.R.

A big part of the problem is focus. We diffuse our focus by try-ing to do too many things. Waaaaay too many. We have to-do lists a mile long.

Shrinking My To-Do List

In December of 2014, I did one of the most courageous things I've ever done in my life. I sat down and removed literally 80 percent of the items from my to-do list. That's right, 80 percent. Gone. I left only three things remaining:

1. Get a publishing deal.
2. Increase my speaking engagements.
3. Lose twenty-five pounds.

That's all. I took ownership of those three things only.

Anything that didn't align with, support, or add to those three things came off my to-do list. That meant there were some worthy goals that had to be cut. In truth, though, none of those things were really getting accomplished anyway. Because the way I'd been working was by juggling twenty balls. I was keeping them all in the air, some-how, but I wasn't really getting anything done. And I was exhausted.

I had to get focused. So I did.

Cutting down my to-do list allowed me to discover three impor-tant things:

1. The majority of the items on my list were never missed once they were gone. There was absolutely no effect from taking them off! This told me they didn't need to be there in the first place.

71

2. Timing matters. Many of the items I had on my to-do list in December 2014 couldn't really be tackled until months or years later. By putting them on my list too soon, I was allowing them to weigh on my psyche unnecessarily.

3. Many of the items on my list could be delegated.

All of these lessons applied to both my personal life and my professional life.

When I removed the extraneous things from my to-do list, here's what happened with item number one, get a publishing deal.

Books are sold based on proposals, and I'd been working on the proposal for the book you're reading for seven years. That's right, seven years! It was one of the twenty balls I was juggling. Every time I submitted a new draft to my agents, they'd say, "Nope, Sheri, that's not it." Back to the drawing board.

The proposal went through at least half a dozen major rewrites, and each time the book would drift further and further away from my original vision.

Then I took the 80 percent off my to-do list. Without all of the distractions, I was able to get focused. With this clarity, I wrote from my heart and my true vision was captured in my book proposal. When I submitted this version to my agents, they called me, ecstatic. "Sheri, this is it! You've found your voice. This is a great proposal!" I literally wept with gratitude. Four weeks after that, I had offers on the table from four major publishers. I chose to go with Penguin Random House.

The power of focus.

The power of ownership.

I strongly recommend you look at your to-do list and pare it down to the essentials. Do this every six months and you won't believe what you will accomplish.

Wisdom

Wisdom is the recognition that positive change doesn't happen without a plan. It is the ability to discern what should be done now versus what should be done later, and to recognize areas where you might need help. It is also the ability to distinguish opportunities from distractions.

The steps you choose to take flow from having a clear Perspective on where you want your life to be going next and Ownership of where you are right now. They are based on your overall vision for your life and on a true acceptance of your skills, talents, and values at this time in your life, as well as your authentic desires.

The simple essence of wisdom is to create a plan for the *one* or *two*—at the most *three*—best next steps. Not the sixty-page business plan, the ten-page marketing plan, or the three-page executive summary—those have their place of importance too, but for now the focus should be on the most important one or two steps to move you forward.

What to Focus On

Wisdom is crucial when you're whittling down your big to-do list. You need to be smart and put your energy where it will do the most good. That means recognizing actions that didn't need to be on the list in the first place. It also means recognizing actions that don't make sense from a timing perspective—those things that can't get done effectively until later this year, or two years from now. Some goals are dependent on getting other things done first.

Focus only on those things that truly need to get done now and can get done now. As soon as those things are accomplished, you can move on to what needs to be done next.

Make a Plan

Do you have a clear idea of where you want to take your life, not just your career? Okay, then, what's your plan? Is it written down? My favorite book says, "Write the vision and make it plain."

Making a plan really comes down to a simple question: What are you going to do differently? You are reading this book because you are ready for change. You are ready for transformation. Change is not just about what you are going to do, but also about what you're going to stop doing. Define success for yourself, determine your one or two— at the most three—best next steps, and then go for it.

As you're making a plan, identify those things you're going to need help with, and start lining up that help. This is especially hard for us high achievers, who tend to take on everything ourselves. Many of us have help we can call on—for example, teenage kids who could be doing many things around the house (if they weren't doing twenty-five extracurricular activities).

Protect the Plan

> The doors that are opened may not be yours. That's why we need perspective.
>
> —DEXTER GODFREY

As important as it is to make a plan, it is equally important to protect that plan. For high achievers that often means learning to distinguish opportunities from distractions.

I am a founding partner of the global John Maxwell Team. John is the world's number one leadership expert—not only for the sales of his books, but for the sheer number of people he has trained (he recently trained leaders in Fiji, which culminated his vision to train leaders in all 196 countries. Mission accomplished!).

In October 2014, a fellow John Maxwell Team member and I hosted a location for John Maxwell's inaugural Live 2 Lead Simulcast. The following month, I signed the contract to host again in 2015. This simulcast was being televised in only three hundred locations around the world, and I was granted the exclusive right to serve as the host for the only venue in Atlanta proper. Not only would this be a great marketing opportunity for me and my brand, but it also expanded my public alignment with the greatest leadership teacher of our era. Added bonus: I could also keep all the profits myself. Needless to say, this was a tremendous opportunity.

Or was it? As I thought about it, I realized that as great as this opportunity was, it did not align with my new focus. In fact, it would have been a monumental distraction. I needed to be promoting speaking engagements for Sheri Riley, not my wonderful friend and mentor John Maxwell. So I removed this "opportunity" from my to-do list.

An opportunity is only an opportunity if it serves the goals you are presently working on. One of the biggest challenges for high achievers is to recognize distractions wrapped up in pretty bows to look like opportunities.

Engagement

Engagement is your pledge to commit yourself to implementing the changes you identified in the Wisdom step. And remember, you're going to be making changes in many areas of your life, not just your career.

Life is a constant journey of victories and defeats. Victories are easy to handle, of course (and the Oscar goes to . . .). Setbacks and challenges, not so much. How you deal with setbacks can either make you stronger or cause you to give up, give in, or feel defeated. If you wish to remain engaged, you must be properly prepared for hardships from the get-go. That means expecting obstacles, great big NOs and major smackdowns. Entering the battle unprepared is like playing professional football without pads and a helmet. Your body will not survive the constant assaults you receive playing the game. *Preparation* is the key to getting through the NOs, and getting through the NOs is the key to victory.

Preparation equals expectation.

To prepare is to have a plan. That means thinking about the obstacles you might face ahead of time, and having contingency steps ready to implement when those obstacles arise. You *will* face obstacles; the key is to not let those obstacles come as a shock to you. If you do, you will find yourself feeling defeated and disengaging from the process. On the other hand, if you mentally prepare for obstacles and have a plan in place for dealing with them, you'll be able to remain engaged.

A good example of this is investing in the stock market. If you don't have a financial plan and you are unprepared for the inevitable volatility that occurs in the market, then you will panic the first time you see the price of your stocks going down, and you will sell them at the worst possible time. If, however, you have a good plan in place and are mentally and emotionally prepared for the natural ups and downs of the market, you will stick to the plan when volatility occurs. You'll remain engaged with your investment and ride out the storm.

A plan is not a rigid set of predetermined responses; it is a flexible and evolving mind-set that anticipates pushback and helps you find the courage to work through it.

High achievers often know how to get through NOs in business but not necessarily in other areas, such as relationships and personal empowerment. In these areas they turn the NOs they receive into solid obstacles. "I can't pursue my true calling because my wife won't support me." "I can't start a business now because I need to pay my kids' tuition." In business, they would trample such false obstacles to dust, but in more crucial areas of life, they let the NOs win.

Getting through the NOs requires only one thing: *having a little more courage than fear.* It requires having just enough courage to push through the next NO. Worry about the next obstacle later; for now, you only need to get through the one in front of you. And I know you can find enough courage for that.

Reward

The final P.O.W.E.R. step is Reward.

It is essential, when tackling change, to have a specific, tangible, and satisfying reward in mind. Otherwise you'll run out of gas. If the only reason you're making a change is because you think you "should," or "it's the right thing to do," that motivation—although admirable—will eventually break down. The reward you are aiming for must feel intensely rewarding to you personally. And you must take care to savor it when it arrives, as well as savoring each small reward along the way.

Denise Hendricks, a client of mine, is an award-winning television producer and writer. She is currently a senior producer for HLN (CNN Headline News) and has been in the news and entertainment business for twenty years. She told me this:

> *Going through the P.O.W.E.R. process helped me see all the ways that I was giving my personal power away—to my job, to my relationships, to my community commitments, to everyone but myself. . . .*
>
> *Since doing a P.O.W.E.R. review of my life, the changes have been astounding, on many different levels. In general, I can say:*
>
> *I trust myself more.*

I love myself more.

I believe in myself more.

I am more confident.

I am more powerful.

I now say YES to things I was fearful of saying YES to before. I say NO to things that I know won't further my purpose, my passion, or the work I am doing to bless/help others.

In my spiritual life, my daily prayer and meditation is now "consistent and crucial." Healthwise, I had already lost about fifteen to sixteen pounds, but now I've lost twenty-four pounds and have managed to keep it off.

I am more confident in my relationships with men—in asking for what I want and being honest about my feelings. . . .

I also made some changes in how I approach my finances and in the type of energy my thoughts bring to this area of my life. This has brought an undeniable sense of peace.

And those are just a few of the changes she shared with me about the life-changing and enduring rewards she has reaped with Exponential Living. The key to getting to Reward is consistency. And the key to consistency is to recognize your triggers. . . .

Healthy and Unhealthy Triggers

Each of us has mental and behavioral triggers—things that "set us off" in a reflexive, almost unconscious way. Some of these are healthy and some are unhealthy. These triggers either support (healthy) or sabotage (unhealthy) our plans. For example, I have a psychological relationship with food. Many circumstances in my life lead back to my good old friend, food. When I'm happy, I celebrate with food.

When I'm sad, I console myself with food. When I'm anxious, bored, tired, frustrated, I . . . You get the picture.

Every emotion can be a trigger for me to eat. As you can imagine, this is not helpful, especially when my goal is to—oh, I don't know— *lose twenty-five pounds*!

On the healthy side, I can allow emotional situations to trigger my innate sense of competition. I'm a born athlete, and I have a competitive streak a mile wide. When I want to make a change, first I stage a competition within myself to set a goal, and then I envision myself in a competition to achieve that goal. For example, I enjoy the challenge of competing with myself to eat healthy, balanced meals. Each time I fit into a pair of jeans I couldn't wear before or catch a glimpse of my body taking on a toned shape feels like a victory. The immediate reward I get from that is the deep satisfaction I feel at the end of the day knowing that I defeated my negative triggers and supported myself toward gaining the long-term rewards I am seeking.

So my healthy trigger defeats my unhealthy trigger . . . usually.

The key to staying consistent in your behavior is to recognize and acknowledge both your unhealthy and healthy triggers. Name them. Call them out. Look them in the eye. Knowing your unhealthy triggers prepares you for the challenges you will face. Knowing your healthy triggers tells you what weapon you can pull out when the demons are dancing.

To consistently make healthy choices, it's vital to spend time thinking about the long-term rewards you expect to get and imagining the way your life will *feel* when you achieve those rewards. Do this imagining on a daily basis—when you get up in the morning, when you go to bed at night, and at other times throughout the day.

None of us can remain motivated toward a long-range goal unless we believe in the real rewards that will come from reaching that goal. Making a change because we think we "should" is not enough. It is the eager and passionate anticipation of great rewards that allows us to override the short-term buzz we get from giving in to our negative triggers. Reward is the fuel for consistency.

The ultimate rewards for living in your P.O.W.E.R. are peace, clarity, and courage.

When you make the choice to live in your true power, your definition of success begins to change. Suddenly the exterior success you were chasing in order to validate yourself to others no longer seems so important. That doesn't mean you grow lazy or unambitious. Far from it. What it does mean is that you expand your definition of success to include things like passionate relationships, soul-nourishing work, and the fulfillment of making a true contribution to the world. As you stop wasting energy on things that don't really matter to you, you find you have far more energy and resources for pursuing the things that do matter.

These are some of the things we'll explore in upcoming chapters.

Vision, Action, Results

In each chapter, this **Vision, Action, Results** section will offer you exercises that I use in my coaching practice and workshops. Each one is designed to crystallize one of the 9 Principles of Exponential Living in your mind and in your life.

Here are two exercises aimed at living your P.O.W.E.R.

Exercise 1: Write Your Obituary

This three-part exercise has been extremely effective in preparing clients to get the most out of the P.O.W.E.R. process.

STEP 1:

Write your obituary. Yes, that's right. Write an obituary about yourself, but write it from the point of view of someone who knows you well and is very honest. This might be a spouse, a child, a best friend, a business partner, a coworker . . . Write whatever you think they would really say about you, even if it's . . . well, unflattering. Don't censor, analyze, or critique your thoughts. (Time limit: take five minutes to complete.)

STEP 2:

Now . . .

Write a second obituary for yourself. This time write what you would *want* to see written about you when you die. Don't hold back. Write the things you truly would want people to remember about you. Include accomplishments, but also include personal qualities you want to be known for and ways you want to affect the lives of others. Include the interests you want to have pursued with passion. Again, be totally honest and don't overthink it. (Time limit: take five minutes to complete.)

STEP 3:

Now answer the following questions. Again, writing the answers down is recommended.

>> What are the differences between the two obituaries?
>> What do the obituaries say about what is most important to me?
>> How much time am I spending working toward or doing the things I identified as important in obituary number two?
>> Who are the people that mean the most to me?
>> How much quality time am I spending with these people now?

>> If I continue to live my life as I am currently living it, do I think obituary number two has a good chance of coming to pass?

>> What am I doing in my life right now that is helping obituary number two to unfold?

>> What are three to five changes I can make now to help me have the obituary that truly represents the life I desire to live?

>> What three to five things am I presently doing that align with my desired obituary?

Exercise 2: P.O.W.E.R. Diagnostic and Tune-Up

When you want your car to perform more powerfully, you ask your technician to run a thorough diagnostic and tune-up. The following questions are designed to help you diagnose where your P.O.W.E.R. leaks are and to help you make the choice to live in your true power.

P PERSPECTIVE: WHAT IS MY VISION?

>> My dream is where I want to go. My vision is seeing the steps I must take to pursue my dream. What is my vision for my life?

>> What major obstacles/problems am I facing in my life right now?

>> How can I change my perspective on these problems in order to see them as opportunities?

O OWNERSHIP: HOW WILL I FOCUS?

>> What do I need to remove from my "to-do" list?

>> List three to five areas of my life where I need to take ownership.

>> List three negative outcomes in my life that are results of my failing to make courageous choices.

>> What are my top five values, principles, pursuits, and ideas that I consider essential to a good life for me and my loved ones?

>> How much time do I spend per week on each of these values?

>> List three reasons I have not spent quality time living the values that are most important to me.

W WISDOM: WHAT IS MY PLAN?

>> What are the top three goals I want to achieve in the next year?

>> What are the one or two or, at the most, three most important next steps for each of these goals?

>> List three current opportunities that are actually distractions in my life.

E ENGAGEMENT: WHAT ADJUSTMENTS DO I NEED TO MAKE?

>> What do I need to do to hold myself accountable for taking these actions?

>> What help do I need with my plan?

>> Who can help hold me accountable for my new choices?

R REWARD: HOW WILL I STAY CONSISTENT?

>> What are the triggers that stop or hinder me from staying consistent?

>> List three to five things I am presently doing that align with my desired obituary. What rewards am I gaining from these actions?

>> What are five important rewards (payoffs) I expect to gain from pursuing the goals I identified in the Wisdom step?

>> How important are these rewards to me "living in my power"?

EXPONENTIAL CONVERSATION

For this chapter, I had the pleasure and privilege of sitting down with Ceasar Mitchell, president of the Atlanta City Council. For the past fifteen years, Ceasar has been a tireless advocate for public safety, economic revitalization, and education for the city of Atlanta. As an attorney, politician, husband, parent, and churchgoer, he knows a thing or two about putting it all together exponentially.

I chose him for this chapter because, to me, he is a great example of living one's power from the inside out. Though he is an accomplished and externally powerful person—prominent attorney in a global law firm, city council president of a major city, and running for mayor of Atlanta—he does not derive his power from his job titles or political positions. He would be the same powerfully centered person if he were working in a homeless shelter or as an elementary-school teacher. He is someone who leads others by leading himself.

SHERI RILEY: When you think about your personal perspective, your personal vision, what do you see?

CEASAR MITCHELL: Perspective is really . . . how you see the world when you get up in the morning. The biggest thing for me when it comes to perspective is staying positive, always looking at things through a positive lens, if at all possible. Now sometimes you have to look at things very, very realistically, but there's still always a way to look at it from a positive perspective. And that's something I have to do every morning. You can't take for granted that what you saw on Monday morning when you woke up bright and early—that what you wanted your week to look like and what you wanted your month, or year, or next five years to look like—will stay the same. It's something that you're going to have to go back to and work on and bear down on the next morning. I think it's a daily process of just staying positive, and visualizing, and moving that vision forward in a very positive fashion.

SHERI RILEY: Ownership is what we choose to focus on. What do you focus on that allows you to live in your power?

CEASAR MITCHELL: What I focus on really are my daughters and my wife, simple as that. When I think about what it is I have to do every day, when I think about what it is I must say and do and how I must treat people, I think about my daughters. And I think about the fact that everything I do is creating a legacy for them, and that legacy is either going to be a positive one or a negative one.

SHERI RILEY: What comes to mind for you when you think about wisdom?

CEASAR MITCHELL: Wisdom really is the product, or the sum, of knowledge and understanding, and the first thing you must have knowledge and understanding of is yourself. And you have to know what your strengths are, you have to know what your weaknesses are, and you have to make a commitment to be in growth mode. The third thing beyond knowing yourself and being in growth mode is understanding that every day ain't gonna feel good.

SHERI RILEY: Right.

CEASAR MITCHELL: And you've got to be accountable to yourself and accountable to others, because there's no mission that is accomplished in a solo fashion. You might be able to get a couple things done, win a couple of battles by yourself, but no great things have happened in the history of mankind without having a team of people who work together. And working together requires accountability. So all of those things kind of come together when you're putting that step forward to execute your plan. And executing your plan really is about being out there, being present every day, having a vision for where you want your work to be, and how you want it to serve and make a difference for people.

SHERI RILEY: I say there are four pain points we come up against: "What's next?," "Now what?," "Is this it?," and "How do I live?" Have you encountered any of those four pain points yet?

CEASAR MITCHELL: What you're really talking about is this notion of change. A buddy of mine said, "Ceasar, dynamic people have to 'repot' themselves every seven years or so." If I didn't have that little nugget of wisdom, then when I came to moments of change, which naturally occur, I would just freak out, rather than say, "You know what? This may be a 'repotting' moment. I may have to take all the old soil out—knowing all the nutrients have been pulled from it—and put in some new soil." Refresh and renew.

SHERI RILEY: I love that.

CEASAR MITCHELL: That's something that's given me a lot of guidance and solace over the years. And encouragement. You've got to have the courage to actually make the change, and then go ahead and make the transition.

SHERI RILEY: What do you do that is centered around your personal development?

CEASAR MITCHELL: Well, a couple of things. Number one, personal development is about self-reflection and meditation and continuing to pour knowledge into yourself, and also, frankly, about putting yourself in scenarios of growth. And what that means is putting yourself around people who are smarter than you, people who have license to challenge you and tell you that your "poo-poo" doesn't smell that good.

I'm a fellow with the Aspen Institute, the Henry Crown Fellowship. And it's a fellowship program that brings together young people under the age of forty-five who have excelled in the business sector—in leadership—in some way. It's a very small group—every year it's about twenty people—and we go through basically what is two years' worth of leadership development and personal growth. My point is that you would look at it from the outside and think that it's all about making you a better leader, like, in whatever field you are in—whether you're an entrepreneur, an elected leader, a general counsel, or a businessperson. What I found, though—because this is a fellowship experience, with relationships that will last for a lifetime—is that we didn't just have a journey of how to be better leaders; we had a journey of self-exploration. I learned that people want the same things out of life—that is, peace, wisdom, clarity, energy, and resolve. And, as much as the people in this group have accomplished, they also want confidence and security.

SHERI RILEY: When I say "Exponential Living," what do you think?

CEASAR MITCHELL: What comes to mind is living such that one plus one doesn't equal two. One plus one equals something more than two, and finding those things within ourselves and within those around us and within our environment and community that will add to that equation such that one plus one doesn't equal two; it equals something infinitely more.

I AM CEASAR MITCHELL AND I AM EXPONENTIAL LIVING.

Key Takeaways

> » There is always a way to view things from a positive perspective.
> » To have Wisdom, the first thing you must know and understand is yourself.
> » When you live in your true power, you don't have to try to be the most powerful person in the room. You can surround yourself with people even more talented than you are, knowing that nothing of great value is accomplished solo.
> » Sometimes you need to "repot" yourself so that you can continue to grow.

Healthy Living Is More Than Just a Diet

I realized I wanted a life outside of my work. I was doing three films a year. I didn't have a family. I didn't have a social life. Once I put value on my life, which I didn't before, I think my work got better.

—SANDRA BULLOCK

When most high achievers think about healthy living, they focus in on two narrow areas: diet and exercise. That's probably because it's easy to set quantifiable goals in those areas. Progress can be tracked. Objectives can be measured. Many high achievers can be good at diet and exercise (if they choose to be). But still their lives are not healthy. That's because they don't include in their health consciousness *the most important* aspect of healthy living: relationships.

Several studies have shown the connection between relationships and health. People who have active, meaningful relationships in their lives live longer and have less depression, serious injury, and illness than those who do not. They heal faster and enjoy life more. Thriving, loving, active relationships—with ourselves, with our loved ones, and with God—are essential to human health.

And yet, relationships cannot be measured or quantified, which helps explain why many high achievers do not give them a tenth of the attention they deserve. For high achievers, relationships often become "background noise," while their business and career goals become the foreground.

A Question of Values

Virtually everyone I have ever spoken to—and this includes both high achievers and non–high achievers—rates relationships with family, friends, spouses, and other loved ones as one of their top values in life. But high achievers typically spend their time and pledge their commitment elsewhere.

A friend of mine, Kidada Muhammad, who's an entrepreneur and owns the event-planning firm Simply the Best Events, is also a wife and a mother. One day we met for tea to discuss business opportunities. At that time, I still had my consulting firm, GLUE, and was looking for an event planner to collaborate with. As we discussed business opportunities, I sensed a heaviness in Kidada.

"How's everything going in your life?" I asked.

It was as if a pressure valve had been released. Words came tumbling out of her mouth in a torrent. She shared with me the truths and challenges of being a wife, a new mom, an entrepreneur, and a woman trying to develop herself. It was clear that, like most high achievers I talk to, she was feeling overwhelmed.

I asked, "Kidada, what do you value?"

She gathered herself and said, "What do you mean?"

"What are the top five things that you value in your life?"

She started with the expected list toppers. "I value my husband and my daughter."

"What else?" I asked.

She sat for a minute, really thinking. Then she said, "Laughter. I feel like I don't have enough of it in my life. I feel like it's reserved for children and as an adult I just want to laugh and have fun with people."

"Now, tell me how much time you commit to each of those values," I said.

I knew my question had a major impact on her, because she became emotional as she pondered. "I don't spend any time on most of the things I value most and the ones I do spend time on, it's definitely not enough."

Her answer was sad but expected.

We all know that relationships are the most important thing in life. Then why do so many of us spend so much time chasing work goals and so little time nurturing our relationships and laughing together like children?

I think it comes down to the way we value *outcomes*.

Value and Outcomes

High achievers value career outcomes more than "personal life" outcomes.

For example, we often *say* we want the best for our children. We *say* we want our children to grow into amazing, productive adults. But in reality two things typically happen: either we don't spend time with our kids, or we do spend time with them but we are mentally checked out when we do so. We're thinking more about the cake we need to bake for the birthday party than the child whom the party is celebrating.

It all boils down to the fact that we don't really value the *outcome* of time spent with our families. "Kid time" does not produce a "hard" result we can measure or see plotted out on a line graph. Time with our children can become an obligation, another thing we have to check off our to-do list. We dutifully put ourselves in the presence of our families, but we are not present *with* them. This is not a truth that we want to admit, but it's the truth that robs us of our peace because it's one of our biggest internal conflicts.

By contrast, the time we spend on business projects leads toward hard outcomes we can get behind. We win the contract. We impress the boss. We get the promotion. We get the raise.

Think about it and be honest. Does your behavior say that you value relationship outcomes as much as career outcomes?

Of course we all want our children to feel important and our spouses to feel desired. Or maybe we want to meet someone special that we enjoy spending time with. But somehow we convince ourselves that those things will just *happen*. Spontaneously and without our effort. We take them for granted. We even tell ourselves that our heavy focus on career advancement benefits our loved ones as much as us. "When I focus on my career I earn more money, which means I can buy more things for my children and take more vacations with my spouse." Or maybe we tell ourselves, "More success will put me in a better position to find the right partner and eventually get married."

True, but if your success is constantly coming at the expense of being *present* to your life and your loved ones, then something has gone adrift.

You must shift your mind-set regarding how you value both the time you spend with loved ones and the *outcome* of that time. If you look at "relationship time" as an obligation to check off your list so you can get back to your *real* work, that's the energy you will bring to it. Instead you must *truly value* relationship time and be present for it. And you must learn to value "soft" outcomes such as building self-confidence in your children, creating trust in your marriage, and solidifying your friendships. These outcomes can't be tracked with metrics like you use at work, but they are real nonetheless. In fact, they are *the most real thing.*

Hit film producer Will Packer, whom you'll meet in the Exponential Conversation in the "Stop Working, Start Maximizing" chapter, recently spoke to me about the "sacrifices" he makes to live with his family in Atlanta rather than in Hollywood:

> *Many people in Hollywood say I can make more money if I lived in LA instead of keeping my home and family in Atlanta. And yeah, I could make more money or have a few more meetings, but what they don't understand is my family is my everything. Coming to Atlanta, being with my family and friends in Atlanta, revitalizes me, gives me my creative energy, my insightful edge, and refreshes me to maintain my ability to engage and connect with people. See, this is what keeps me aligned with my values and my goals, which makes me a better businessman and producer. And I'm doing pretty well for myself. [Seven number one movies to date.] What wouldn't work for me is to make another million or ten million dollars and lose my core, my connection to my family, or the joy I get from the life I've created in Atlanta.*

Will makes the choices he does because he values the outcomes.

Redefining Success

If you wish to value relationship outcomes as highly as career outcomes, you must redefine success. Most of us, sadly, don't have our own definition of success. We have unthinkingly accepted a societal definition that regards only material achievement as valuable and meaningful.

Not too long ago, if you had asked me, "Sheri, are you successful?" my answer would have been no. Why? Because I was not at the financial level I wanted to reach. For the first several decades of my life, I equated success with my net worth and my bank account. It never occurred to me to do otherwise.

I now define success much more broadly. I look at the whole picture. I take delight in the fact that I am from Richmond, a small town in Kentucky, yet have worked as a record label executive and run my own company. I take equal delight in the fact that I have a man who adores me and works to have a great marriage. I have two amazing children. I have a mother who is healthy and vibrant in her seventies. I have dear friends, like Camay Davis, I can call at four a.m. who will pray with me or talk to me just *because*. Both of my girls have been able to attend a private school. In other words, I am living the *whole life* that I have always wanted. That is real success, I now see.

Why didn't I feel successful before? Because I accepted a second-hand definition of success instead of writing my own. And so anytime I wasn't chasing income or status, I felt anxious. I felt like I was being unproductive. Today, success is the feeling I get not only from career and professional achievements and reaching financial goals, but also from spending a quiet evening with my mom, from having a heart-to-heart with my daughters, or from going out to dinner with my husband.

Do I desire more, financially? Always. But that doesn't mean I am not successful if I haven't yet reached certain financial benchmarks. And it doesn't mean I can't love and enjoy the time I spend with those I love. Do I still pursue career goals? Absolutely. But I have learned to say "both/and" rather than "either/or." I now realize that

I can have *both* personal success *and* professional success, not *either* one *or* the other.

When we broaden our definition of success to include not just career achievements but things like quality time with our children, an emotional connection to our spouse, caring for our aged parents, sitting quietly in meditation, dating, and doing activities we deeply enjoy, we begin to unleash the hidden 90 percent of who we are that is obscured when we give 100 percent of ourselves to the 10 percent.

This, my friend, is Exponential Living.

Are you ready to define what success means to you? Are you ready to include relationships in your definition of success? Are you ready to start treating your key relationships as the *very cornerstones* of healthy living?

Five Key Relationships

When we accept the definition of success society hands us, we put most of our energy into our *work* relationships. But Exponential Living—true success—flows from nourishing five other key relationships:

1. Relationship with God
2. Relationship with self
3. Relationship with spouse (or love partner)
4. Relationship with children
5. Relationship with friends

Relationships with our community and with the world at large are also crucial, but we'll talk about those in another chapter.

Each of these five key relationships has different rewards and requirements, and each must be given time and attention—not because it's on our to-do list, but because we truly value both the experience and the outcome.

Let's look at each of the five.

Relationship with God

> Seek first the kingdom of God and His righteousness and
> all these things will be added unto you.
>
> —MATTHEW 6:33

A few years ago I spoke at the California Women's Conference, and Immaculée Ilibagiza, a survivor of the Rwandan genocide in 1994, was one of the keynote speakers. She shared her ordeal of spending ninety-one days hidden in a bathroom no larger than three by four feet with *seven other women*. As they hid from their would-be attackers, the women could hear screams from the killings that were taking place in the streets outside—killings that would come to include most of Immaculée's family.

She said about her excruciating ordeal, "The killers never found me, but I found myself." Instead of giving in to fear, anger, hatred, and fantasies of retribution, she surrendered to prayer. Every day she prayed for hours, and managed to find love, peace, and tranquillity in the midst of horror.

When she went into that bathroom to hide, she weighed 165 pounds. Ninety-one days later, when she emerged, she weighed 65 pounds. She was nothing but bones, but her heart was whole, full, and healed. Even though she had lost nearly everyone she loved, she found forgiveness for those who had committed the killings. She now travels around the world as an inspirational speaker.

Mind Is Not Enough

Had Ilibagiza relied only on her own mind to sustain her during this three-month descent into hell, she surely would have lapsed into terror, anger, and despair. But because she was able to surrender to a greater truth and power, she found a fresh perspective and transformed the worst experience of her life into a blessing.

High achievers often live in a state of great stress and inner turbulence because they rely on their minds only. They believe it's "all on them" to juggle their many priorities and solve every problem that crops up in their lives. The greatest discovery high achievers can make—and I do mean *the* greatest—is that they can "lay their burdens down." They can relinquish the tight control they exert on every facet of their lives and allow a greater wisdom to manage the details.

An absolutely essential component of Exponential Living is developing a relationship with God. Without this relationship, we never experience the deepest expression of joy and peace, nor the power that comes from this experience.

Start the Day with God

One of my clients runs several prominent and successful businesses. He does not awaken every morning with a head full of to-do lists and worries, as many high achievers do. Rather, he begins his day in stillness and quiet. The first thing he does every morning is meditate. He considers "time with God" to be his primary tool for business and life. He then spends some quiet time with himself. Only after spending time with God and himself does he feel prepared to deal with the demands of the day. Without this peaceful morning ritual, he says, he would be absolutely ineffectual at his job and would be a basket case mentally.

I am the same way. I cannot imagine trying to manage my life alone. It simply wouldn't work. I absolutely *rely* on God. My personal spiritual practice is to pray, thank Jesus through worship, seek fellowship with others, and read the Bible. That's what works for me. No matter what situation I am in, I find the answers I need by praying and reading. The support I get from this practice allows me to go with the flow of God. When I do this—rather than resisting God's plan—my life unfolds magnificently and purposefully. However, when I try to coordinate and micromanage all the details with my mind, I am stressed, anxious, and always working to gain control.

Without a connection to our spiritual truth, we are like cells in a petri dish, struggling for survival, but with no greater purpose. When we connect our spirit with the Spirit of God, we become like cells in a *body*; we still have individual concerns to deal with, but we now serve something greater than ourselves.

It is critical for high achievers to have some kind of spiritual practice, some way of tapping into their inner power, some way of accessing a deeper truth. This can be prayer, meditation, silence, contemplative walks in the woods, or whatever centers them in a place of peaceful stillness. We will revisit this topic more comprehensively in the next chapter.

Relationship with Self

Almost as important as our relationship with God is our relationship with ourselves. Many high achievers have very poor relationships with themselves. They elevate career achievement to such a high place in their lives that they fail to take care of themselves in the most basic ways. Worse, they rationalize this as necessary. Their career then becomes more important than their health and their emotional and spiritual needs. As a result, they do things like eat poorly (lots of junk food, gobbled on the fly), miss exercise, absorb tons of stress, lose sleep (and have no value for sleep), sacrifice family time, subject themselves to grueling commutes, endure humiliation and spirit-breaking job demands, omit their spiritual practice, and abandon personal hobbies and interests. All in the name of the endless hamster wheel called work. Many even view this personal neglect as a badge of honor, bragging about how little sleep they get or how late they stay at the office.

A shift to Exponential Living means a shift to making YOU an important person in your life, not an afterthought. In order to develop a healthier relationship with yourself, you must

1. Stop minimizing and devaluing who you are.
2. Clear your mind of all self-defeating thoughts.
3. Eliminate the need for validation from others.

In short, you must love, honor, and believe in yourself. You must put yourself first in all matters—not your ego, but your true self. Putting yourself first means speaking your truth with firmness and boldness. It means understanding that "No" is a complete sentence and it's one you are entitled to deploy when you need it. It means not martyring yourself with work, family, and friends, and not taking on the burdens of the whole world.

Only by having a mature, loving, respectful relationship with yourself can you have meaningful relationships with family, friends, and colleagues and achieve long-term success in both your personal and professional spheres.

Physical Health Is Vital

Though healthy living is more than diet and exercise, you *must* take good care of your physical health.

In my twenties I gradually became very unhealthy. By my late twenties I weighed almost two hundred pounds. I wasn't just physically unhealthy; I was mentally unhealthy too. I was so focused on my career path that I lost my connection with myself and hence my connection with everyone else. My relationship with me became one of feeling sorry for myself because I was overweight, unhappy, and stressed-out.

One day I got into a huge argument with a guy I was dating and started blurting out remarks that made me sound like a victim. After this disagreement, it clicked for me. I realized I was riddled with self-pity and had been for a long time. In that moment, I made a commitment to stop feeling sorry for myself. I made a shift in my mind-set and decided I would treat myself with the same love, dignity, and respect I consistently showed others. I committed to my own spiritual, mental, psychological, and physical wholeness and well-being.

I started walking at a track near my house. An athlete throughout high school and college, I had now gotten so out of shape I could barely walk one lap. But I committed to that. One lap. Even that small exertion caused my legs to throb with pain.

I committed to adding a quarter of a lap each day, and I built from there. During my walks, I talked to God to get me though. This was the first quiet time I'd had with myself, ever! My prayer walks became my central tool in rebuilding my long-lost relationship with myself. I was building my spiritual strength along with my physical strength. Finally, another shift happened and I began to *want* my health the same way I wanted food, water, and air.

Today, no matter how busy I get, self-care remains a priority. During the writing of this book, for example, I was committed to a minimum of five hours of writing per day, keeping up with my speaking engagements, servicing my clients, and building my business. I was also committed to being a spouse, parent, daughter, and friend. But even with all of these responsibilities, I still made sure I got my three to four days a week of exercise and eight hours of sleep. Hard? You bet. But doable by paring away the nonessentials and staying fully present to each task and relationship.

Self-pity? No chance.

The Gift of Sleep

Sleep is an essential element of self-care that many high achievers ignore or minimize. In fact, they often wear their lack of sleep like a badge of honor—proof that they're committed and getting things done. This is insane.

As high achievers, we are constantly going and getting less and less sleep. And many of us are so filled with anxiety that, as we say, "our brains never turn off." And so we need assistance—sometimes pharmaceutical assistance—when we do try to go to sleep. We have this false notion that we're getting more done when we go on three to four hours of sleep, but we are actually much less productive and make poorer decisions.

For most of my life, I was a person who didn't value sleep. I thought it was a waste of time and a drain on my productivity. One day, I flew back to Atlanta on a red-eye from LA and went straight into my regular routine: shower, dress, and start working. My husband, who was my boyfriend at the time, couldn't comprehend why I was trying to work when it was obvious that I was beyond wiped out. Somewhere around eleven a.m., he *made* me lie down. Within seconds I was asleep. That was some of the best sleep I've ever had. I woke up a few hours later, rejuvenated and recharged—and with plenty of workday left to "get things done." The power of those few hours of sleep made a convert out of me.

When I began to value sleep, not only did my work improve but my health did too, along with my disposition, my critical thinking, and relationships with my family and friends. Added bonus: I no longer do the late-night-snacking thing.

Destroy Destructive Habits

Constant growth is what makes our relationship with ourselves fresh and vital and dynamic. Each of us has habits that stunt our growth and keep us living small. In order to experience Exponential Living, we must break these patterns. We do this by reminding ourselves that *who we are* is more real and fundamental than any habit we've learned. That allows us to move out of our comfort zones.

One of my clients recently said to me, "Sheri, I have to stay angry because it's the anger that allows me to be successful."

"Listen to that statement," I said to him. "You're negating your experience, decision-making ability, vision, people skills, creativity, problem-solving, and self-confidence, and giving all of the credit for your success to your anger, which is in fact the one thing that causes you damage in your career."

"Yep," he said proudly.

I replied, "You will never go further than you have unless you own who you truly are, which is a brilliant businessman. You will minimize your success and you will always be in a cycle of confrontation, instead of living the fuller version of you."

Success blinds many of us because, while we think our destructive habits are propelling us forward and giving us an edge, we are actually achieving wealth and fame *in spite of* these traits, not because of them. But we are convinced it's the other way around. So we continue living a personal untruth that creates emptiness and pain in our lives.

My destructive habits were being controlling and sarcastic and talking to people (mainly my children and my mom) in a harsh tone. I asked God to show me a better way. I vowed that the next time a moment arrived when I would normally revert to one of my destructive habits, I was going to make the conscious choice to identify the negative and unhelpful behavior and take a different tack. My habit is not who I am.

Most people defend or deny their bad habits; that's why they don't grow. They say: "That's how I was raised," "It's been okay up till now," "I'm too old to change," or "That's how I've always handled things." We're so focused on defending our negative behavior that we block our access to the power and grace that would enable us to identify those destructive habits and create new, healthy habits.

Relationship with Spouse or Love Partner

After our relationship with ourselves, the most important relationship we have is with a loving spouse. This relationship can be with any "significant other," but it reaches its highest expression in marriage. A spouse is more than a companion, a friend, and a lover. A spouse is someone who is committed to our growth as much as to his or her own. Marriage is a physical, emotional, and spiritual bond like no other. It is based in trust—ideally—and it accelerates our growth in ways that enhance what we are able to manage for ourselves alone.

The majority of humans choose to enter a close love relationship at some point in their lives, or at least hope to do so. While there are some people whose mission in life calls for them to remain single, these folks are in the small minority. Most of us crave the intimacy that a committed relationship offers.

Single and Seeking

Single high achievers often deny their need for intimate love. I've had clients say the following to me:

"I don't want to be married."

"I'm forty-two. It's too late for me to be married."

"I don't have time to date."

"I'm too set in my ways to be married."

The list of untruths high achievers have told me about being single goes on and on. I realize that not everyone wants to be married, but too often it is the ego that makes these claims, not the heart. When most of us own our truth, we realize that our heart wants love and companionship.

What I have learned from coaching high achievers and serving as a life strategist is that if you want a spouse and/or a family, you must put this goal first in your life, not last. You must be intentional about it—at least as intentional as you are about your career goals.

That means making room in your life for a mate *before* you meet one. High achievers often say, "I don't have time for dating or a relationship." But the reality is that they choose not to make time. When I was single, I would remind myself, "My future husband is not the Avon lady. He's not going to walk up to my front door and ring the bell. I must spend time in new environments with new people, and be open."

Many single people take the attitude "I'll stay busy for now. Later, when I meet someone, *then* I will make room for him/her in my life." Hello? Cart before the horse! When a man feels there is no space in your life for him, he will look for a woman who *does* appear to have time. The same is true for anyone seeking a romantic partner.

In order to find the relationship your heart desires, you must:

1. **Choose to be vulnerable.** Stop being so guarded and so *serious*. Lower your defenses and, for heaven's sake, smile! It won't kill you, and it will attract a hundred times more interest than your business face.

2. **Move outside of your comfort zone.** Pursue a new hobby. Get into some new environments. Try some things that have no relationship to work. *Do* stuff. Meet people.

3. **Open up to the possibilities of love and a broken heart.** Just as you can't succeed in business without risking loss, you can't succeed in love without risking hurt. Love is a no risk/no reward proposition. Is it worth it? Well, no one on their deathbed ever says, "I wish I had played it safer with my heart."

Many of my clients openly receive my coaching when it applies to their careers, but not when it aims to help them invite healthy intimate relationships into their lives. In fact, I've had several of my single clients, male and female, admit they wanted to be married, but I've only had one single client admit she wanted to be married and then commit to doing the work needed. During our sessions, she learned to stop spending time with dead-end prospects. By the end of our time together she was seeing a quality gentleman regularly, and they were getting pretty serious. The reason she succeeded in love was that she *owned her truth*—that she didn't want to remain single—and then did the transformational work.

If you want love in your life, you must own that truth, and then go through the P.O.W.E.R. steps as you would with any other desire. Love doesn't just *happen*. It is sought, received, given, and nurtured.

After "I Do"

Marriage is a river so wide and deep that I won't pretend to offer comprehensive advice about it in just a few paragraphs. We'll dive into this topic a bit more in my conversation with "exponential couple" Boris Kodjoe and Nicole Ari Parker at the end of this chapter. For now, I'll just offer a couple of key points.

Commitment is ongoing. All married people take vows as part of their wedding ceremony, but commitment is not a "one and done" phenomenon. It must be renewed constantly. I am convinced that if every married person took even ten seconds—yes, *ten seconds*—every morning to purposefully renew their commitment to their spouse, two-thirds of all divorces would be eliminated.

Many married people fall into the *habit* of being married, but do not recharge their *commitment* to marriage. In the midst of parenting and working and pursuing individual goals, the marriage becomes a fading priority. Husbands and wives who have been married longer than five years, especially, must commit to being *interested* in their spouses.

Committed interest means being aware of our spouse as a complete, living, breathing human being with a spirit, a heart, and a mind, not just part of the furniture of our lives. That means paying attention to their needs, keeping tabs on what's important to them, doing random acts of kindness for them, sharing observations and laughs with them, touching them lovingly, and treating them as if they are the most important people on earth. Imagine if you found out your spouse had only twenty-four hours to live. What would you want to tell your spouse? Show your spouse? Share with your spouse? Do it today. That's what marriage should be.

Get the ego out. It is often said that communication is the key to a healthy marital relationship. This is certainly true. But what is the key to healthy communication?

Getting the ego out.

Too often, what happens in marriage is that spouses become adversaries rather than friends. In the majority of conversations I've had about people's marriages—personally and professionally—the main thing I hear is complaints about the spouse. The universal mantra of most married people seems to be "Everything would be fine if my wife/husband would stop (or start) doing *x*, *y*, or *z*."

In many marriages, the partners are more interested in being right than in being happy. That's because these couples relate to one another through the ego. When the ego is all you bring to the table, a healthy and happy marriage is impossible. Why? Because the ego must constantly *win*. What's really needed in marriage is *radical humility*.

Surrender to the covenant. My husband and I went through some extremely turbulent times together. The only way our marriage survived was that we both turned to God and placed our egos aside. Marriage is what *brings* couples together, but what *keeps* them together is *covenant*. A covenant is a sacred agreement with God. It is not based on winning the daily battles with your spouse; it is based on a silent promise you make deep within yourself to grow and to serve. It is rooted in your true peace and power.

A marriage rooted in and of the flesh cannot last. To make marriage work you must surrender to a deeper covenant. You must choose the marital bond over your selfish moment-by-moment needs. Remarkably enough, when you do this your needs are met and exceeded tenfold.

Relationship with Children

Virtually every person who has children will tell you that family is their number one priority. But how many of us put our money where our mouths are?

I remember a key moment when I realized, with some shame and shock, that I wasn't fully living up to my role as a parent. It happened when my youngest daughter was in first grade and started playing lacrosse. While watching her first game from the stands, I decided to call one of my girlfriends I hadn't talked to in a long time

ONLY ONE CHANCE

In 2013 Ben Jealous resigned from his position as CEO of the NAACP, the nation's largest civil rights organization, because he realized he was missing out on something more important—parenting his seven-year-old daughter and eighteen-month-old son. "During the first year of my son's life, I was on the road 155 days," he said. "There's no way for me to be both [a parent and CEO of the NAACP]. You get many chances to serve, but you only get one chance with your kids" (*Jet*, January 27, 2014).

and catch up. I continued to watch the game as I made the call. I had my Apple earbuds in, I saw every play, and cheered each time my daughter's team scored. But I was on the phone at the same time, at least for the first quarter of the game

After the game, I was bursting with excitement because Dominique had played almost the entire time. And she had done really well. As I was approaching her for a hug, with my arms open wide, she stopped, looked me straight in my eyes, and said in a voice crushed with disappointment, "Mommy, you were on the phone for my first lacrosse game."

As she walked away to join her team for an after-game meeting, I really *got* for the first time how important my full presence was to her. As her team meeting went on, my ego was telling me all of the things I could say to her. "Mommy was only on the phone part of the time. Some of the other kids' parents didn't even show up. You should be thankful. Mommy took time out of her busy day to be here. . . ." Fortunately, when the team finished and she walked over to me, I shut down my ego, the rationalizations fell away, and I allowed my heart to speak its truth: "Baby, Mommy is so sorry. I will never be on my phone again during one of your games." My daughter hugged me and said, "Mommy, thank you, and I accept your apology." And three years later, I have never been on my phone during my daughter's lacrosse games or any important activity she is involved in.

A New Mind-Set

We have to change the mind-set that spending time with our family and loved ones is an obligation. We must stop feeling that doing homework with our kids, for example, is an unwanted interruption to our workday. When we begrudgingly help our kids, rushing through their work so we can get back to ours, they feel it. Why would they want to do homework with us when our irritated, impatient energy makes it clear that we have more important things to do?

If you wish to experience Exponential Living, you must commit to investing in those enriching aspects of your life that aren't related to work and career. That means valuing both the *time* you spend with your family and, as I said earlier, the *outcomes* of that time.

This really hit me during my youngest daughter's first-grade parent-teacher conference. The first thing her teacher said to us was "You have Dominique well prepared." She said this many times and wrote it as her note to us in her paperwork. I realized—happily—that this was an outcome of the time and presence I had invested in her. For the first time, I was able to appreciate a family outcome in the same way I appreciated career outcomes. It was a real *aha* moment. Not only because I realized how little concrete value I often gave to outcomes like the growth of my children, but also because it took an outside person to point this out to me. High achievers often don't recognize their own true successes.

Preparation and engagement with our children is important in every stage of their development. Jini Thornton, our featured Exponential Conversation in the "Your 10 Percent and Your 100 Percent" chapter, said she had to be even more intentional and give more of her attention to her boys when they were teenagers than when they were toddlers. My dear friend Karen Mason, whose daughter, at age twelve, launched a successful national magazine, *Blackgirl*, that landed her on the couch talking to Oprah Winfrey, told me that she established "engagement" traditions with her daughter throughout her life—from the many years she homeschooled her to annual trips to Jamaica together. She shares her insights:

We created certain rituals in our lives. When she was about nine or ten, we started to go to Jamaica every December. I wanted her to meet and know about her Jamaican heritage. When she went to undergrad at Howard University, on full scholarship, I went there regularly. I just showed up to find out what her class schedule was. I needed to know how she was living, and I needed her to be comfortable that no matter what she was doing at any given time that it was okay, that she didn't have to hide it. When she graduated, she became press assistant to the Senate majority leader, Harry Reid, who is now the minority leader; I visited her there too. When she went through her master's program, I visited and familiarized myself with her curriculum. Our children are influenced by so much. I needed to always see where she was in her growth.

We must give our kids—and all of our family members—the same level of excellence and dedication we give to our clients and work responsibilities, instead of giving them our "leftover" energy, time, and mental space. We must give to our family from our "overflow," not from our "fumes." That means keeping something in the tank for our families, not running ourselves empty at the office every day. It means setting aside work at a reasonable hour and not answering e-mails at night. Even when my office was in my house, I learned to separate my office space from my home space. I got up in the morning, got dressed, and went to work, like everyone else. I just had a shorter commute. At the end of the day, I left "the office" for good, and if someone called me with a work request, my response was "I'll get that to you tomorrow when I'm in the office." Setting firm and clear parameters around your work life tells your family that they are as valuable as your job.

Relationship with Friends

Among the first relationships to disappear in the lives of high achievers are friendships. Busy achievers just don't have time for them. There are always more important things to do, it seems, than hanging around with a friend enjoying a leisurely glass of wine or stroll in the park. And yet friends play a vital role in our lives that can't be filled by anyone else.

We all *think* we have friends and *say* we have friends, but often that's because we misuse the word. *Friend* is the most overused word in the dictionary. A friend is not just someone you like and occasionally spend time with. A friend is not just a coworker who makes you laugh. A friend is not just a business associate with whom you have a pleasant, positive relationship.

A friend is someone who deeply values you for who you are. A friend is someone you confide in and share your life with. A friend accepts you fully, with all of your flaws and quirks. A friend has an open ear and gives you a fresh perspective on your problems. A friend wants what is truly best for you and is willing to give you a kick in the pants when you need one (who, *moi?*). A friend cares about your life and your family and your work. A friend—especially a longtime friend—knows you in ways that even your family and spouse don't (and we all have a deep need to be *known*). A friend helps you sort out right from wrong and clarify your value system. Friendship is a true, honest, and reciprocal relationship. To know you have a trusted ally who will help and support you *no matter what* goes wrong in your life gives you a sense of personal security that no insurance policy or bodyguard could ever provide.

A recent CBS poll revealed a troubling truth. The average person today has only two close friends, down from three only twenty years ago. That's quite a change in just two decades. That means, in this era of Facebook friends, LinkedIn networks, and mile-long contact lists, we have fewer actual friendships than we did before the Era of Connectivity began. Today's cyber-"friendships" too easily satisfy our need to check the "friends" box without too much trouble or extra effort on our parts. These relationships are efficient, fast, tech-based, superficial, quantifiable, and totally on our own terms, but they don't satisfy the needs of our 100-percent selves.

Real friendships are vital to Exponential Living. You must have people you love and trust—and who aren't involved in your daily work or family life—whom you can talk to honestly about your needs and struggles. You must have people with whom you can let down your guard and take off your mask. You need people you can laugh with until your bladder leaks.

It's time to recognize friendship as an essential component of health, not just one of life's "extras." That means you must value both the *time* you invest in friendship and the *outcomes*. It also means you must choose carefully who you call a friend. None of us has time to waste on pseudofriendships. So what do you do when you give some-one your heart, your time, and your ear, and they don't give it back? You forgive them. You let it go. And you move on.

I urge you to start expanding your definitions of both *success* and *health* to include rich, loving relationships. Relationships are the food of the soul. No amount of wealth or achievement means anything without them. So stop putting achievement first and relationships last. There are people all over the world who have little wealth but who are happy.

What makes them happy? Family and friendship and the strength, support, and love they draw from them. There are also wealthy and famous people all over the world who are miserable. What makes them miserable? Lack of loving relationships. End of story.

Vision, Action, Results

Exercise 1: Write a New Definition of Success

We all say that relationships are among our highest values, yet many of us don't reflect that in our actions. That's because we accept a societal definition of success that is all about income and career achievement.

1. Write a *definition of success* that is expanded beyond income goals and career achievements. Make sure it includes key relationships.

2. List five daily and/or weekly actions, big and small, I can be taking right now to achieve success according to my new definition (e.g., institute "game night" with my kids or "date night" with my spouse).

Exercise 2: Relationship with Myself

» What do I like about me? What are five things I appreciate about myself?
» When do I feel the most vulnerable?
» What do I do to "protect" myself at these times? Is this my true self or my ego at work?
» What are three habits of mine that are rooted in my ego, not in my true self?

>> How would breaking these habits empower me to live more truthfully, and with more self-respect in my relationship with myself?
>> What are three *new* habits I will begin in order to live more truthfully in my relationship with myself?

Exercise 3: Relationships with Others

>> What are the five most important things I need in my relationships?
>> Name some relationships that give me each of these things.
>> In my relationships with my loved ones, what am I not doing or not doing enough of that I need to do?
>> What qualities do I exhibit or actions do I take that weaken my relationships?
>> What positive role do I play in my most rewarding relationships?
>> What have I contributed to the healthy relationships in my life?
>> What are three qualities in my current relationships that frustrate me?
>> List five specific actions I can take to have better relationships.

EXPONENTIAL CONVERSATION

Boris Kodjoe and Nicole Ari Parker were both successful actors when they met in 2000 on the set of the Showtime series *Soul Food*. They fell in love and were married in 2005. They cohosted their own talk show on Fox in 2015, a lifestyle talk show that tackled everything from current events to parenting and relationships. They also served as co-executive producers of the show. They live and work in Los Angeles with their two kids and their dog, Max.

Boris and Nicole epitomize the concept that healthy living is more than just a diet. Not only do they take good care of themselves, through diet, exercise, meditation, and other "healthy" practices, but they also recognize that their relationships—with each other, with their children, with their friends, with their work colleagues—are the true bread of life. Their ego-free style of communicating with each other stands as a model for healthy couples engaged in Exponential Living.

SHERI RILEY: Working at LaFace Records, I loved my job, I loved the people I was working with, but I was miserable, and I realized later I wasn't the only one who had this amazing life but was completely overwhelmed with trying to manage it all.

BORIS KODJOE: I think it's because when people don't have a basic sense of who they are and work becomes their only identification, it brings with it so much stress and anxiety, because you literally feel that work is the only thing that defines you and so success becomes a lifeline: if I'm not successful, I'm nothing. And I think that's when people fall into those patterns.

SHERI RILEY: Communication is the key to marriage, but I believe it's one step further. I believe that communication *without ego* is really the key to a healthy relationship, especially marriage. Tell me about a time that removing ego really helped you in continuing to have a healthy relationship with each other.

BORIS KODJOE: I think when you're in a relationship you slowly become aware that you don't have to fight for position anymore, and you don't have to justify your actions, your decisions, who you are. You don't have to prove anything to the other person anymore. And once that settles in, that gives you a great sense of comfort, protection, confidence, and I think that's when the ego leaves the room. Because there's no more fear or anxiety that you have to make a point. The other person accepts you; the other person embraces, loves you, and knows that you have their best interests at heart. And once that settles in, I think fears go out the window, as well as ego.

NICOLE ARI PARKER: I think my development in this ten-year marriage is that I did the opposite. I used to fight by using my ego. As I have gotten older and done more spiritual work, I think that I can start a discussion having done a whole lot of work before I even open my mouth. I know that I am taking this personally. I know it isn't the end of the world that I am having this issue. I know that he's not doing it intentionally. He's activating something in me, so it becomes a gift, in a way, to help me grow. So I do all that now before I storm in the room. We have these really short discussions about issues now. They're not screaming matches, fighting, slamming doors, "Forget *you*, then." Stuff can *seem* big, but now we can sit on the steps and talk it out. And I can listen, and he can listen, and then we're done.

SHERI RILEY: So how did you get to that point of recognizing that working on you first is what's going to always help make the marriage better?

BORIS KODJOE: I think everybody has to do work on themselves first. Some people do it later in life, and some people do it early. I was fortunate that I was forced to do that work very early in life, so that when we got married, I was already very solid in knowing who I am and why I am here. And I wasn't threatened, and I wasn't insecure.

SHERI RILEY: What would you say is the key to the ten-year marriage, and the ten-plus-year relationship?

BORIS KODJOE: Well, I think the first thing is that we want to be here—we don't need to be here. We want to be together because life is better when we're together, and now we have two beautiful kids; that certainly throws challenges your way that were completely unforeseen. But I think going through those times of adversity sort of reinforced my belief that she is my partner and we're supposed to do this together. Because the stuff that we went through, most people don't survive that. And for us to sit here with you now, and be more in love than ever, and have such great knowledge of each other and the friendship that we have, is amazing.

NICOLE ARI PARKER: I think the key, like it should be worked into the marriage vows, is . . .

BORIS KODJOE: Shit's going to happen.

NICOLE ARI PARKER: . . . And my vow to you is, I forgive you already. My vow to you is, I want to wake up the morning after the hurricane hits.

SHERI RILEY: You can't just roll out because the hurricane hit.

NICOLE ARI PARKER: I read in a spiritual book that your partner is your chosen teacher. That person has been assigned to you to accelerate your growth, and you to him. And so when I took all this other social pressure off what he's supposed to do, and looked at him as my teacher, a whole world opened up. Number two, shit's gonna happen, and you will always be better after that. It's always an opportunity to grow. Number three, no matter where you go, no matter where you run to, you still take yourself with you, so pick somebody that you want to learn that lesson with.

SHERI RILEY: How do you guys take the time to individually work on yourself or spend time with yourself, with all the responsibility of parenting, career, husband-wife? *Do* you take that time?

BORIS KODJOE: Yeah, absolutely, you have to. I start out in the morning right when I wake up, with stretching and meditation and prayer, and then I make sure that I have a physical outlet; that is very important for me. I want healthy living: the physical, the mental, and the spiritual; for me [they all] go together. And if one is lacking, then you can't possibly reach your full potential.

SHERI RILEY: And you, Nicole?

NICOLE ARI PARKER: For me, I need time to do nothing. Sometimes I just need to sit with a book, read some of it, and then put it down. I don't need a lot, just a little bit every day—thirty minutes of nothing, to sit there, stare out the window, make my favorite tea. Because I'm constantly going, and that thirty, forty-five minutes is like heaven.

BORIS KODJOE: You have to schedule it. Even the doing-nothing time. We have to schedule everything, because with two kids, and the business, and the shows and everything else that we're up to. Otherwise you're behind the eight ball all the time.

NICOLE ARI PARKER: What I've been doing, Sheri, is every few minutes, or every hour, take a breath and tabernacle with God. Even if it's for sixty seconds when you are driving, you just have a moment of rest, peace; let whatever God means to you just *be* with you. No other thing. No other thought. Trust that He's gonna take care of everything in this sixty seconds and you can let everything go. I've been doing that, and miracles have been happening. I'm calmer. I'm not controlling, and stuff falls into place. And it's cumulative. You do it a little bit every day. You start out 98 percent on the hustle and 2 percent with God. You practice and you get to 80-20. You keep going and you're at 50-50. Then you get to a place where it's 20 percent hustle—in terms of energy—and 80 percent peace.

SHERI RILEY: Yes!

NICOLE ARI PARKER: And there's nothing like it. It's happened maybe once or twice so far—'cause I'm still in practice—those days when I'm 80 percent in the light. The phone calls, the agents, the work, the business: everything's perfect. The kids flow and are "Mommy, I got my homework done"; somehow the salmon comes out perfect; I get my little workout in. It's literally like the hand of God orchestrated that whole day.

BORIS KODJOE: But the key is to still be 80-20 even when it doesn't go right, and not try to jump in and control . . .

NICOLE ARI PARKER: That's very true.

SHERI RILEY: Exponential Living is pursuing peace, choosing clarity, and living courageously. That's all I'm teaching; that's my whole purpose. Peace is our power. Peace is the new success.

NICOLE ARI PARKER: It really is. It's pursuing the peace that passes all understanding. Peace is not a weak position. You feel fortified, you feel ready, you feel vibrant and capable.

BORIS KODJOE: We've been conditioned to make peace conditional. Peace comes . . .

NICOLE ARI PARKER: . . . Like when I get a car or something.

BORIS KODJOE: It's an external satisfaction. When I get this, when I reach that, when I'm successful . . . then I will have peace. That's what we've been conditioned to believe, so we always look for outer things, manifestations to give us that peace. . . . You get it temporarily, but you have to keep running, because the triggers come from different places. When you win the Grammy, you want the Oscar. When you win the Oscar, you want the money. And it never stops, unless you stop it. When I go to work, there are a lot of people who are chasing their aspiration and are less about the journey and more about getting to that place. Getting to the next. They haven't realized that they are on this perpetual sort of hamster wheel that's taking them away from peace, that's taking them away from confidence.

SHERI RILEY: When I say "Exponential Living," what do you think? What comes to mind?

NICOLE ARI PARKER: I think for me Exponential Living seems like the 80-20. Seems like if you incorporate this teaching that you're writing about, you're gonna be in this 80-percent bubble. It's not materialistic; it's a feeling, although there might be some beautiful material things in your life. It feels like 80 percent appreciation and 20 percent action because your action is going to be efficient now. It's like an all-inclusive, paid, five-star vacation. The food, the fun, the family, the peace, the neighbors, the school, the future, peace with your past, present in the moment; it feels full.

SHERI RILEY: Yes, and it doesn't eliminate the career, the wealth . . .

NICOLE ARI PARKER: Oh no. All-inclusive.

BORIS KODJOE: To me it's maximizing your physical, spiritual, and mental potential as a human being. Living in that peace, comfort, and confidence. And that in itself is the relationship with God.

I AM BORIS KODJOE AND I AM EXPONENTIAL LIVING.

I AM NICOLE ARI PARKER KODJOE AND I AM EXPONENTIAL LIVING.

Key Takeaways

» Communicating without ego is the key to strong relationships.

» Your partner is here to accelerate your growth. You are here to do the same for your partner.

» It may sound like a cliché, but you must work on yourself and care for yourself before you'll be any good to a partner.

» Take time out throughout the day to "tabernacle with God."

Pursue Peace and a Positive Mind

Follow effective action with quiet reflection. From the quiet reflection will come even more effective action.

—PETER DRUCKER

At the age of fifteen, I had my first colonoscopy. Seems I had a "nervous" stomach, brought on by worry, stress, and anxiety. What did a fifteen-year-old have to worry about that would cause enough anxiety to require a colonoscopy? Well, I was a dedicated A student, I worked twenty to thirty hours a week at Wendy's, I played basketball, and I had an active social life.

But even still, a colonoscopy at fifteen?

I later realized that it wasn't my external pursuits that caused the anxiety I was experiencing both mentally and physically. It was my mind-set. For much of my life, I believed my sense of peace was tied to my accomplishments. If and when I accomplished x, then peace would follow. I tried various remedies to remove the anxiety, worry, and stress. Some of them calmed me down temporarily, but nothing eliminated the cause. What I finally discovered is that choosing peace is a cause, not an effect. It doesn't happen when you check something off of a list, but when you choose to pursue and value peace directly.

Throughout my life's journey, nothing *outside of me* has ever given me peace—not my bank account, not nice vacations, not a good marriage. It wasn't until I began to say this phrase aloud to myself every day, "I pursue peace with a positive mind-set and I live in the power of peace," that my stress and anxiety began to abate. It was only through the power of managing my own thoughts and through prayer and meditation on scripture that I found the peace I was so desperately seeking.

Peace is the medicine that healed my hurt, built my confidence, corrected my thinking, and has given me boundless strength.

Peace is possible. Peace is our power. Peace is the new success.

The Pursuit

High achievers are always pursuing. In the beginning they pursue material and financial success. When they attain that sort of success and realize it can be more of a burden than a blessing—or that it doesn't make them happy or fulfilled—they find themselves pursuing validation. They constantly try to prove or affirm that they have importance and value to others, looking outside of themselves to find approval and acceptance.

The mind of the typical high achiever is almost never content. After all, when you pursue approval and validation, your mind is forever on goals that—even if they *can* be achieved—are temporary and unsustainable. And so the inner life of even the highest of the high achievers is often turbulent and anxiety ridden. The endless pursuit of something that can never really be "caught" and "held" is exhausting.

Pursuit seems to be an essential aspect of being a high achiever.

But what is really needed is a pursuit of peace. By "pursuing" peace, I don't mean chasing it like a goal that you can reach and then forget about once you've checked it off your to-do list. I mean continually bringing your mental and spiritual focus back to peace, over and over.

To pursue peace means to make it your intention every minute of every day. It means to consciously and deliberately choose peace instead of letting anxiety, stress, and urgency hijack your thinking. It means to recognize that the time you spend resting, praying, and meditating—or anything else that activates your sense of peace—is just as important as the time you spend working. This is a very hard idea to grasp because it goes against all of our high-achieving tendencies as well as our logic.

But when you train yourself to pursue peace you realize that peace, in fact, is a place of maximum efficiency. Peace empowers you to have not only external success but also a satisfying life. It allows you to achieve your goals without stress and anxiety, while also remaining fully engaged, attentive, and loving with your friends and family.

Pursuing peace allows you to release your past and live in the present moment while planning and working toward your future. The pursuit of peace puts you in a much better frame of mind to achieve the future you desire than a frantic, tunnel vision–style "future focus" does.

Peace is a difficult state to describe; it must be experienced. But let's try. . . .

Peace Is Not a Destination

Many high achievers believe that peace is a result, a payoff, a destination. Deep down we believe that when we achieve a certain level of success, a desired income bracket, a beautiful home, or the ability to take nice vacations, we will achieve peace. Peace is the thing we desire, yet peace eludes us. So instead we pursue titles, money, access, and approval, thinking that these things will *bring* us peace.

You know the drill. You go after money because you think it will give you freedom. And freedom will give you peace. "I will be at peace when I can pay all my bills comfortably," you imagine. You go after a beautiful, comfortable home because you think it will provide you a sanctuary, a safe and quiet place to lay your head. Which you believe translates to peace. You go after a mate—someone who will always have your back—because you believe this psychological security will give you peace.

What we really desire is the one thing we don't pursue because we think it is not available to us directly. Peace itself. And so we pursue an endless series of go-betweens.

We have the process backward. We need to pursue the peace directly. When we do this, we gain the power and presence to achieve all of the other goals we want.

The world is full of high achievers who are broken because, at their core, they wanted peace, but instead they pursued the money, the access, the titles, the career, and the companionship. And when they achieved those goals, they did not find peace. Quite the opposite, actually. I have heard this story from clients over and over and over: "I've spent my life chasing [money, fame, sex, power, victory, love, excellence . . .] because I thought it would bring me peace, but instead it brought me emptiness, misery, and shattered relationships." Or "I achieved everything I desired, except peace."

But when we pursue the peace *first*, not only do we achieve our goals more efficiently, but we thoroughly enjoy the journey and all the steps along the way. And we remain fully engaged in our lives and the lives of our loved ones.

Peace is not a destination; it's a lifestyle, a moment-by-moment choice. It is not a state you arrive at when you go on vacation or when you open the door to your home after a day at work. It is not "quiet time." It is not lying on a beach. It is not becoming so intoxicated that you "forget your problems." It is not having heaps of money so you don't have to worry about your bills. And, surprisingly, it is not the absence of turmoil and strife in your life.

Peace is a mental and spiritual focus and a state of being. It is a mind-set that says regardless of what's going on around you, your mind, spirit, heart, and soul will remain settled and calm. It's a state in which your thoughts are clear, your soul is open, and your spirit is engaged—where you are grounded, centered, and unshaken by life's realities. Peace is an active choice to dwell in the place where your true power lives. It's a moment-by-moment, daily, hourly practice.

Peace Is Not External

Peace is not dictated by what's going on around you; it is found within.

When I was working on the early development of this book, my dear friend and Soror Jacquie Lee agreed to do monthly "vision calls" with me to help me refine my message. When I sent her the initial definition of Exponential Living, she loved everything except the word *peace*.

"Sheri, you've nailed it, but I recommend you remove *peace* from the definition," she said.

I knew peace was the core of Exponential Living but I was open to her insight, so I asked, "Why do you feel I should remove it?"

"Peace is just not possible in this day and age," she answered. "There is so much noise all around us; there's never a place of peace. Pumping gas used to be a moment of quiet, but now there's always music blaring at the station. Riding in a taxi was my quiet place. Now every city cab has videos and commercials playing. Even if you try to have a quiet walk in the park, you hear the sound of engines and radios. There's so much noise around us these days, *peace* sounds lofty and unattainable. I love the idea that Exponential Living will give me less stress, more clarity, and a more fulfilling life. But what word can we use instead of *peace*?"

My reply was "In my favorite book, there's a story where Jesus and the disciples are riding in a boat. It's a small boat, and suddenly a big old storm kicks up. The waves are huge and the boat is rocking violently. The disciples are upset and frightened, and yet Jesus is just peacefully sleeping. Afraid that the boat will go under and they will die, they wake Him up, frantically saying, 'Lord, have you not noticed the storm we are in? Do you not care if we die?' And Jesus calmly and powerfully says, 'Peace, be still.'

"What I take this story to mean is that peace is always available to us, no matter what is swirling around us in the world. Regardless of our external circumstances, we can always choose internal peace. The biggest hindrance to peace is our attitude. We must first believe peace is possible. Then we must choose only thoughts that activate peace in our minds, and allow peace to permeate our thoughts, spirit, and soul. We do have control over this, despite what we may tell ourselves."

When Jacquie understood that peace was an inner state, she was all on board.

Peace is always available to us; it never goes away. When we are stressed, worried, angry, or anxious, this means we are not choosing to allow peace to be our primary focus and pursuit. Peace is not dependent upon everything going smoothly in our lives. We can choose the power of peace, regardless of our circumstances. I'm not saying this is easy. It takes practice. We have to overcome our conditioning that says peace is an effect that happens when everything goes our way.

In our society, the majority of us are not raised understanding this most basic truth—that peace is within us. When I worked in the entertainment industry, we made sure our artists had the best makeup artists, choreographers, fashion and hair stylists, nutritionists, trainers, and acting and vocal coaches, but there was little to no focus on their personal development. Instead we encouraged them to pursue more and more external "stuff," to fill the void that can be filled only by peace. I have experienced up close the pain of achieving everything you've ever wanted and still feeling empty. And I have seen this happen to countless other people in the worlds of music, sports, business, and acting. Nicole Kidman has said of her Oscar win for the 2002 film *The Hours*, "[Winning an Oscar] can show you the emptiness of your own life."

No amount of money, fame, fortune, or even spouses, sex, children, or the love of others can give us peace. Peace is already there; we just need to learn to choose it.

Peace Is Trust in God

Many people experience a state of calm and relaxation through meditation, but what I have discovered is that true and lasting peace is rooted in a deep belief in, and relationship with, God.

When we operate under the illusion that we are separate, disconnected hunks of biology fighting only for our own survival, then of course we have trouble finding peace. But when we accept that we have an immediate, intimate, and personal relationship with God, peace becomes not only possible, but inevitable.

The key to peace—for me and millions of others—is trusting

that God has a perfect plan for our lives, that God knows what we need better than we do. Once we accept that, we begin to trust His plan and process more than our own. This relieves us of a huge burden. It means that when "things go wrong," or we don't seem to be getting closer to our goals, we can tell ourselves that everything is as it should be. We pursue a deeper understanding of God, engage with our inner power, and let go of all worries and doubts. And we are flooded with peace, knowing that the journey we are on is not always a simple one from point A to point B, and there is value in the detours and speed bumps we pass on the way.

How do we go about doing this? By listening to the small, quiet voice deep within us that urges us to believe. By allowing our spirit to become the CEO of our lives. For me and many people I coach, this happens through prayer, meditation, and reading and believing the Word of God. Others use mantras, time spent in nature, and/or other inspirational readings and rituals.

The central message God wants to speak through me is peace. Of this, I am certain. And so I now represent that message *at all times*—with my husband, my kids, my family, my friends, my clients, my business associates, and now with you. Of course, I had to live it before I could teach it. And for me that meant learning to choose peace every minute of every hour. No more stressing about business worries. No more putting business goals ahead of people. Today I *am* peace, not a fake replica of peace where I speak and teach it but fail to embody it.

Learning to do this has not been an overnight thing. It takes a lot of openness and a lot of humility. It takes acceptance that every day anxiety and stress are waiting for me and that they will probably win unless I make the decision to pursue peace the moment I wake up, throughout my day, when I lie down to sleep again, and throughout the night.

Not long ago, I realized that my morning meditation and dialogue with God were off base. It always centered on my to-do list. It revolved around either fighting my fears of not getting it all done or seeking peace around what I might or might not accomplish that day. I saw that my entire relationship with God, and the whole focus of my daily prayers, was still 100 percent about my "10-percent me." I was consumed with what I had to *do*, rather than with being who I am. This was a critical realization in my journey to unveiling the hidden 90 percent of me.

One day God spoke in my spirit, telling me this wasn't full communion with Him. My focus should not be about my to-do list for the day, He said; it should be about my love for Him and His love for me. Period. So I had to ask myself, "Am I going to trust in deadlines to provide for me, or am I going to trust in God to provide for me? Is my life about just what I *do* or about my love for and fellowship with God?"

I realized it was time to give God my thoughts and my mind-set. I had to stop looking to the world to tell me what fits for my life and my family. I had to learn that my identity is not tied up in my performance; it is rooted in God. I had to come to believe that God has already worked out everything He wants me to do. I just need to be a *confident, bold, and open vessel for Him to speak to and through.* I have to stop stressing and trust God, believe God, seek God, and receive from God.

God loves me. God has a plan for me. God works all things for my good. Nothing else matters. This is the essence of peace.

Can you receive it?

Stillness

There is great power in stillness. In the stillness of God, all things are possible. Action is not always needed. This is hard for high achievers to grasp.

When we are drowning, we tend to fight the water. We panic and flail our limbs, which makes it impossible for a rescuer to save us. It is far better to get still and center ourselves. It's stillness that allows help to wrap itself around us and bring us up safely. In the same way, it's mental stillness that allows us to receive the gifts of power and clarity. This clarity empowers us to move with authority when the time is right.

These days, God is teaching me how to trust that He is working on my behalf even when it appears I am not doing anything. This requires me to believe in God's plan for my life more than my own skills and my own busyness. This is not an easy task. But I've learned I needn't be pressed with *where* I am when I know *who* I am.

As a business owner, I have people who work with me, and I trust them to handle the areas that they are responsible for. That's what I am learning to do with God. I am learning to see His hand working beyond my ability and the skills that I have honed and depended on for so long. I'm learning to see that I am not capable of doing all that needs to be done to elevate my life to the levels that God has in mind for me and that I have the potential to achieve. Much work is being done on my behalf, and sometimes stillness is all that is required from me.

This is a hard lesson for high-achiever types like me to learn. I'm always worried that I'm not doing what I'm "supposed to be doing." But God finally gave me a breakthrough in this area. I asked myself,

"Are you spending your life looking or waiting for something and missing out on what you already have?" I came to see that if the *all-powerful Creator of the universe* is truly helping and supporting me, I don't have to spend 100 percent of my time laboring in order to be successful. If I insist on trusting only in my own abilities, then yes, stillness will always feel like wasted time. But when I *know and believe* God is working on my behalf, then I can be at peace in stillness, knowing that God, with one wisp of intention, can accomplish infinitely more than any human being can.

Even if you prefer not to adopt a spiritual perspective, there are plenty of scientific studies that show how taking time in silence and stillness can clear your mind, increase your health, and enable you to approach challenges with a new mind-set.

There's a difference between doing nothing and being still. When you're doing nothing, your mind-set is that nothing is changing. When you're being still, you are present with God, living in the power of peace, open to receive beyond what you have conceived, and trusting that important shifts are occurring in your life. All things move in stillness.

THE SOUNDNESS OF SILENCE

My very first coaching client, Tanya Forrest Hall, resisted every attempt I made with her to sit in silence and stillness. She absolutely refused. A little over a year later, she shared with me that she finally trusted herself and was able to spend quality time with herself in silence. And from this, her life had taken off. She was able to easily shed some long-standing issues that were anchoring her soul, and now she was free and truly experiencing Exponential Living.

Exercise the Muscle

The way to choose peace is by gently controlling your thoughts and emotions.

Most of us allow our minds to run wild. We focus our attention on whatever "shiny object" our mind finds compelling at the moment. This is a very destructive habit. Why? Because the mind is lazy, habitual, and drawn to negative and worrisome thoughts. And one negative thought quickly leads to a cascade of other ones. We believe these thoughts represent reality—and so we become fearful or depressed or defensive—but they are really just thoughts.

When you learn to control the flow of your thoughts, you gain control of the quality of your life. We all know that we *can* control our thoughts, in theory, but many of us don't know *how* to do this. It's not difficult at all, if you make the effort. The practice simply needs to be made into a habit.

When I was a teenager, overcoming some difficult challenges showed me the power of controlling my thoughts. I learned that the mind is a muscle and, just like with our biceps and quads, we can control and shape it through conscious exercise. I learned how to arrest thoughts that led to troublesome mind-sets such as anxiety, depression, and paranoia. Whenever these "seed" thoughts would begin, I would *immediately* say out loud, "Stop! I am not going to think about that." Of course, to change a habit, you not only have to stop the "bad" thing you are doing; you must replace it with something "good." So after stopping the troublesome thought, I would *force* myself to think a more empowering thought that I chose to be my truth. I was amazed to discover that with a little effort I could retrain my mind. And that changed everything.

A Shift of Focus

One of my clients, Lisa Tanker, who is a fitness-and-lifestyle expert, was under consideration for a TV show. The casting process was dragging on for weeks. She was wearing herself down mentally and physically, worrying about whether she would get the gig or not. Anytime her phone didn't ring for twenty-four hours, she would need to be talked off a ledge.

She and I discussed the realistic worst-case and best-case outcomes, and how neither necessarily represented a life change for her. We talked about how her being on the show (or not) was only a small part of her lifetime-success strategy. I pointed out that it was only hurting her to waste time and mental energy thinking about the show. I then taught her how to exercise the muscle of her mind, training herself not to obsess about the casting process when there was nothing she could do about it.

Two weeks later, during our next session, she reported that she had been exercising this muscle, and instead of stressing about the show, she was focused on creative thinking around the brand opportunities she had control over, which led to several great ideas that she implemented on her social media platforms. She began posting more exercise and nutrition tips, which increased the engagement level with her current followers and also brought her new followers. This led to a great opportunity with a prominent radio station to provide lifestyle, health, and fitness tips on its website, which broadened her audience even more and has led to other media opportunities.

Changing Tracks

As I mentioned earlier, during the writing of this book, I had to put my schedule on lockdown. I was writing four to six hours per day. Other than write, the only work things I did with my time were launch my redesigned website, work on my speaking engagements, and plan the strategy for my book release. This meant there were many other opportunities, meetings, and events that I could not participate in. Having spent my entire career *doing* a zillion things a day, I began to hear my thoughts saying I was not being productive.

For example, around six p.m. on the day I received the final version of my publishing contract, thoughts saying that I had wasted my day (because I had not done any writing) began to creep into my mind. If I had allowed these thoughts to build and multiply, they would have brought on stress and anxiety. During dinner with my family, that anxiety would have changed my mood and made me cranky and short-tempered. This would have caused my family to stop talking and laughing, and everyone would have been walking on eggshells, trying not to set me off. And instead of having the amazing evening with them that I did, I would have mentally beat myself up about all the work I didn't get done, and made everyone else miserable in the process.

But before these thoughts could gain momentum, I said out loud, "Stop," and began to mentally list all of the things I had done that day. From kissing my youngest daughter good morning, through the two-hour process of renewing my passport (confirming a potentially lucrative collaboration via text as I waited), through the quality time I spent with my husband, who was only in town for a couple of days, through taking my mom to the doctor to begin her next knee replacement, through enjoying dinner with my family, to signing my publishing deal for this book, it had been a *very* productive day. After I reviewed all of these accomplishments, I realized, "I am living exactly the life I've always wanted to live. Not the life I thought I was supposed to live in order to identify myself as successful, but the life that is actual success for me."

All of the choices I was making through my commitment to the 9 Principles of Exponential Living were allowing me to *truly experience* Exponential Living.

I came to this joyful realization only because I took the steps to control my thoughts rather than let my mind climb onto a runaway thought train.

A Positive Mind-Set

If you pay careful attention, you can actually observe the mind's habit of chasing negative thoughts. Tomorrow morning, when you first awaken, notice how, for just a moment, the world is a blank slate to you. For just an instant, you might not even remember what day it is, or even what period of your life you are in. For one glorious nanosecond each morning, anything seems possible. Then, almost instantly, your mind starts trolling for problems. It says, "Now what should we be worrying about today?" A moment later it serves you up a ready menu of anxieties. Before you have a chance to get your bearings, the day's worry avalanche has begun.

What I encourage you to notice is that the *urge to worry* precedes any actual worries themselves. The fact is, if you didn't have today's set of problems, your mind would find another set to worry about. No matter how many problems you solve, the mind will always find something new to worry about, if you let it.

Maybe this is an ancient survival pattern. Maybe back in the days of saber-toothed tigers, the mind had to habitually scan for threats in order to ensure our safety. But today this habit is more destructive than helpful. It creates the illusion of danger where no danger exists. The great thing is, if you notice this habit, you can stop it. You can nip it in the bud. Before your mind finds a worry to zero in on, you can divert it to positive thoughts instead. And you can do this throughout the course of the day.

One Negative Can Trump a Hundred Positives

The mind's capacity for negativity is astonishing. Very often we allow the one thing that is bringing us sadness to rob us of the joy and satisfaction we could get from the hundred things that are going great. High achievers are particularly vulnerable to this trap. We are driven to achieve, and so that one "off" thing, that one thing that is not exactly how we think it should be, can throw us into a funk. Our mind then takes us on a grand tour of everything else we've failed to do perfectly. Which makes us lose our confidence and question whether we are even capable of performing the task we are currently attempting. Before long, we are completely down on ourselves. Which creates negative interactions with others. *Their* negativity then comes back on us, creating a vicious downward cycle. Sound familiar?

The tragedy is that it's a situation created entirely by the mind.

During a recent event I worked on, there was an aspect of the lighting production that wasn't planned and executed effectively. One of the producers knew this would be a problem and tried, prior to the event, to get her team to change this part of the event. They didn't take her suggestions and this element of the event was not lit very professionally.

As the event was wrapping up, this producer had become so upset she was close to tears. I shared with her that, yes, this poorly lit element could have been handled better, but the rest of the event was great. Everyone was having a fabulous time and the client objectives were being met. But she couldn't take her mind off this one detail that wasn't done in excellence. And others were picking up on her energy. It was obvious to me that if she continued to allow this one thing to rob her peace, her negative energy would infect the client's entire attitude about the event. It would make them see issues they hadn't even noticed. Fortunately, the producer was able to hit her mental "refresh" button.

One person's mental energy can affect the experience of thousands of people, positively or negatively.

That's why it's so important to pursue a positive mind-set. You must commit your thoughts to those things that are going right. You must stay focused on the blessings and positives in your life. That is where your peace and your power lie. No matter what challenging circumstance you may be facing, you *must* speak and reflect daily on the positive elements of your life. Are your children healthy? Do you have a roof over your head? Do you have a job? Are you physically and mentally able to read this book? Open your heart to gratitude for these things. Gratitude instantly ushers in a positive mind-set. We'll talk about gratitude more in a later chapter.

Many of us speak words that steal our joy. We come into agreement with the negative in our life instead of aligning with the positive. It is far better to speak from a positive place. For example, instead of saying, "I'm exhausted," which is negative and draining, and makes us feel defeated and robs us of our joy, say, "I've given my all." This prompts a sense of accomplishment and satisfaction. It is a more empowering way to express your truth. It also sets the stage for you to move positively into rest and restoration instead of feeling a need to do more. Say what you want, not what you don't want.

Triggers That Rob Our Peace

We all have triggers that lead our minds down negative pathways. For some this might be watching the nightly news—we get caught up in pessimism and worries. For others it might be listening to talk radio—we get drawn into "I'm right/you're wrong" debates. For others still, it might be social media—we become jealous of the lifestyles of our peers—or talking to negative people. There may be certain subjects that continually act as triggers for us—money, relationships, health concerns. Every time the triggers occur, our mind predictably spirals into negativity and turbulence.

The first thing we need to do is recognize these peace-robbing triggers. Become aware of them. The second is to make simple changes to our environment so as to lessen these triggers. Turn down the jarring music; shut off the talk show. I have clients who stopped watching TV news years ago. They still manage to keep up with current events, but they no longer start and end each day with images of crime and warfare. Instead, in the morning and evening, they bring in positive triggers that stimulate feelings of peace and well-being, for example, prayer, scripture, exercise, music, meditation, or inspirational literature.

Though the ultimate goal is to be able to find peace in *any* situation no matter how turbulent, this job becomes much easier when you remove the major peace robbers from your external environment.

Hopes and Dreams

It's very hard to have peace and a positive mind when you have lost hope. Many high achievers are struggling with hope but don't recognize this as their issue. They feel a void in their lives so they set larger goals and work even harder. But the fuel that's missing is hope. And many times, it's not in their career achievement where they've lost hope; it's in every area outside of their career—a satisfying marriage, a happy family, a sense of true purpose . . . So they double down on the one thing they *are* good at achieving.

Hope is essential. Hope gives us energy to do what we would ordinarily quit doing. When we lose hope, we don't even plant ourselves to take the shot because we already know we're going to miss.

What many of us don't realize is that hope is a choice. It can be deliberately cultivated. How? Here are a few ways:

1. Spend time with God. God is hope. Trust in God's plan.
2. Recall times when God came through for you, when doors opened in the middle of what appeared to be solid brick walls. Allow for the possibility that now is another such time.
3. Declare the future you aspire to—boldly, loudly, and clearly.
4. Stop your mind from dwelling on the disappointments. You can control your thoughts. You can turn your mind to recalling the triumphs instead.

5. Talk about your hopes and dreams with people who will affirm that all is possible. It's vital to talk with hopeful people. People who say no are a dime a dozen. People who say yes are treasures.
6. Breathe deeply. Soak in the present moment. Notice that there are few problems in reality; there are only situations. Most "problems" you obsess over are only in your mind.
7. Learn to dream again.

Let's spend a few moments on that last one.

High achievers need to believe in dreaming again—not just strategizing, not just goal setting, not just planning, but dreaming. Dreaming is something we all do as children, but then we forget how. We grow up and we dismiss dreaming as pure fantasy, as a waste of good, productive time. We replace dreaming with planning and strategizing.

The problem with planning and strategizing is that, while in many ways they are necessary and essential to our lives, they are also dry; they have no flavor; they bring no delight. They involve our head only, not our heart. Dreaming, however, involves our whole being. To dream is to boldly imagine our fondest hopes coming true. It's to savor the sweetness of what life would be like if we had the things we deeply desire. To dream is to *feel*, not just to see. Dreaming comes from a positive mind and releases peace. Dreams allow us to connect to who we really are, because they tap into what genuinely delights us as unique individuals. Dreams allow us to connect to our emotional and spiritual truth. Dreams allow us to embrace 100 percent of who we are and what we desire for our lives, not just our narrow 10 percent that usually only includes career achievements.

Somewhere along the way we decide that dreaming is for kids, but I think one of the great killers of hope is that we stop allowing ourselves to dream. Dreaming is not a waste of time. To dream is to envision the future in such a way that our emotions are ignited. And when we ignite our emotions, our goals become real to us. So real we can taste them. And it's by making our desired future real to us that we regain hope.

Fill yourself with dreams each morning when you wake up; take moments throughout your day, and each night before you go to sleep. Just let your mind roam free, in a completely unstructured way, and gravitate toward things that feel good to imagine. I guarantee you will begin to notice hope being reborn in your life.

Yes, Surrender, and Acceptance

To pursue peace and a positive mind, we must conquer resistance. Most of us spend the bulk of our lives in a state of resistance toward *what is*. In our minds we define what a successful life looks like, and when reality doesn't measure up to that, we go into resistance mode. We refuse to fully accept *what is*. We say no to reality. We adopt a state of anger, blame, bitterness, defeat, frustration, or denial.

Anytime there is resistance, friction is created. Friction slows us down and gets us stuck. The greatest way to overcome this blockage is to say yes to whatever is happening right now. The faster we make peace with *what is*, the better we feel and the faster our lives move forward.

To do this we must acknowledge that life will never be perfect. It will always be in flux. It will always be messy. We will never have all of our goals perfectly met at one time. There will always be waxing and waning, failing and succeeding, and these will occur simultaneously. Perfection can only be found in the imperfection itself.

There are three stages we go through in making peace with messy reality: Yes, Surrender, and Acceptance.

To say Yes means to declare faith in what you want. It is to commit to something affirmative instead of just dwelling in disappointment and resentment. There is immense power in speaking aloud those things we desire. The angels perk up and listen.

When we say Yes, we become hungry, eager, and focused. For a while. Then we learn the power of surrendering. Yes and Surrender are not the same thing. Surrender means coming to understand that we don't control the process. And that we can't do it all on our own. We need others, and we also need rest and rejuvenation. We need patience. We need humility. My true power was released when I surrendered my definition of success and the timing of success in my life. I didn't give up hope, but I quit worrying about how and when achievements would manifest for me. And I realized I didn't have to be miserable and unhappy in the meantime.

There is yet a deeper level of surrender, and that is acceptance. Acceptance means fully embracing the *outcomes* that show up in our lives. Acceptance means getting to the place of realizing that our true success resides in our peace—that all of the accomplishment in the world doesn't make for a good life. Peace does. Acceptance means we are empowered to give thanks for everything that is going on in our lives because we recognize that all things are working together for our overall good.

The Yes, Surrender, Acceptance process is as much a spiritual process as a practical one. I'll share an example from my professional life, but this process applies in our personal growth and maturity as well. I've coached my clients through these three stages for many different transitions in their lives.

When I knew I was ready to become an empowerment speaker, I said Yes to that new career and started doing the prep work I needed to do. I began to educate myself, joined the global John Maxwell Team, hired several coaches, worked on my presentation skills, and did other things to ready myself as a speaker. I believed I could still maintain my business, GLUE, while I did this.

As I started to make progress I had to Surrender to the truth that it was going to be a lot harder to do both things—run the business and serve as an empowerment speaker—than I first imagined. A greater time commitment and a more singular focus were required to reach my goal, and I had to Surrender to that fact. I also had to Surrender to an even deeper truth—that I no longer had a passion and desire in my heart for the business and career to which I'd dedicated almost twenty-five years of my life. It had turned into more of a burden.

Finally, I had to reach a point of true Acceptance. I had to make the real and substantive changes in my life that I knew were called for, including closing my business—which took me three years to accept—and setting up my life so as to better focus on becoming exactly the kind of speaker I wanted to be. It meant, for example, adjusting to the fact that I might not have the level of income that I was accustomed to for a few years and making the lifestyle changes to accommodate that, such as selling my home, reducing my family vacations, and having only one vehicle.

Saying Yes is relatively easy, until you realize the costs involved. To Surrender means to really *get* that this thing is going to take longer, require more work, and necessitate a deeper commitment and personal growth than you first thought. Acceptance means peacefully making the changes to accommodate the hard truths of what you've said Yes to. That may mean, for example, changing the timeline for achieving your goal, which almost always takes longer than you first thought. For me, Acceptance also included realizing that some elements of my life that I wanted to maintain had to be changed and, in some instances, removed. My entire previous career, for example, was built on relationships and connecting with people. A major component of my lifestyle and business practice was attending several local events every week and traveling to major events in other cities, such as the NBA All-Star Weekend, Grammy Awards week, and various conferences. I had to accept that this was no longer an effective use of my time and finances. I had to accept and trust that new and unfamiliar steps, such as spending several hours a day in quiet study and writing, were leading me to an unknown future that was better than the great life I was leaving for it. This also meant that some relationships with people who could not support my new mission were going to have to change or end. Tough stuff.

But ultimately Yes, Surrender, Acceptance is the path of peace and greater rewards. Everyone I know who has trusted this process has received more in every aspect of their life—financial, spiritual, social, psychological, and mental. All things are doable through the peace that empowers us. Peace gives us the clarity to see that our lives are worthy of celebration exactly as they are.

Hallelujah.

Vision, Action, Results

Exercise 1: The "I Am Peace" Meditation

Here is a very powerful meditation you can use to find peace on a daily basis and also to change your entire relationship with peace. I have had people report life-changing results from doing this very simple meditation.

1. Sit quietly in a comfortable position with your eyes closed.
2. Take several slow, deep breaths. Pay attention to your breathing.

3. Give your mind permission to release all thoughts. Now begin to notice your thoughts. Each time a thought pops into your head, simply let it go. Don't worry about it. Don't get annoyed by it. Just release it, like a helium balloon.

4. As the frequency of your thoughts begins to lessen, start to become aware of the "empty" space between your thoughts.

5. Notice the quality of profound peacefulness in that space between your thoughts. Notice this space expanding and deepening as your thoughts become less frequent.

6. As you become more deeply aware of the peaceful space between/beyond your thoughts, say to yourself, "I AM peace; I AM joy." Gently shift your sense of identity—your sense of "I am"—away from your head and onto the peaceful space between/beyond your thoughts. Feel your sense of "I am" emanating from within that peaceful space.

7. Hold your sense of "I am" in that new place for as long as you can.

8. When you are ready to return your consciousness to normal, say "I am peace" three times. As you open your eyes, allow your sense of "I am" to remain rooted in that peaceful, silent place. If possible, allow this new place of "I am" to carry forward into your day.

Exercise 2: Pursuing Peace

MY DEFINITION OF PEACE IS . . .

» What are three "triggers" that lead me away from living my definition of peace? Am I willing to consider eliminating these sources of negativity?

» What are three to five "positive triggers"—things I find uplifting—that I will incorporate into my daily routine?

>> What are three to five things I am anxious, stressed, or worried about?

>> In what ways has the lack of peace had an impact on me and my life? On those around me?

>> The following five thoughts always make me feel good . . .

>> Am I willing to substitute these thoughts for the negative thoughts that usually occur when I'm "triggered"?

>> How might my pursuing peace have an impact on those around me?

>> What tools and resources do I believe will help me develop more positive thinking?

>> How will positive thinking increase my peace and productivity?

EXPONENTIAL CONVERSATION

I chose Bert Weiss for this chapter's Exponential Conversation because he is someone who has been able to find peace in the midst of the "storm." There was a period in his life, which he talks about in our conversation, when his father was dying, his marriage was dissolving, and his longtime radio cohost decided to leave the show for a competitor. Bert found peace during this part of his life, but not by accident. He found it by *pursuing* it, by making conscious, loving, positive choices.

Bert, by the way, is the radio host of the nationally syndicated *The Bert Show*, which has been repeatedly voted Atlanta's number one morning radio show. Bert and his cohosts have been bringing listeners a unique blend of lifestyle advice, national entertainment news, celebrity interviews, and humor for over twelve years.

Bert is deeply involved in philanthropy. He has his own nonprofit organization, Bert's Big Adventure (BBA), which provides a magical, all-expenses-paid, five-day journey to Walt Disney World for kids with chronic and terminal illnesses and their families, and supports them with year-round programs. Bert has been recognized for both his career and philanthropy achievements, with awards such as the 11Alive Community Service Award and *Atlanta Business Chronicle*'s annual "100 Most Influential Atlantans" list. He is the proud father of two sons, Hayden and Hollis, who can always make him laugh.

SHERI RILEY: One day a young lady called in to your show, and she was twenty-four, and she said she wanted to kill herself because she couldn't find contentment. You said to her, "The toughest thing you will have to do is change yourself." You told her that through your time with your therapist, you had found this place of joy, of peace. What has been your journey to get there?

BERT WEISS: I had to completely re-create the foundation that was built for me as a child. There really was no family in my family. There were disconnections; there wasn't a lot of value placed on family whatsoever. We were all just kinda living our lives, going through the days, but there wasn't a lot of caring involved. When I first realized I really needed to make a change for myself was when my firstborn, Hayden, came to life and I didn't have a connection with him. I wasn't getting on the floor with him. I was kind of pushing him aside. I was working a lot, he was fourth or fifth on my list, and I just didn't have an emotional connection. I felt myself becoming my dad, and I had always said to myself that was never going to happen. I realized this was not acceptable.

SHERI RILEY: How old was he when this started to come to you?

BERT WEISS: We were probably eight or nine months in. And I'm saying to myself, "Wow, I really don't feel like a dad; he's more of a hassle than anything else." And that's exactly how my dad treated me pretty much my whole life. So I decided to see yet another therapist and make that change. I worked super hard to become the best Bert I have ever been. My father even told me on his deathbed—and it was the greatest gift I ever received from him—that I became the man he never could be.

SHERI RILEY: Wow.

BERT WEISS: I had to re-create who I am. I had to learn how to feel and how to care. The thing is, when you're from a family [where there's no caring], it seems so foreign to do it a healthy way. One of two things was going to happen: I was going to continue this cycle of dysfunction in my own family, or [I was going to realize] I had the power to change myself. But here's the awesomeness of it: when you change and you have kids, you get to change your entire family tree all the way down.

SHERI RILEY: What were some of the hardest things you had to face and do to make those changes? Because it's not easy.

BERT WEISS: I think for me it all came down to losing ego. Really digging inside who you are and who you want to be and what you're perceived to be. These are very different things. You've got to move ego aside. I think in any relationship, whenever you have ego in the way, it's always the biggest obstacle. So when you lose that ego—and I continue to do it every single day—I think that's the biggest challenge and the most rewarding thing you can do. We all want to believe we've got it together and when you get a little older, you realize you really don't.

SHERI RILEY: And you need help.

BERT WEISS: Right, you need help. That was another part of this journey for me. I grew up very independent because my parents really just didn't show a lot of caring. So even now, asking friends or family for help is still very difficult for me. It's easier to ask for help when I'm paying for it, so going to a therapist was easy.

SHERI RILEY: How important has inner peace become to you?

BERT WEISS: I'm still searching for it every single day. This last year, though, I have taken gigantic steps toward that. It's been a tough year. My dad passed away, and we were estranged for years. This has been a year filled with a lot of obstacles and a lot of growth. But it's also brought me closer to peace than I have ever been.

The key I have learned this year is that if you handle your business at the level of integrity that you expect of yourself, then you will find that peace. You will be able to walk away from any situation and say, "I really did give it everything, and there's nothing I would have changed." Let me give you two examples.

With my dad, as I told you, our relationship was just messed up and his relationship with *his* dad was way worse. In my family, you have just a little bit of an argument and you cut each other off for ten years. Literally. So my dad and I had an on-again/off-again relationship, and it was never very loving, never very intimate. I got a call about a year and a half ago from his wife, saying, "I'm leaving your dad and I don't know what you're going to do with him. I know you don't talk to him a lot, but in a couple of months he's gonna be alone." So I had to make a decision. Do I help out? This man doesn't deserve anything. He brought me into the world and then pretty much gave up. But I made the decision, "I'll bring him to Atlanta, put him in a retirement community, and I'll visit him from time to time."

I didn't realize how bad his medical condition was. He was suffering from dementia, COPD, colon cancer. Anyway, my theory was, handle this as if he's dead. How are you going to live without any regret? Everything I did over the course of his last seven months, he certainly didn't deserve it, but I handled it with a level of integrity that I am super proud of. I spent a fortune taking care of his retirement. I visited him and hung out with him, got to know who he was, took him to doctor's appointments. I didn't want to have any regrets. He finally passed away.

SHERI RILEY: That is so powerful.

BERT WEISS: It may have been the first thing I had done in my life where I looked back at the entire time and said, "There's not one thing I would do differently. Not one thing." I took the high road even when my ego was saying, "He doesn't deserve it, he was never there for me, he never showed up for a baseball game, he made me drive myself to the hospital when I broke my hand." But as he said to me, I became the man he never could be. My dad taught me so many lessons by watching him do things the wrong way that he really ended up, in the strangest way possible, the best role model I ever had.

SHERI RILEY: Wow.

BERT WEISS: And in the same year my wife and I separated. We hadn't been happy in a very long time. We worked and worked and worked, super hard, on trying to make it work out, and by the time we ended it I walked away in peace saying, "This is sad, but I did everything I could; I handled it the right way." And I think when you do that, it brings you closer to inner peace.

SHERI RILEY: What value have you personally received in this pursuit of peace?

BERT WEISS: I think the value is the peace itself.

SHERI RILEY: Is there a role that spirituality, or God, or faith, or belief, plays in your journey of peace?

BERT WEISS: Absolutely. I would say that I'm religiously confused, but spiritually clear. I spend a lot of time praying and appreciating the things I have, the places I get to go, and the things I get to do. I feel like I'm being guided. I don't know what that form of God looks like, but I do think that there is a purpose, a reason why things have happened to me. There's a reason why God made me the person I am. Even my therapist has said there's no reason, psychologically, that I should be where I am right now, considering the background I have, my childhood. The only answer is that I'm being guided.

SHERI RILEY: How do you define success?

BERT WEISS: Success is finding that journey of peace. Those small, little nuggets of peace. You can't put a money price on it. You can't say, "When I retire, or when my kids are the capable, responsible gentlemen I'm trying to make them, that will be peaceful to me, and that will be a success." I learned a while ago hanging out with people of affluence and influence—I don't want to say you can't have it all; you just have to adjust what your definition is. I think the people I was hanging out with, their definition of success was money, money, money, and they weren't taking care of their family at all. They were miserable, three-quarters of them, including myself. And I definitely was guilty of this in the beginning of my relationship, not making sure that the framework of my marriage was taken care of because I was working so much.

SHERI RILEY: One of the core things I say with Exponential Living is "Personal development fuels professional growth," and you have so epitomized that in this conversation.

BERT WEISS: I thought I was a good manager ten years ago. I wasn't. I wasn't a good manager of people until recently. The same things I applied with my staff that applied with my kids years ago, and I'm still working on this, that is, investing in my people, timewise. I wasn't raised to really care for people except myself, so I wasn't caring for my kids. I should have cared more in the beginning of my relationship with my wife, or shown it. I just didn't have the skill set. I have it now. I'm not even close to the manager I want to be, but I'm much better now than I was ten to thirteen years ago.

SHERI RILEY: And that's from your personal development?

BERT WEISS: Definitely from the personal development. Through therapy. In trying to get closer to my kids, I realized I need to be more intimate with everybody around me. My friends—and I'm still working on this—my friends, family members, and co-workers, it all kind of blends together. It's really difficult to fight your history. It has to be fought every single day for those of us that came up in a dysfunctional family. And for me it still doesn't come easy. I fight it every day, but every day I get a little bit closer to that peace.

SHERI RILEY: Share with me a time you knew you were challenged with fear, and how you overcame it.

BERT WEISS: Agreeing with my wife that the relationship was over. We were working on it and working on it and we went out for a date night on a Wednesday night. I had printed off this list of things that happy couples do, and I was going to go over it with her at dinnertime. She said to me, "I see you trying so hard, but I just don't think you love me anymore." She was waiting for an answer back. I remember just saying to myself in the back of my head, "If you can just get the words out, it's only gonna take five seconds." But actually saying the words . . . "You're right. I don't love you anymore." Somewhere in the back of my head, somebody was telling me, "If you can just get over the fear of saying those words, then your life is about to change," and that's scary. Life completely changes after you say those words. That was the huge fear, saying those words. I had been with that woman for twenty years; we grew up together pretty much.

SHERI RILEY: What release did both of you guys have after that?

BERT WEISS: Living with authenticity. I think that I was numb for a while and I was tired of pretending. I think she was tired of pretending also. When the words came out, finally, we cried a lot together, and we still have been crying through the holidays together . . . but living authentically, I think, is what came out of that.

SHERI RILEY: I often talk about truth and reality. A lot of times we live in our reality, but we're not living in our truth.

BERT WEISS: I've never thought of it that way. Don't you always feel like you know what your truth is, though?

SHERI RILEY: You always know. I never let my clients say, "I don't know," because the reality is, we do know. We may not want to deal with it, we may be in denial, we may not want to accept what will happen afterward, but we always know.

BERT WEISS: Or you're too scared. It's always that fear that everything's gonna fall apart on you, and I think it rarely does.

SHERI RILEY: When I say "Exponential Living," what comes to mind for you?

BERT WEISS: I really think it may be about that last piece we were talking about. It's about the pursuit of peace; it's the pursuit of authenticity. I wasn't sure of the definition before I walked in here, but in talking to you I think that defines success. Your peace, your authenticity, and the pursuit of both.

I AM BERT WEISS AND I AM EXPONENTIAL LIVING.

Key Takeaways

» Though peace is the most natural thing in the world, it doesn't necessarily *come* to us naturally. We have to work on ourselves to find it.

» When you change yourself, you change your family tree all the way down the line, forever.

» Getting past our fears allows us to live our authentic truth.

» The value of pursuing peace is the peace itself.

Have a Servant's Heart and a Giving Spirit

I have everything that they say you should have to be happy and I'm not happy. You could die tomorrow and you've done a few movies, won some awards—that doesn't mean anything. But if you've built schools or raised a child or done something to make things better for other people, then it just feels better. Life is better.

—ANGELINA JOLIE

I can't think of a better way to open a chapter on service than to share a conversation I recently had with my dear sisterfriend Shanti Das. Shanti is a music industry executive, marketing expert, philanthropist, and author of the book *The Hip-Hop Professional 2.0: A Woman's Guide to Climbing the Ladder of Success in the Entertainment Business*. I got to know Shanti when I worked at LaFace Records and we have been friends ever since. She has managed marketing campaigns for Outkast, Prince, and TLC, among others. I know she has a true servant's heart so I asked her to tell me about how she discovered that service needed to be an integral part of her life. This is what she said, in her own words, which I have edited for length:

> *I think it was the year 2009. I was at the height of my career, executive vice president of marketing at Universal Motown. A lot happened in my life that year. My uncle passed; he was like a dad*

to me. My mother's Alzheimer's got worse that year and also I had developed some health issues myself. I felt like God was trying to tell me something because . . . you know how it is, working in the entertainment industry. We are constantly working to help everyone else to fulfill their goals, and sometimes we tend to lose sight of our own personal journey. So, I prayed about it and talked to friends and family and realized that it was time to make a change in my life.

One night, at work, I was surfing the Net and I came across an article on CNN.com about how broke the city of Detroit was and how they lost a lot of funding for the local morgue. I was mortified when I read that deceased family members were literally stacked up in body bags in the morgue and families couldn't afford to bury them. I thought, "Oh my God, here I am, worried about trivial stuff, and some people can't even afford to bury their family members." That night, at my office, I wrote a heartfelt letter to my colleagues in the entertainment industry and I came up with a name for the initiative, which was May We Rest in Peace. I know this was all God's doing because I've never really organized any sort of charitable efforts. The next morning, I woke up, went to the UPS Store, and suddenly I was kind of leading the charge—with the same sort of excitement as if I was marketing an Outkast album back in my early days.

The response was overwhelming. Within six weeks, I raised six thousand dollars. I negotiated with a local funeral home, and they were able to cremate some of the family members or help bury them for about one thousand dollars per burial. Then I sent a note to one of my colleagues at Atlantic Records to try to reach out to Kid Rock for me because he is a native of Detroit. I thought they would just put me in touch with his management, but, lo and behold, Kid

Rock actually called my cell phone and said, "Hey, I hear what you are doing for my city. It's great. I want to help." He gave five thousand dollars.

I ended up raising thirty thousand dollars to bury thirty people in Detroit, and I thought, "Okay, I get it, God." I decided to move home to Atlanta shortly thereafter, and then the earthquake happened in Haiti. So, I put together Happy Hour for Haiti and I raised five thousand dollars for one of the villages.

Since then, over the last six years, staying back home in Atlanta, I have really been able to pour back into the community through my No Reservations Needed annual Thanksgiving dinner. For that, I partner with the Atlanta Mission; I'm in my fourth year. I've also done six or seven "day of pamperings" with the Genesis Shelter to pamper moms who are homeless with newborn kids. . . .

It's an overwhelming feeling just to know that we are serving others and doing God's work. It's a real blessing, and I never really had that in my life. It just feels right. Sometimes I wake up and I have really tough days, because I suffer from depression. So there might be a day when I'm supposed to go to speak or go serve and I don't know how I'm going to get out of the bed. I'm sure on those days it's God—plus knowing that I'm changing lives and helping others—that gives me the energy to get there.

It really is a purposeful life now. It's the true meaning of Exponential Living. The reward is—I mean, I can't put a price on it. It's priceless, the love I feel in my heart because I know it's the right thing to do, serving my community and my village.

I think it's important, though, that we not only write those checks but that we go out there and roll our sleeves up. Because serving is more than cutting a check. Unless you put yourself out there, you do not get that joy and that feeling of love and compassion. You don't see the light that comes on in someone's heart and mind.

   But I really think service starts in the home and it's about respect and compassion and the ability to see someone through their struggles. Sometimes you take things for granted, especially family members, but God wants us to serve them just as we would serve any stranger. If I can go out and be really kind to a stranger, but I'm not taking care of home, then I'm a hypocrite.

   [When I serve others] it's just an overwhelming feeling knowing you're making somebody else happy for unselfish reasons. I think I get more out of it than the person I'm helping. It sparks a light inside of me that shines bright for the rest of the week, the rest of the month.

I couldn't ask for a better encapsulation of what it means to have a servant's heart and a giving spirit.

A Secret Source of Energy

Many high achievers live in a cycle of depletion and replenishment. They work long hours and subject themselves to constant stress, which takes a toll on them physically, spiritually, psychologically, and mentally. Then they renew themselves—partially—by doing things like taking vacations, going to the gym, drinking, having sexual encounters, or going shopping. These renewal measures work to some degree, but their effect is limited and short lasting. Soon the high achiever is back in the pressure cooker again. There's a relentless ebb and flow to their lives. Depletion, renewal, depletion, renewal.

   What many high achievers do not realize is that they have a bottomless supply of "life fuel" available to them that far exceeds what any short-term fix can offer. And it comes from a most unexpected source. That source is giving and service. Yes, giving is an energy *source*. I have talked to countless individuals who have discovered that, rather than draining them, serving others actually provides them with non-stop energy and power. It seems that serving other human beings is fuel to the human soul—as well as the human heart, body, and mind.

When you learn to have a servant's heart and a giving spirit, the person who ends up gaining the most is you. That's why giving and serving is an essential principle of Exponential Living.

Service Is Right Here, Right Now

Many high achievers do service mainly through charities. They write lots of (tax-deductible) checks. Maybe they spend some time working at a local soup kitchen or a women's shelter, or doing fund-raising activities. Those who have a high enough public profile may even start their own charitable foundations. All of these are valuable endeavors—make no mistake about that—but what many of us tend to forget is that service begins and ends where we are planted, in the here and now. It is not reserved for a few hours a month that take place "over there" in the special space reserved for charity work. It does not happen only when the cameras are rolling and the service recognition awards are being handed out. In order to experience Exponential Living, service must be a constant motivation, an everyday, every-hour type of thing.

Often, it is our families and friends who are the last on the list when it comes to receiving our giving heart and spirit. Many classic high achievers work hard all week, spend their weekends at charity fund-raisers, then come home too tired and grumpy to give to their spouses, children, and family. They miss the point about what service really is.

Though philanthropy is a *very important aspect of giving*, what *really* ignites Exponential Living is how you serve yourself and those around you on a day-by-day basis. You must have the heart of a servant toward those people you love the most. That does not, of course, mean behaving as a paid servant would, or doing things for them that they could do for themselves; it means constantly asking yourself what they truly need—this moment, this day, this year, this season of their lives—and how you can help them achieve it. What your loved ones need might be praise, teaching, security, your undivided attention, encouragement, discipline, tenderness, appreciation, or love (always love). And to give it to them requires more of you than cracking open your checkbook.

Here's a note I keep on my desk: "What we really leave behind us is not what is engraved on stone monuments, but what is woven into the lives of others."

Time and Attention

What the people we love want *the most* from us is not things, money, privilege, or paid bills. It is our time, our attention, our presence. To be fully present to another human being—whether for fifteen seconds or for an entire day or week—is *the greatest gift* we have to offer. My daughter, for example, appreciates all the things my husband does for her, but what she really craves is Monopoly time. She *loves* to play board games with her dad, and nothing else he does comes close, at least at this time in her life. And so he has a choice. When he comes home from a business trip or a long day of work, he can either give in to exhaustion or he can find some energy to play Monopoly with his daughter. Each time he does the latter, he makes an investment far more valuable than money can buy, or sleep can restore.

I often hear high achievers actually *bemoaning* the fact that their families want their time and attention. "Why do they make me feel guilty when I come home tired and want some 'me' time? Can't they see that everything I do at work is for them? When I work fifteen-hour days, I'm doing it so they can have all the things I never had, and a better life." They sometimes come across as if they resent the fact that their loved ones value their presence.

If you catch yourself thinking this way, in any capacity, it's time to get a fresh perspective. Think about how *fortunate* you are to have people who love you so much, they want your time and attention more than the contents of your wallet. Instead of seeing this as a burden, see it as an honor. You have the power to light up the lives of your loved ones simply by giving them your time and attention. It is tragic to view that as anything less than a blessing. Not just for them, but for you. You have such importance to the people around you that all you have to do to make them feel like a million bucks is *be* with them. Amazing.

Think about that the next time you are feeling overwhelmed because your loved ones want your attention. Flip it around and be deeply, deeply thankful. Not everyone in this world is so fortunate.

I guarantee that if you get in the habit of thinking "it is my honor" instead of "it is my obligation" each time you give attention to those you love—or to anyone at all, in fact—you will experience a break-through in your heart. You will be flooded with humility and ap-preciation, rather than with resentment. You will discover a joy, an inner glow, a power, that cannot be matched by any goal attained, possession acquired, title earned, or accolade received. Like Ebenezer Scrooge on Christmas morning, you will feel as if you've been reborn.

Time and attention are the currency of the soul. They are the keys that unlock the hidden 90 percent of who we are.

The Power of Fifteen Minutes

When I was in college studying business, the professors used to tell us, "Identify several people who can serve as mentors or help you in your career, then contact them and request a fifteen-minute information interview." Yeah, great idea. Until I tried it. During my third year in college, I started sending my résumé out to every top-level executive in the music industry and making follow-up calls, asking for informational interviews. Surprise! No one would even take my call, never mind grant me a fifteen-minute informational interview.

Well, that's not completely true. Two VPs did briefly take my call and spent ten minutes on the phone explaining to me that a kid from Kentucky had no chance of working in the music industry. Thanks, guys.

Fast-forward four years. I had now moved to Cleveland, Ohio, and was still trying to break into the industry. *Finally*, I got an account executive at a local radio station to agree to give me a fifteen-minute informational interview, *in person*! I was thrilled beyond reason. It didn't matter that she had no power to hire me—she was working in the music business; that was all I cared about. Sitting in that chair, during our conversation, I felt so overjoyed and encouraged. Why? Because she was only the second person, in all those years of weekly calls and résumés sent, who was willing to give me fifteen minutes of her time. Fifteen simple minutes. I have no memory of what we talked about, but I do know that her agreeing to talk with me was what gave me the strength to persevere when my faith was the size of a mustard seed.

While I was sitting in her office, waiting for our interview, I made a promise to God and to myself: "God, if you bless me to live my dream, I promise you I will always take fifteen minutes to talk with someone, anyone, who needs my time." And throughout my career, I have honored that commitment. Sometimes it might take me six months or even a year to talk with that person, but I always find the time eventually. Not surprisingly, this commitment has brought some of the most brilliant people on planet Earth into my life.

The Rhythm of Service

Giving is one of the great paradoxes of human life. Common sense would seem to tell us that giving is a subtractive process. If I give to you, then something I once possessed—my time, my energy, my money— is now in your hands. Therefore, I should now have less. Right? That's certainly how the ego sees it. But the fact is that giving is an *additive* process for both parties. The recipient gains something, but so does the giver. In fact, giving—when it is done with a servant's heart and a giving spirit—adds more to the giver than it does to the receiver.

A glorious secret I have discovered—and so have many of my clients and colleagues, as you'll learn from the conversations in this

EXPONENTIAL EMBRACE

Mata Amritanandamayi is an Indian spiritual teacher better known as Amma or "the Hugging Saint." For over thirty years she has traveled around the world embracing people in a spirit of blessing. So far she has hugged over thirty-four million people and shows no signs of slowing down. The crowds that line up to hug her can number in the tens of thousands, yet Amma wholeheartedly embraces every last one of them, often going for days with little or no sleep. When asked where she gets her impossible supply of energy, she always replies that she gets it from those she hugs.

chapter—is that giving creates its own kind of energy, its own kind of power. And this is truly an exponential power. It multiplies and remultiplies itself. It starts within the giver, then goes out into the world, then returns to the giver in multiplied ways, feeding him/her more energy, then goes out into the world again, then returns to the giver yet again, and on and on in a virtuous cycle. Those who give of themselves in service to others discover that giving creates its own life rhythm, its own flow. And this rhythm is self-perpetuating. The more we give, the more we are energized to keep on giving.

I find that I can identify giving spirits simply from the light in their eyes. Givers have a presence about them that is unmistakable and an energy level that is unmatched. I used to think that some people were just naturally buoyant and energetic, and that was why they had so much to give to others. I have since learned that it is giving itself that gives people an unbounded supply of energy. Service begets service. Selfishness begets selfishness.

We are all interconnected and share the bond of humanity. What impacts one of us impacts us all. When I give to you, I am truly giving to me. This is not just Hallmark-card sentiment; it is reality. When we adopt this awareness, we become thankful when we have the opportunity to give, and develop a sincere appreciation of all that God has blessed us with. We develop a spirit of gratefulness that infuses every aspect of our lives.

Don't believe me? For one week, try starting every day with the thought, "How may I serve?" As you enter each new environment every day—your family kitchen, the train station where you commute to work, the office—ask yourself afresh, "How can I serve?" and approach everyone you encounter with a servant's heart. At the end of the week, see if you feel drained or energized.

Rinse and repeat.

No Expectations

There is no doubt that the greatest beneficiaries of giving are givers themselves. But even if it weren't for the spiritual and emotional benefits, giving has some business benefits that can't be minimized. One of these is the "law of reciprocity."

It is well-known that people who receive gifts or acts of service feel a sort of obligation to repay the favor. Robert Cialdini writes about this in his book *Influence: The Psychology of Persuasion*. He offers several examples of people and organizations that performed acts of generosity and were amply rewarded for them.

One of these was a well-known religious organization that once raised money by having its members dance on the streets and "beg" passersby for donations. Many people considered these sect members to be a public nuisance, and frequent jokes were made about them. So the group decided to change tactics. It began giving out flowers as gifts to pedestrians. No strings attached, no obligations. The organization's donation level immediately began to rise. According to Cialdini, this new strategy, based on giving before getting, brought in enough money for the group to acquire temples, businesses, houses, and other types of property all around the world.

Have you ever gotten any "free gifts" in the mail from a charity organization—things like stickers or mailing labels or coins? Organizations send out these gifts in hopes of activating the law of reciprocity in you.

Reciprocity is a powerful dynamic. But here is a crucial point to remember: this doesn't mean you should give with the *intention* of getting something in return. If the main reason you're doing a service for someone is so that they will reciprocate, then you are engaged in an act of commerce, not in an act of giving. Your heart is not in the right place. This applies in the home as well as in the business environment. A husband who brings his wife flowers in the hopes of getting something in return—you *know* what I'm talking about, ladies—is not really engaged in the act of giving. True giving, true service, is done without any expectation of thanks, returned favors, recognition, or other benefits. That's why Principle 4 is called "Have a Servant's *Heart* and a Giving *Spirit*." Only when you serve *for the sake of serving* do the inner walls of stinginess and self-interest come tumbling down. And that's when the blessings start to flow for everyone involved.

No Control, No Conditions

Many of us high achievers do wish to serve our families, friends, and loved ones, but we limit our effectiveness because of our controlling nature. We strive to control the outcomes of our "generosity," and so we set conditions on our service. For example, we might tell a jobless friend, "You can borrow my car for two weeks, but you must promise to go on at least one job interview per day." We believe we know what's best for the recipient, so we try to use our giving as a crowbar to leverage their behavior.

Even prayer can often include a desire to control the outcome for another person. What we are really saying is "Please, God, make this person act the way I want them to act."

I speak as a recovering control freak, so I know this trait very well. It does have some positive aspects. For example, you tend to be proactive instead of waiting for others to do things for you. But there's a fine line between being proactive and having an agenda for every situation. When we are constantly trying to control those around us, we interfere with the giving intention and the giving process. This creates resentment and pushback in the recipient.

A good example is my oldest daughter. There were so many areas in her life where I *knew* that I could help her grow and take advantage of the amazing opportunities presented to her. Whenever I would do something for her, it would be with an intention to nudge her toward the greatness of her capabilities. But this desire to "fix" things about her, even though I felt I was helping her, caused friction in our relationship.

I had to learn to release my control and allow her to grow at her pace into who, how, what, and where she wanted to be. Even though my judgment told me there were greater things she could do, I realized I couldn't control her desire to go after those things.

Similarly, with my husband, I wanted his growth to move at the pace that I believed was best for him and for our family. So the things I did for him were always steeped in that agenda. But the reality is, I can't control the timeline for his development or his desire either. I had to cease my attempts to control his responses to growth opportunities in his life.

I have finally learned that when it comes to serving your family, all you can do is encourage them, inspire them, hold them accountable, and, yes, communicate your desires to them. But then you must release yourself from the outcome.

Of course, if a seriously disruptive situation arises—such as a child who is taking drugs or a spouse who is cheating—you need to steer that situation toward a defined outcome. But in the normal course of events, you must serve your family and friends with the understanding that they have a right to do whatever they wish with your input, and that includes completely ignoring it.

When I finally understood this, I realized that my desire to control my family had kept me focused on the 10 to 20 percent of them that (I felt) needed to change as opposed to honoring the 80 to 90 percent that was wonderful. And, of course, the more I tried to control their outcomes and behaviors, the more resistance they developed. By releasing my control, I was able to take my focus off *them* and place it on me. This allowed me to honor and serve them more purely. I then found I was able to engage with their 80 to 90 percent rather than being upset about the 10 to 20 percent. This also allowed me to be more honest about my own needs.

One of the most powerful ways we can serve those closest to us is to accept and honor who they are right now while praying for and supporting those things that will help them become even better versions of themselves. But this must be done without trying to control them or the outcome. Control is exhausting for everyone, and it weakens, rather than strengthens, relationships. Why? Because it is based on external power, not inner power. When you try to control others, you become the external power exerting itself on *their* inner power.

Not for the Ego, for the Other

Another way of saying this is that service to others should not be done primarily to satisfy *your* emotional needs. Service should always be done with the good of the other person in mind. That means it should be based on the true needs of the other person.

For example, it might feel good *to you* to serve a meal at the local homeless shelter, but maybe if you talked to one of the residents, you would find out that what he or she really *needs* is shoes. It might be fun to toss a ball with your son in the backyard, or to play a game with him on the Xbox, but maybe what he really *needs* from you is help understanding algebra. It might satisfy *you* to donate to the local food bank, but maybe what that *organization* really needs is someone with your expertise to serve on its board.

When you have the impulse to be of service, make sure your service meets the real, felt needs of the person you are helping. When we focus on what the other person needs, rather than on our own emotional rewards, we typically find that service can be rather challenging and inconvenient. For example, it's relatively easy for a movie star to attend a fund-raiser for a nonprofit organization that helps single mothers, but it might be harder for that star to actually babysit her single sister's kids. It might be fun for a rock star to play a benefit concert (that coincidentally also helps him promote his new CD), but it might be more challenging for him to give guitar lessons to his nephew who recently suffered a brain injury. It's easy to give your daughter a cookie, but it's harder to read her a bedtime story when you're dog-tired.

Real giving often has a cost to us. If it didn't, the gift wouldn't have real value. But think of it as an investment in something you value. One way or another, that investment *will* pay dividends. They may be dividends you can see and feel, or they may be hidden dividends that will never be apparent to you. But no act done with a servant's heart and a giving spirit is ever in vain. It always gains interest and creates value of some kind.

In college, when my friends and I would discuss what we wanted to do after we graduated, I would always say, "I want to make a difference." I wanted to affect things on a global scale, because I wanted to believe I mattered profoundly. But what I finally learned is that "making a difference" isn't just about helping the sick, underprivileged, and war ravaged; it's about helping those in need who are standing right beside me.

The Miracle of Giving When You Have Nothing

The biggest reason people offer for not giving and not being of service is lack of resources. They don't give money because they're behind on their own bills. They don't volunteer their time because they're working sixty hours a week. They don't give of their spirit because they're feeling burned out. But I am here to tell you that when you give of exactly those things you *don't* think you have, you open the door to miracles.

Earlier, I mentioned a period in my life a few years ago when everything had fallen apart for me, financially and emotionally. During that extremely trying time, I facilitated three mastermind groups for high achievers. I felt I had absolutely nothing to give, but I did it anyway. Before each meeting I would sit in my car and cry, then pray for the strength to serve.

As I look back on that time in my life, I realize that it was those acts of service and pouring myself into the lives of others that saved my life. Having a reason, outside of my own pain, to pull myself together, hold myself accountable, and find my inner strength empowered me not just to "go through" this hard time in my life, but to "grow through" it. Being committed to serving the personal and professional needs of the men and women in these groups was what forced me to find power within myself. And that is what got me through. If I had contented myself by saying, "I can't do these groups right now because I have nothing to give," it would have been a self-fulfilling prophecy.

When you give what you don't think you have—time, money, energy, love—you make the strongest commitment possible to increase that very thing in your life.

Service Starts with Serving Yourself

Even though there are times in our lives when serving from our broken places empowers our healing, you can't continually serve others, at your highest level, if you are always running on empty. That is why YOU must be a main recipient of your service and giving. As I stated earlier, serving and giving to your loved ones must come from your overflow, not from your fumes.

Often we high achievers push ourselves to keep going and going, like the Energizer Bunny, because we see it as a badge of honor to always press through. We insist on being superheroes and minimize our own need for sleep, nutrition, entertainment, and nurturing. We put ourselves last. Even when the world takes a break from beating us up, we continue to kick our own butts.

We need to flip this around. There are times as parents and as spouses that we must say to our families, "I can't mother or father you today; I need you to love on me. I need to receive your love."

This is not selfish; it is healthy and necessary. As important as it is to be of service to others, it is equally important to *receive the giving and service of others*. Otherwise we shortchange ourselves. We also shortchange those around us by depriving them of the privilege to serve. Not *accepting* service is just as destructive as not giving service. It stops the giving cycle in its tracks.

We need to give both ourselves and others permission to love us and love on us. Loving ourselves well is how we show those closest to us how to love us.

For many years, I wanted my husband to express his love for me in a certain way. I wanted him to speak up on my behalf to family and friends. I wanted more of his support in work situations that I felt I was handling alone. I wanted him and my bonus daughter to show me a higher level of appreciation. For many years, I felt they took me for granted. They loved me and expressed their love for me but not as consistently or at the level I desired.

By giving love to myself, I showed them the types of expressions of love that I really needed. When I let go of trying to control how *they* loved me and began expressing appreciation to myself in the way I needed, I *showed* them what I couldn't tell them. They eventually joined me in this expression of love and we all felt better giving and serving one another.

Part of serving yourself is knowing how to say no. Many of us, when we adopt a giving spirit, fall into the trap of saying yes to every request that's made of us. But spreading ourselves too thin does no one any favors. It just means that we fall behind on our commitments and run ourselves into the ground. One of the greatest acts of service is the act of saying no. *No* says that we honor ourselves and our current commitments.

Saying no isn't a personal jab against anyone else; it's just saying yes to you. It also gives your *yes* more power when you decide to use it with others.

Service on the Job

Service-mindedness should be part of what we do, all day, every day. Not just at home, but at work.

If you work with customers or clients, your primary focus should be on providing service to them, not on what you are getting *from* them. If you are a public figure, your main focus should be on serving your audience, your readers, your fans, your constituents. If your work does not put you in contact with the public, your main focus should be on serving your organization in its mission.

Of course, it helps if that mission is one that brings positive value to the world. If you truly want to experience Exponential Living, you should work only for organizations that have a mission you absolutely believe in. That way, you can fully give of yourself every moment of every day, with a servant's heart and without inner conflict. If you own your own business, find a way to infuse it with a meaningful mission, so that every hour of work feels like an act of service toward something bigger than yourself. My mission, for example, is to empower people with the tools to pursue peace, choose clarity, and live courageously. I know this is my purpose in serving the world. My heart and spirit are completely aligned with my work. Thus, everything I do, every hour and every minute of my workweek, feels like an act of service. I encourage you to feel the same way about what you do for a living.

The Sequence of Giving

In my experience, there is a flow of giving/serving that aligns with Exponential Living. When the below are woven together like a tapestry, flowing fully in your life, you create a robust "rhythm of service":

1. God
2. Self
3. Family
4. Career
5. Community/the world

Serving God and yourself first "fills your cup" so that you have an overflow you can give to others. Trying to serve from an empty cup is pointless for all concerned; you must have something to give.

After taking care of yourself, you give to your family, your career, and to your community/the world, in that order, which ensures that you are prioritizing your service correctly. You are serving where you are most needed first, not last.

Vision, Action, Results

Exercise 1: The "How Can I Serve?" Challenge

» List some of your favorite environments that you regularly spend time in. These might be, for example, your bedroom, kitchen, living room, neighborhood, office, favorite lunch restaurant, grocery store, parents' home, etc.

» List at least three things you can do in each environment from a servant's heart and a giving spirit. For example, in your neighborhood, you might pick up trash on the street, shovel snow in front of your neighbor's house, or start a conversation with a neighbor.

» Make a seven-day commitment to ask yourself, "How can I serve today?" At the end of each day, answer these questions in a notebook:

> » What acts of service/giving did I perform today?
> » How did the people involved respond?
> » How did I feel after each act of service/giving?
> » How successful was I at serving/giving today?
> » What can I do better tomorrow?
> » What opportunities to serve/give did I miss?
> » How do I feel now?

Exercise 2: Developing a Servant's Heart

Please write answers to the following questions:

» In what areas do I have a heart to give and serve?

» Outside of my profession/career, what do I love to do? How much time do I devote to serving myself in this way?

» When I spend time with my family, I feel . . .

» Of all the time I spend with my family, what percentage of that time (based on 100 percent) am I . . .

    » fully engaged? _____
    » distracted/thinking about work? _____
    » so tired I am not really present? _____

» Write the (applicable) names of your parents, spouse, children, and at least three friends/relatives. Beside each name, list at least two ways you could be better serving this person.

» What do I need to change in myself/my habits to serve my loved ones more?

» Looking back over my life, what have I done to serve people consistently?

EXPONENTIAL CONVERSATIONS

Tracy Wilson Mourning

For this chapter I spoke with *two* "Exponential Pioneers" instead of just one, Tracy Mourning and Darrell Griffith. I guess you could say that Tracy represents the giving spirit and Darrell the servant's heart, though they both exemplify both traits.

Tracy Wilson Mourning is a designer, broadcast journalist, motivational speaker, author, mother, and wife to retired NBA All-Star Alonzo Mourning. Tracy and her husband have enjoyed wealth and success since their early twenties, but Tracy's giving spirit is not born of the dutiful responsibility that goes along with fame; it is a fundamental part of who she is. It radiates from her every cell. Tracy founded the Honey Shine Mentoring Program, dedicated to enriching the lives of young women, but she gives to those around her in ways too numerous to count.

SHERI RILEY: The premise of the chapter is to have a servant's heart and giving spirit. You and Alonzo have this teamwork. You have this essence and this purity of your heart, and he has this commitment to serve.

TRACY MOURNING: Alonzo was a great example for me because when he was first drafted to the NBA, and we went to Charlotte, automatically he wanted to give back. There was this group home there called the Thompson Children's Home, and that was his mission, because he was in a group home at one point in his life. And from that point on, he was a great teacher for me in that.

All my life I've been blessed. I've been aware of those blessings. I've watched others around me that maybe didn't receive what I have received all my life. I knew I was called because I was meant to do something with it. I was given so much because I was to share and make a difference in someone else's life.

SHERI RILEY: Tell me about a moment that service really touched you.

TRACY MOURNING: God placed on my heart Honey Shine, my mentoring program, when my husband's job took us back to South Florida. I grew up in South Florida, and Miss Annie Lou Johnson was this amazing woman who took care of me when my mom worked. Cleaned houses and worked at the jail. She lived in a neighborhood where individuals walked down the street looking like zombies, and no one messed with them. She'd have coins in her pocket, and anyone asked, she'd give. And it was in visiting her [later] that I saw these groups of girls walking around the same neighborhood I grew up in with babies on their hip. Little girls, house shoes on their feet, in the middle of the street. And it was then that God placed it on my heart: you're to do something about that.

I didn't listen right away, and that voice kept getting louder and louder. So one day I gathered a group of girlfriends around my table and said this is what we're to do. And here we are, going on fifteen years later. It was one of the many moments that I knew I was here to make a difference.

SHERI RILEY: I say this all the time to you. You have the most beautiful spirit. What do you attribute that to?

TRACY MOURNING: It's a reflection of you. That's why you see it. It's God.

SHERI RILEY: What's the legacy that you and Alonzo want to leave for your children?

TRACY MOURNING: Well, that's big. To serve. To give back. To make a difference in someone else's life. Our children's lives have been blessed in so many ways. We've had our challenges, as a family and as individuals, but we're so blessed in so many ways and you have to pay it forward. And our children know that too. . . . You have a responsibility to pay it forward. To make a difference in someone else's life, because it comes back. You don't do it because it comes back, but I'm a witness that it comes back.

SHERI RILEY: What is the legacy you want to leave in the world?

TRACY MOURNING: If my children are good people and making a difference in this world, then I'm all good. And I want women and girls to know that they can be and do anything they want in this world. And that we're bosses. We got this. Even when we don't feel like we do. Because when we take care of our women and girls, I feel like we change this world.

SHERI RILEY: What's a success story of yours? I know there are many.

TRACY MOURNING: When we started Honey Shine summer camp—it was only one week long back then; now it's six—and I went home the first day crying. I said to Alonzo, "I'm not going back." I was praying and he was, like, you gotta go back. I was like, "God, I'm sure you want me on a beach somewhere. Umbrellas and drinks. I know that's where I'm supposed to be."

I was praying and the next morning I went to camp. I was in my car praying, and I got out and went inside. Soon as I walked in, a Honey Bug runs up to me and hugs me, and she says, "Miss Tracy, I told God thank you for Honey Shine." It was over. That was that moment for me that just said, this is what you're supposed to be doing.

SHERI RILEY: As a family, you guys serve. You serve during tragedies. You serve at home. You serve through your charities, through your foundations. How do you determine where you're going to give your time?

TRACY MOURNING: It's all about kids for us. For me, it's all about women and girls, and education. My mother would always say, "Tracy, if they can keep you uneducated, they can control you." And I never knew who "they" were until I had children of my own, until I was educating my own children and working with kids in communities where two out of twelve are graduating from high school.

SHERI RILEY: With all the service you do in the community, how do you honor your family? How do you serve your family?

TRACY MOURNING: Giving of time. Giving of attention. Undivided. Sundays are our day. It would be great if my children thought that Sundays meant church. But my children think Sundays mean Houston's. That's our time together, family dinner. That's how I honor them. And I honor them by being true to who I am, being honest about my feelings, being honest with my thoughts. My kids and I have some amazing conversations, at every single age. . . . So I honor my family by respecting them as individuals, and loving them exactly where they are, because they do the same for me.

SHERI RILEY: How do you define success?

TRACY MOURNING: Peace. Success for me is not necessarily a degree. I have that. It's not necessarily financial freedom. I have that. It's not an abundance of friends or relationships. I have that. Success, for me, is peace.

SHERI RILEY: When I say "Exponential Living," what does that mean to you?

TRACY MOURNING: That's a new word you introduced to my vocabulary. Thank you. Give me the definition.

SHERI RILEY: Exponential Living is pursuing peace, choosing clarity, and living courageously.

TRACY MOURNING: That's me! How did you know!

I AM TRACY WILSON MOURNING
AND I AM EXPONENTIAL LIVING.

Darrell Griffith

Darrell Griffith, aka "Dr. Dunkenstein," is a retired NBA player who spent his entire career with the Utah Jazz. He's also the owner of Griff's, a popular sports-themed restaurant in Louisville, Kentucky, and special assistant to the president of the University of Louisville.

Given his many accomplishments, you might think Darrell would have reason to put on airs. But he is one of the humblest, most service-minded people I have ever met. After his basketball career ended, Darrell returned home to Louisville, Kentucky, where he started the Darrell Griffith Foundation to help those in need. For over twenty-four years, his foundation has hosted the Darrell Griffith Foundation Experience, which is one of the largest and longest-running events during the Kentucky Derby. But it's the way Darrell behaves when the cameras *aren't* rolling that most impresses me. Whenever he sees someone in need—whether it's a colleague or a homeless person on the street—he quietly moves in to help. And he is wise enough to know that he himself is the greatest beneficiary of the service he gives.

SHERI RILEY: In the twenty-plus years we have worked together, you have so exemplified having a servant's heart. You have the Darrell Griffith Foundation. Did you always know you wanted to serve?

DARRELL GRIFFITH: Well, I think we're all given examples of giving as a child—we just don't realize it. The first example is Christmas. We get gifts on Christmas when we are young kids. As we get older, we start being able to *give* gifts and to know the meaning of Christmas and why the most important words in the Bible are to love and give. "For God so *loved* the world that He *gave* His only begotten son."

No matter who you are, someone has helped you along the way. Someone has given you something. And if you came up in a good household, you recognize what has been given to you, first by your parents. And you understand the sacrifice that comes with giving, and it sticks with you. Our parents would always point out the people who were less fortunate than we were at Christmastime, and that stuck with me. Being in a community and seeing people on the corner with signs saying they need help for food. I told my kids if you ever see that and you have money, don't ask questions—give them the money. And to this day if I see someone at a corner, I always stop. I don't even question what their motive is. That's between them and God. I put the money in the bucket and keep moving.

As a kid I was blessed. Even in college people went out of their way to make sure I got my education. They directed me in the right way to be able to achieve the goals that I wanted to achieve. I was blessed that a goal of mine (playing basketball) came true, but I knew it wasn't going to last forever. God blesses you with the resources to help your family, help yourself, and help your kids.

I always wake up in the morning, wondering what I can do to help somebody. And really, Sheri, money is not the most important way of giving. The most important gift you can give someone is your time.

SHERI RILEY: It was natural for you because of the example you had. How did you try to expand that to your peers, to other men around you?

DARRELL GRIFFITH: Well, it's easy, Sheri. What you end up doing is you get them involved. It's that simple. If I'm in the car with my friends, and I see a lady on the corner with her grocery basket with all her belongings in it, I stop my car and I tell my friends, "Here is one hundred dollars. Go over and give it to that lady." It just happened about six months ago and my friend Rob got out of the car and went over and gave the lady the money. And to me, sometimes the things that you do in silence have the most powerful impact. Didn't say anything to Rob. The only thing I said was "I hate seeing people do without." But I guarantee you it had an impact on him. Now he can start seeing things like that.

You know, when I feed three hundred homeless people for dinner, I try to get everybody as involved as possible. I do it at a college here in town; I use their cafeteria. I get the local transit authority, TARC, involved. They go around and pick people up at all the different shelters. We bring them over to Spalding College cafeteria and I have the youth in my church serve them dinner.

SHERI RILEY: Oh, I love it.

DARRELL GRIFFITH: And the homeless people come in and I have them sit down. They're not going through any lines because they've been going through lines all day long. The youth from my church, they go through the line, get the meal, and serve the people. And I tell the kids to always be friendly and always look the people in the eye.

SHERI RILEY: We both know, as people of faith, that the Bible says you reap what you sow. I know you don't do any of this in order to get back, but how has serving benefited you personally?

DARRELL GRIFFITH: When you have a servant's heart, the benefit you get out of it is one simple word; it's just joy. To see that people are able to be in a better place from something that you've done to help them. I don't do anything for publicity. My Derby event—if it wasn't for the fact that I have to advertise it, I'd rather nobody knew. I don't need a big picture of me with a big check. That's not important to me.

SHERI RILEY: When you give, the joy you get is beyond anything you could express. And it's joy that really fuels our soul. There are so many people who have these foundations and they do great work financially, but they're not living a servant's heart. What would you share with them?

DARRELL GRIFFITH: Eliminate the financial part and ask yourself how you give your time. Because, as we talked earlier, time is the most important thing you can give someone. Financially, that's the extra stuff. Time comes first. You need to figure out how you're going to fit with the need in your community, or your family, or whatever. And it could be as simple as advice, or just being an ear, giving someone direction. Sometimes in family conflict or friends conflict, we tend to run away because we don't want to be a part of it, instead of seeing how we can zero in and help that person—if they want to be helped.

SHERI RILEY: When I say "Exponential Living," what comes to mind?

DARRELL GRIFFITH: I think for me it's just being able to be at peace with where you are with yourself and being able to tackle things in your life with peace.

*I AM DARRELL GRIFFITH
AND I AM EXPONENTIAL LIVING.*

Key Takeaways

» When you "pay it forward" you are always paid back.

» Giving to your family—or to anyone, really—means giving them your time and attention.

» No matter who you are, someone has given you something along the way that has helped you.

» The service you do in silence, without recognition, often has the greatest impact.

» The benefit you get from having a servant's heart is joy.

Stop Working, Start Maximizing

There's more money in what I know than what I do.
The longer I stay tied to what I do, I miss the abundance
of what I deserve.

—ALLYSON BYRD

The principle I am going to share with you in this chapter can change your life in a hurry. In a way, it is the very *engine* of Exponential Living. To master this principle, you must understand the other eight. And when you set Principle 5 in motion, it *activates* the other eight.

The principle is this:

Stop working. That's right. Stop working. Abandon the idea of *work* altogether, along with all the baggage that comes along with that word. Start *maximizing* instead. Maximizing opportunities instead of working is the secret shared by many who experience Exponential Living, such as my friend Scooter Braun, the music and media mogul behind the careers of megastars like Justin Bieber and Ariana Grande. All day, every day, Scooter focuses on maximizing opportunities. As a result, he is one of the most successful people in the entertainment industry.

I suggest you try it. From the time you awaken in the morning till the time you go to bed at night, invest all of your energy in maximizing your life in every area. Sometimes hard effort is involved in maximizing opportunities; sometimes it isn't. But one thing I can tell you for sure is that busywork does not equal productivity and does not guarantee forward movement. Labor and effort have value only if they are serving to maximize your opportunities.

You must stop thinking that just because you are working hard, you are accomplishing something. You must give up the tyranny of the to-do list and invite a whole new paradigm into your life.

Are you ready?

Light Dawns on Me

I can remember the moment like it was yesterday. It was back when I worked at LaFace Records. I was sitting at my desk with my head down, working, as usual. That was my constant MO. Always working. Always slogging through my to-do list. No nonsense. Head always down.

Antonio "LA" Reid, the co-owner of LaFace Records, walked up to the door to my office. It took me a minute to even realize he was there. When I finally looked up, LA gave a little laugh, with a knowing glint in his eye.

"Sheri, you are a marketing superstar," he said, "a freaking marketing genius. Your campaigns have allowed my artists to sell millions. But your head is always down. Do you realize that? Always down."

I looked at him uncomprehendingly. What was his point?

"That head-down thing, it's going to limit your career. See, while your head is down, opportunities are passing right on by you, and you don't even see them."

I still didn't get his point. After all, if my head was down, that meant I was working. He was my boss; wasn't that what he wanted? Wasn't I proving my value to his company by always working hard and getting the job done?

LA smiled and walked away, leaving me to think about what he'd said.

I did. But only for a few seconds. I had work to do.

It wasn't till over a decade later, in 2009, that I finally *got* what he was trying to tell me. I was on an airplane heading back to Atlanta from Miami, where I'd been helping out at an annual event.

For fifteen years, Alonzo and Tracy Mourning hosted this *extravaganza* called Zo's Summer Groove. It was a weekend in July where activities included a golf outing, a comedy show, teen empowerment sessions, a concert, a gala, and an NBA-sanctioned basketball game, with all the proceeds going to charity. Many of the best players in the NBA participated every year, and every event sold out.

Every year, except for two, I served as a volunteer. This was always one of my favorite weekends of the year. Not only did I get to serve with my friends and other amazing people but I also had the privilege of helping raise money to help children from underprivileged neighborhoods.

Every year, this weekend involved a lot of work, a lot of fun, and little to no sleep. The year 2009 was no different. On the plane coming back I was physically exhausted. At this time in my life, my youngest daughter was three years old and, because I now had the added responsibility of being a mom, my exhaustion level had reached an all-time high. As I was flying toward home, I prayed for the strength to jump straight back into mommy mode, after having been away from my daughter for almost five days—as well as catch up on all of the "work" I needed to do for my clients and business. I didn't think I had the strength or energy.

Suddenly, my anxiety melted and gave way to an overwhelming sense of joy. Even though I had "worked" all weekend, I realized this was the one weekend that I "kept my head *up*" and accomplished a great deal. I so loved what I'd been doing that it was hard to call it work. I realized this was true of being a mom too. I said to myself, "I can't use the word *work* anymore. Let's say I 'maximized opportunities' all weekend." I realized that was how I needed to look at every aspect of my life—my coaching and speaking, my parenting, my marriage. I needed to lose the whole idea of work. I needed to shift to a mind-set of maximizing opportunities. Work drains you; maximizing elevates and energizes you.

In that moment, it became official. I resigned from working. I literally said out loud, "I resign," and declared, "I will never work again. I will only maximize opportunities." Work had been good to me, but that season in my life was over. I loved my career and loved my family so much, I could no longer allow myself to have the mind-set that attending to them was work. Flying home to focus on my clients and the responsibilities of my company, and to meet a three-year-old ball of joy who was going to jump into my arms the second she saw me, I realized that the time I was going to spend getting caught up with my professional commitments and with my family, even in my exhaustion, couldn't be considered work; it was everything my heart desired. Since July 2009, I have not worked—all I have done is maximize opportunities. It has been a huge relief.

Working Vs. Maximizing

It took me many years to understand the wisdom LA Reid had imparted that day in the doorway. When you spend your days with your head down, busily knocking things off of your to-do list, you cannot see opportunities popping up around you, opportunities that might allow you to powerfully and gracefully leap forward in all of your endeavors. By contrast, when you are open to seeing *opportunities* as your primary concern, and then do *only the work needed* to maximize those opportunities, your life takes a quantum leap in both productivity and joy.

Many high achievers are so focused on working that work becomes an end in itself. They become addicted to the demands, the stress, and the sense of accomplishment they get from working hard, even if their hard work isn't leading them anywhere they want to go. Often, high achievers don't even realize they have achieved what they are working for and that it's time to move on to something else.

Work is labor, folks. That's all it is. It has value only to the extent that it accomplishes something you truly desire. Many of us high achievers operate under some version of the Puritan work ethic. That is, we believe that work has value in and of itself. So therefore, if we do a lot of it, *we* must be valuable. So we take on lots of work, and keep ourselves very busy, but not necessarily as productively as we could. We exhaust ourselves because we confuse work with value. At the end of a tiring workweek, we look back and say, "Well, at least I did *that*." We may not be any closer to our dreams, but we sure did work.

Of course, sometimes maximizing opportunity requires a great deal of effort. I'm not suggesting that success just happens without taking action. What I am saying is that action done intentionally, with the goal of maximizing an opportunity, has an entirely different character from work for work's sake.

A major key to Exponential Living is to think in terms of *opportunities* rather than *responsibilities*. There is a huge difference between the two.

Opportunity Vs. Responsibility

An opportunity is something you actively desire and strive toward; a responsibility is something you are required to take care of. A key to Exponential Living is to be alert for new opportunities, every hour of every day, and when opportunities arise, to respond to them effectively. You also need to reframe some of your current "responsibilities" as opportunities.

Here are some examples of reframing responsibilities as opportunities:

Instead of viewing your day at the office as drudgery, see it as an opportunity to build your career as a company leader. If you see it this way, new opportunities will reveal themselves many times a day. Writing a routine intraoffice memo, for example, suddenly becomes an opportunity for you to demonstrate your writing skills, your value system, your grasp of the company's strategy, and your sense of humor. That stack of forms you need to review? That suddenly becomes an opportunity to teach an aide how to do the job. Not only does this help you develop your managerial skills, but now you can take the hour and a half you gained and use it to make strategic phone calls and work on your idea for a new product.

Instead of thinking of parenting as a duty, think of it as an opportunity to build a relationship with your children and to help sculpt them into future global citizens. That attitude gives you a powerful and purposeful outlook. It means if you have only forty-five minutes to spend with your children today, you will use it to do something that brings you all closer together and that models good values, rather than just yelling at your kids, impatiently helping them with homework, or passively watching TV together.

Instead of resentfully fixing the porch because your wife keeps bugging you about it, see the task as an opportunity to improve your home's value. Instead of dutifully calling your mom every Sunday because you promised her you would, think of it as an opportunity to practice your listening skills. Instead of dragging yourself to your spouse's company dinner, see it as an opportunity to invest in your marriage and make your spouse look good to his/her boss.

When you learn to look at life as a series of opportunities to maximize, a few things happen. You begin to realize that many of your present "responsibilities" actually contain life-enhancing energy. You've been robbing them of their vitality by seeing them as things you "have" to do, rather than as privileges you are blessed with. You begin to open up to new opportunities you hadn't even noticed before. You start to use your time *much* more efficiently. Maximizing opportunities creates a very different mind-set toward work itself. You gravitate toward doing those actions that accomplish the most with the least effort, rather than those that generate the greatest amount of busywork. Sometimes making one phone call, for example, accomplishes five times more than writing a hundred memos or e-mails.

Of course, some responsibilities can't be reframed as opportunities. In those cases, you may need to just drop those responsibilities altogether.

Maximizing opportunities has a very different character from working on responsibilities:

WORKING ON RESPONSIBILITIES ...	MAXIMIZING OPPORTUNITIES ...
Feels heavy.	Feels light and exciting.
Is a burden.	Is a privilege.
Consumes energy.	Produces energy.
Can seem meaningless and rote.	Feels purposeful and meaningful.
Is driven by a sense of duty; it's something we *have* to do.	Is driven by a sense of optimism; it's something we *want* to do.
Leads to routine, repetition.	Inspires creativity.
Discourages efficiency; we tend to drag tasks out unnecessarily.	Inspires efficiency; we want to get the most bang for our buck.
Puts us in a negative mood that makes others want to avoid us.	Magnetizes others to us.
Gives us a sense of completion.	Gives us a sense of openness and possibility.
Is associated with a "pushing" type of energy; we have to push ourselves to get through it.	Is associated with a "pulling" type of energy; it pulls us forward.
Leads to success only in the "10-percent" part of our lives.	Leads to success that opens up the hidden 90 percent.

To shift to the mind-set of maximizing opportunities, it helps to use that actual phrase. Instead of talking about work, talk about maximizing opportunities. Yes, say it out loud, every morning (or at least to yourself). "What opportunities am I going to maximize today?" Try saying it and see what a difference it makes.

Less Is More

> The less effort, the faster and more powerful you will be. It's not the daily increase but daily decrease. Hack away at the unessential.
>
> —BRUCE LEE

To maximize opportunities is not to DO more, but rather to AC-COMPLISH more. In many ways it is the opposite of working hard. To maximize means to use your time and energy efficiently. It means asking yourself every day, "What are the two or three things I can do today that will accomplish the most?" I recently read that Warren Buffett writes down twenty-five things that he needs to do. He then whittles the list to his top five and discards the other twenty things. His philosophy is that the other items are distractions from his focusing, committing to, and maximizing what's most important. Remember the importance of distinguishing distractions from opportunities that we talked about in an earlier chapter?

In football, "yardage gained" is often used as a way to assess how well a team has played. But that is misleading. After all, yardage doesn't matter on the scoreboard. A team that racks up a lot of yards but doesn't score a lot of points is actually playing inefficiently. It is working hard, marching up and down the field, but it isn't scoring touchdowns. *Touchdown yards are the yards that matter.* A more meaningful metric that some analysts are using today is *scoring efficiency*. This metric looks at how many points the team scores *per* yard gained. "Power" teams are those that rack up the *fewest* yards for each point scored. Fewer yards, but more points. That's efficiency. Power teams consistently create good field position for themselves—so they don't *have* to travel long distances—and also score on turnovers and trips to the red zone. In other words, they maximize opportunities.

Imagine how you would manage your workday if your intention, every hour of every day, was to maximize opportunities, not log a lot of work hours.

Your O.N.E. (Overall Navigating Edge) Thing

To maximize opportunities, rather than just fill up time by working, it is crucial to know what your O.N.E. thing is. By O.N.E., I mean your Overall Navigating Edge. Each of us has one essential gift we bring to the world that we do really well and that is a fundamental aspect of who we are. Our O.N.E. thing is what allows us to navigate the world with power that is unique to who we are. Our Overall Navigating Edge is what empowers our gift. When we know our O.N.E. thing, our Overall Navigating Edge, we can leverage our strength and use our energies most efficiently. When we don't know our O.N.E. thing, we waste a lot of time doing "filler" work that keeps us busy, but not fulfilled or at our most productive.

Your Overall Navigating Edge is what powers your purpose. John Maxwell does five things daily that power his purpose. His O.N.E. thing actually has five parts: he reads, files, writes, thinks, and asks questions. Others, like John, also read, file, write, think, and ask questions, but for him, because this is the Overall Navigating Edge that empowers his purpose, he brings a greater impact to the world by doing this five-part O.N.E. thing than others do.

But you don't have to be a global expert to live in the power of your O.N.E. thing. Everyone has this ability. Your O.N.E. thing is that unique signature approach you bring to the world. As a teenager, my oldest daughter is discovering that her O.N.E. thing is her heart's amazing ability to care. I'm excited to watch her grow into a deeper understanding of how to live her O.N.E. thing and power her purpose. It has already allowed her to have a tremendous impact on children through her job with an after-school program, through babysitting her many cousins in Illinois, through her mission work in China, where she served at an orphanage for children with mental and physical disabilities, and positioned her to receive the H. A. Fincher and Jacqulin Long Bible Awards at her high school. These are the highest senior honors given for service. And that's only the beginning of her lifelong journey.

Sean "Diddy" Combs is the master of many enterprises—a successful record label, a fashion line, restaurants, a TV network, and a vodka company. He is also a recording artist, producer, movie actor, and designer. But Diddy started as a promoter, and has always been a promoter. I would say he's a master promoter. His O.N.E. thing is his keen ability to create so much energy around what he's doing that you feel a compelling draw to him and whatever venture he's promoting.

Steve Harvey is a comedian. I've heard him say that being a comic—his ability to make people laugh—is at the core of everything he does. He leverages and maximizes his O.N.E. thing to bring him success as an actor, talk show host, radio host, game show host, book author, public speaker, media entrepreneur, and inspirational figure. Comedy is what gives him his Overall Navigating Edge and separates him from the pack in whatever he does.

While Diddy and Steve Harvey are clear about their O.N.E. thing, you may not be. That's probably because your O.N.E. thing is so natural to you, it's like breathing. You can't even see it, or if you can, you think it's something everyone can do. You take it for granted. For that reason you may need someone else (someone who knows you well) to point it out to you, so that you can start leveraging it more consciously and effectively.

To be honest, I didn't recognize my O.N.E. thing until fairly recently. I was working with a colleague and I asked him what he thought it was. His response was that the O.N.E. thing I consistently do is listen well and consult God before taking action. As I thought about that, I realized he was right. Ever since I was a child, I was the person other people went to with their problems. Why? Because I would listen. Listening has always been second nature to me, so I never saw it as a particular talent. Later in life, as I developed my relationship with God, I got in the habit of intently listening to God as well, before responding to any person or situation. I ask God for guidance, and I listen to what comes up in my spirit. Then I use that guidance to shape my responses.

My husband says I have this essence about me that shines a light on other people's truth, whether they want to see it or not. This is because I am always open to what God is saying to and through me. And to be honest, for many years, I really didn't want this to be my truth, or at least I wanted to be able to "turn it off" when it made people uncomfortable because they weren't ready or didn't want to "hear" their truth.

My clients have told me that I seem to have a way of telling them exactly what they need to hear at any given time. It's not me, believe me; it's God doing the work through me. But I have come to realize that my ability to tap into that power is my Overall Navigating Edge. My O.N.E. thing is listening to God and being obedient at all costs, which empowers me to listen to others and speak words that engage their peace, clarity, and courage.

What is your O.N.E. thing? Maybe it's writing insightfully—you create your advantages through the written word. Maybe it's working with people—your ability to inspire and organize others is what helps you navigate your journey. Maybe it's your analytical approach—your skill at diagnosing and solving problems has always given you your edge.

In order to understand your O.N.E. thing, it helps to know the difference between gifts, talents, and abilities. Your O.N.E. thing is what empowers your gift.

A purposeful life stems from knowing your gift and using your O.N.E. thing as your main way to bring that gift to fruition.

Your Unique Gift

Your talents are things you naturally excel at. Your abilities are things you can do competently well, including things you've picked up through training and education. All of us have multiple talents and abilities. We can do several things well and many things competently. This makes it hard for many of us to know what we should be doing with our lives and our careers. There are many things we *could* be and are good at.

That's why it's important to know what your gift is, as opposed to just a talent or ability. A gift is the anointed power of God flowing through you. A gift is something you know you have, even without training or education. It's as natural to you as breathing. It's more of a calling than a talent. Your gift is a power within you that leads you toward a purpose and plan for your life. Your gift is what draws you toward developing some of your talents, and leaving others alone. Many of us never take the time to listen for what our gift may be. We're too busy getting trained and educated, and developing a career.

Growing up, we train our talents every day. We read, we go to school, we receive certifications, diplomas, and degrees. We educate and mold our talents. But are we truly fulfilled? There are so many successful people who have no peace and no joy, and who live unfulfilled lives. Why? Because they ignore their gift.

Why do so many of us develop only our talents and abilities and never truly engage our gift? There are many reasons. Some of us decide to pursue money as our only goal. Some of us follow others' advice and expectations as to what to do with our lives. Some of us adopt the societal definition of success instead of our own. There's also the fact that our talents are "concrete," so it's easy to recognize them and to see how we can make money with them. But our gifts can be hard to recognize and even harder to "monetize" (at least, that's what many of us think). Our gifts often even challenge our belief that we'll be able to make money. But when we discover and acknowledge our gift, our talents fall into place to serve that gift.

LIVING YOUR GIFT

My dear sisterfriend and angel Patti Webster is the founder and was the CEO of W&W Public Relations before her death in 2013. Her company represents and works with some of the biggest celebrities in the world. Past and current clients include Alicia Keys, Steve Harvey, Patti LaBelle, Jermaine Dupri, Kirk Franklin, Chris Paul, and Janet Jackson, to name a few. Patti's life exemplified the idea of living one's gift. She had a servant's heart and a gift for bringing grace and the power of God's love into the lives of everyone she met. Through that gift, her talents in public relations allowed her to be a successful publicist, build a multimillion-dollar PR company, and enhance the lives of everyone she came in contact with. Because she understood her gift and lived in the power of her O.N.E. thing, her impact on the world was greater than the press coverage she secured for her clients. She left a legacy that will live beyond her precious time on this side of heaven.

Talents Vs. Gifts

Talents can create a mirage of success. We're told we can have a nice career by monetizing our talents. Talents can lure us toward living a 10-percent life. Following our talents and abilities alone, while ignoring our gifts, does not lead us toward fulfillment. Also, remember that talents can have an expiration date. You might possess a skill set that is hot today and then discover you cannot give it away tomorrow. Darkroom technicians, for example, are not much in demand in today's world of digital photography.

But your gift is your eternal "bloodline" to your true purpose. It flows from who you are and never dries up, fades, runs out, or ends. To find out what your gift is, all you really have to do is ask God, "What is my gift?" and then position yourself to "receive" what is already in you. Many people say that to identify your gift, you should answer the question "What would I do if money wasn't an issue?" An even more powerful question I ask my clients is "If there was ONE thing you could do, ONLY ONE, what would that be?"

Your O.N.E. Thing and Your Gift

A gift is that thing you feel spiritually called to do and do well. It is the thing you feel you were put on this earth to do. Your O.N.E. thing—Overall Navigating Edge—is the unique and particular *way* you are empowered to successfully accomplish things. One way to think of it is that your gift is *what* you are here to do, and your O.N.E. thing is how you do it.

For me, I would say my gift is to move people to a place of peace, truth, and fulfillment, and my O.N.E. thing, as I described before, is my ability to listen and live in the power of God for guidance.

One of my clients has the gift of making people feel alive and inspired. The O.N.E. thing he uses to do that is performing: singing, acting, talking to audiences.

Maybe your gift is to bring people together for a higher purpose, and your O.N.E. thing is your ability to use words eloquently and passionately.

It is important that you recognize that you are here to accomplish something particular and to do so in your particular way. Anytime you waste energy doing things that other people can do better than you, or things that pull you off the track of what you are here to do, you are just working, not maximizing.

Rest and Reflect

In order to know what your gift is, and to find the courage and insight to develop that gift, you must stop *doing* so much. You must take time to rest, reflect, and rejuvenate.

Too often we don't take pauses in our lives; we're too busy working. Though we may pray for guidance, our prayer is like calling someone on the phone, asking them a question, and then hanging up before they answer. Constant busywork is like hanging up on God— we don't provide space or silence to hear His answer.

There are times in our lives when we just need to stop. Stop meeting. Stop writing. Stop trying. Stop working.

Stop.

We are told that "faith without works is dead," and so we believe "works equals busyness." But "works" also means taking steps to activate your true power. And sometimes that means sitting still. Being quiet. Sometimes "works" is doing nothing but being, believing, trusting, letting go, living in peace, standing in joy, and receiving what God sends you. It's not about what you do, but what you can receive. And to receive, you must open up space within your heart and within your life for something new to enter.

Rest and recovery are fundamental aspects of growth. This idea is supported by modern sports medicine. Research has shown that both stress and rest are equally important when trying to grow muscles. Stress provides the *stimulus* for growth—the muscles need to be pushed to the edge of their capacity. Then rest and recovery provide the *time and conditions* for growth to take place. Those who go overboard with their gym workouts do not get good results. You can't work the triceps in the morning and then do it again in the afternoon. You need to wait forty-eight hours before stressing the same muscle groups again. Why? Because there needs to be time for the growth to actually happen.

The same principle holds true in any part of our life where we are seeking growth. We must have a cycle of effort followed by a cycle of rest. And we need to be aware that rest is often where the real magic happens.

Input and Output

Life consists of output and input. Output is what we say, do, and create. Input is what we take in from others. Many people today, especially high achievers, are all about the output. They focus 95 percent of their energy on their workouts, their rehearsals, their business presentations, their blog entries, their e-mails, their speeches, their projects. They are in a constant battle to produce a stream of impressive output. What they don't realize is that the rest of humanity is inundated with output—on the Internet, on their smartphones, on TV and radio, in their in-boxes, on the printed page, on billboards, and on bulletin boards. Everyone swims in a sea of output. What people really want is someone who'll listen, truly listen. Listening is the one commodity that is in very short supply these days. Many times the greatest opportunities present themselves when we switch out of output mode and go into input mode. That is, shut our mouths and listen.

Listening means turning off our inner agenda and opening up the space inside us to download what's going on inside another human being and, even more importantly, what's going on within ourselves. This is very difficult for high achievers, who believe their value comes from constantly *producing* in one way or another. Some of the greatest value we provide to others and to ourselves, though, is the simple ability to attentively and compassionately listen to what they have to say and to what's going on within us.

Learning to listen is the greatest business tool on earth. More opportunities present themselves to us when we are in input mode than when we are in output mode. And we can maximize those opportunities by carefully listening.

When you listen, you . . .

» **Learn what others really want and need.** Actually listening teaches you how to truly be of service to your customers, clients, friends, and family.

» **Build trust.** When others know you've really heard them, they gain confidence in your ability to act on their behalf.

» **Create a lasting impression.** People remember those who listen to them, not those who talk at them. Maya Angelou once said, "[P]eople will forget what you said, people will forget what you did, but people will never forget how you made them feel."

>> **Foster peace.** Most of the tensions that exist in the home, the workplace, and the world are a result of people not feeling heard. When you take time to really listen to the people around you, grievances are ironed out, friction is lessened, and conflicts are resolved. As a result, more is accomplished with less effort.

>> **Make yourself likable.** We all like people who listen. And, as Will Packer mentions in our conversation later in this chapter, likability is a major factor in success. People want to work with people they like.

Learning to listen is at the very heart of "Stop Working, Start Maximizing." Want to save a struggling marriage? Learn to listen. Want your kids to respect you and help you? Learn to listen to them. Want to move up the ladder in your company? Learn to listen to your bosses and colleagues. Want to create a thriving, relevant business? Listen to your current and potential clients and customers.

What you *don't* do is as important as what you *do* do. When you get in the habit of allowing the world to turn without feeling the need to crank its handle, you will discover this glorious truth: things start to happen *for* you, things that you didn't directly cause.

Vision, Action, Results

Exercise 1: Discovering Your Gift and Your O.N.E. Thing

Discovering your gift means knowing what you are here on earth to do. Discovering your O.N.E. thing means understanding your unique way of successfully navigating the world. To know both, and to act on both, is to have a purposeful life. This three-step process will help.

STEP 1:

Your O.N.E. thing may be invisible to you. It may feel so natural to you that you can't even identify it. For that reason, it helps to evaluate what has worked effectively for you in the past.

List at least six of your greatest accomplishments in life. More, if possible. These are accomplishments you are personally the proudest of, even if they didn't generate public acclaim or recognition. They are not necessarily awards and trophies and scholarships (though those can count as well).

Study the list for a while. See if any common threads begin to emerge. Was there anything similar about the approach you used in each of these cases? Was there anything similar about the actions you took? What did you do to rise above the challenges and obstacles you faced? What motivated you to succeed? What strategies did you employ?

STEP 2:

Ask five people who know you well the following questions to help you identify your gift:

» What do you think I do uniquely well?

» What are the top three to five qualities I possess? (Note the similarities or common characteristics that come up.)

» In what ways am I most effective in the world?

» What do you see as my most fundamental gift—the power that underlies all my other skills and abilities?

» How do you think I could most effectively serve humanity?

These are tough questions to answer, but encourage openness and honesty, and be sincerely appreciative of the responses you get.

STEP 3:

Using whatever spiritual method you employ—prayer, meditation, silent walks in nature, etc.—ask this question of your deepest self, every day:

"What is my true gift?"

Be open for answers in whatever form they may appear—a quiet voice within, an opportunity that suddenly appears, confirmations from friends and others. No rush on this one. Keep asking until you feel confident you have received an answer. You will begin to feel a peace and power as you acknowledge and intentionally engage your gift.

Exercise 2: Responsibilities to Opportunities

Make a list of the "responsibilities" that currently occupy the bulk of your time. Include responsibilities at work, at home, with extended family, in the community, etc. Then reframe each responsibility as an opportunity that excites, fulfills, challenges, delights, or has important meaning to you.

For example:

CURRENT RESPONSIBILITY	REFRAMED AS OPPORTUNITY
Drive kids to school.	Opportunity to engage, connect, and have a "teaching moment" with the most important people in my life.

Are there any responsibilities you can't find a way to reframe? Can you drop those "responsibilities"? (Hint: If you really *can't* drop it, then you must be gaining some value from it. In that case, there is probably a way to reframe it.)

Exercise 3: "Opportunities" That Are Distractions

Ask yourself the following questions to evaluate new opportunities that you suspect might actually be distractions. For each "opportunity," ask:

>> What is my desired outcome from this opportunity?
>> What is my motivation to reach this desired outcome?
>> How much time will it take to achieve my desired outcome?
>> What resources will it require?
>> How stressful will it be?
>> Does this outcome align with the two or three main goals I am currently prioritizing? How?
>> Do both the outcome and the opportunity align with my values?

EXPONENTIAL CONVERSATION

For this chapter I had the honor of chatting with my good friend Will Packer. Will, as you may know, is a film and television producer. As of this writing, seven—yes, seven—of his films have opened at number one at the box office. His credits include hits such as *Straight Outta Compton*, *Takers*, *Ride Along*, *No Good Deed*, *Think Like a Man*, *The Wedding Ringer*, *About Last Night*, and *Stomp the Yard*. He has several films in production and is a producer for the 2016 remake of the classic TV miniseries *Roots*.

Will is a great example of the art of maximizing opportunities. If you looked at all the responsibilities—or rather, *opportunities*—on his plate, you would say it was impossible for one person to juggle them all, especially when you consider the fact that he spends a lot of quality time with friends and family. How does he do it? Our conversation offers some hints. It also shows him as a person who epitomizes Exponential Living in general.

SHERI RILEY: What are your gifts and talents that allow you to maximize your professional success?

WILL PACKER: I think it's . . . relating to people. I think that I have a better-than-average ability to relate to people, to communicate with people, to feel comfortable around people, and have people feel comfortable around me. That is really important because people work with people who they like. As much as we try to say, "No, I'll work with anybody!" or "I treat everybody the same," the reality is that if you genuinely like somebody, you like to be around them, you like to communicate with them, and be in their presence. Those are the type of people you're going to surround yourself with. We generally don't surround ourselves with people that we have adversarial relationships with if we can help it. So, what that means is that people in power tend to lean toward people who they like. So for me, I definitely have had success by getting along and having good relationships with people who could help me and people who are above me, or people who I could help who are below me. So I would say that relating to people is definitely a trait that I have that helps me in this industry.

SHERI RILEY: I love that. How do you maintain your integrity?

WILL PACKER: I could get a thousand dollars before and now I can get a hundred million. I'm blessed that those are some of the conversations, but it is the same decisions I have to make about "Is this opportunity going to compromise me?" Part of the reason I have an office in LA yet live in Atlanta . . . is because it helps me to stay grounded.

. . . Yesterday was football Sunday so I had a bunch of folks over for football Sunday. I need to do that. I need to have a bunch of folks and very, very few of them have anything to do with the industry. Just sitting around, kicking it. And before that, me and all the kids went to church. You have to have those things that have nothing to do with getting ahead, winning in your particular career field, or things that are material, quantitative elements of success. Because if not, you'll try to get full off of just those accomplishments, accolades, money, material, praise from other people, and those ultimately will not fill you up. That's not stuff that will fill your soul.

SHERI RILEY: To what do you attribute your ability to spend quality time with your wife, your children, your friends, and throw some of the dopest parties?

WILL PACKER: I live hard. I love hard. I work hard. I play hard. It's my philosophy. I think that's how we should do it. I think that we've got this life and it's up to you. Everybody's given the same life; what are you going to do with it? What separates some of the most successful people in the world—and this goes back to your Exponential Living mantra—is the fact that some people do more with their same twenty-four hours a day than others. I know that at the end of the day when God calls me home and I'm no longer on this earth . . . they can say, "He made this movie which made this amount of money. Or maybe he won this award, or . . ." People will hear it, and they'll say, "That's great!" and then it's over and done. What will last, what will really define who I am once I'm gone . . . is my legacy. And my legacy is what I leave behind in the form of people who will actually be influenced by and carry out my thoughts, works, and deeds. People who were influenced by me and are living their lives in a very specific way based on knowing me. People who were affected by knowing me. And that's a lot different than a résumé.

My dad was great. He was so active in his church and community and he was on all these boards, but you know what people really remember about him? Me. His son, and his daughter, my sister—his legacy that he left behind because I am William Packer Sr.'s son. And . . . whatever I do, I do it as my father's son. And the same will be true of my kids.

SHERI RILEY: How important is inner peace to you?

WILL PACKER: Oh, essential, essential. Because we all deal with, and have to overcome, external challenges. No matter who you are or what you do. But at the end of the day your ability to handle all those external challenges is because of what inner peace you have. At the end of the day it is your internal fortitude; it is your internal peace of mind. I have to deal with a lot of adversarial relationships because my industry tends to be like that sometimes. [But] at the end of the day . . . I'm very fortunate and blessed to have a great deal of inner peace that allows me to navigate those shark-infested waters. It doesn't matter when a deal doesn't go my way or . . . does. I never get too high or too low, because internally I am at peace. I am very comfortable with who I am and where I am in my life. I am very happy. I am a happy person. If I never produce another movie or none of my TV shows hit number one, I am happy. Because my internal happiness, my internal peace, comes from things that aren't defined by material successes or industry standards.

SHERI RILEY: Share with me a time that you met a challenge that was just overwhelming, a brick wall. How did the inner peace give you the power to navigate that challenge?

WILL PACKER: On a daily basis I am faced with numerous challenges. Right now I've got a movie set to go into production in just over a month and I don't have my cast lined up. I just had to change the location literally from one country to another country. And I'm in production on *Roots*, the miniseries, which is a huge, huge, tremendous undertaking and there are just a lot of challenges; it's a very difficult project to put together. So as I navigate all those different challenges—because your question is ultimately about how I maintain peace in the face of those challenges—I give it all I have. I have great solace that at the end of it, whatever the end result is, I'm comfortable with it. I'm okay with it. That's a big part of me, being able to have peace. Because as long as I know I gave it my best, if it doesn't work, I honestly will feel like it was not meant to be, and there will be another opportunity presented because this one didn't go the way I thought it would.

SHERI RILEY: How do you keep that from challenging the ego? Because 99 percent of the issue we have is ego. How does ego not step up and go, "But I'm . . ."

WILL PACKER: "But I'm Will Packer! What do you mean, I didn't figure it out? I'm supposed to figure it out! I'm supposed to do anything!"

I have a lot of self-confidence. I try to keep ego out of it, but . . . the other side of me being self-confident is the fact that I am comfortable with my body of work, if you will. And for most people our body of work is our lives. Are you comfortable with your life? Have you given your all within your life? If you've given 100 percent within your life—family, God, wife, husband, work—then you should be able to sit back and, wherever you are, say, "You know, I gave it my all and I'm comfortable." Oftentimes people are . . . looking for a quick fix, or the easy way out, or they cheat. They want to cut corners. And then if you're not happy with where you are, you have yourself to blame . . . You know it inside. So I know that I have put in the effort and the energy, so I know ultimately wherever I end up is where I'm supposed to be. There's nothing I could have done differently. I take solace and I don't allow my ego to say, "But I should have been able to do this because I'm so and so!" I let other people do that. But I am . . . very comfortable with who I am, successes and failures. Warts and all.

SHERI RILEY: What do you do for your personal development?

WILL PACKER: My personal development is all about my family at this point in my life. . . . I am forty-one, married, kids. For me, my personal development . . . is about me being able to affect my kids in a positive way. Me being able to give to my marriage and see it grow and flourish. I think that I am very attentive to my personal development outside of my professional life because it is so much about my family. . . . They give me a lot of strength and they validate me in a way that a number one hit movie never could.

SHERI RILEY: When I say "Exponential Living," what does that make you think of?

WILL PACKER: When I think of Exponential Living, I think of giving 100 percent of you to the parts of your life that mean the most to you. I think of balance. I think of internal peace. . . . I think about making sure that you're giving energy to the areas of your life that will give energy back. And to the areas of your life that are most important. It is not giving a bunch of energy to just the smallest part of your life. It is giving energy to the most important areas of your life. And again, internal peace—I think that's so important because you can't live exponentially if you are only chasing external accolades or material successes or things that will not ultimately . . . feed your soul.

I AM WILL PACKER AND I AM EXPONENTIAL LIVING.

Key Takeaways

» Material success can be truly enjoyed when we are intentional about maintaining our inner peace.

» Before seizing an opportunity, ask yourself if it will compromise you in any important way.

» What will be remembered after you die is not your business success but the legacy you leave behind with people.

» One aspect of peace is not getting too high when things go your way or too low when they don't.

Happy Is a Choice, Joy Is a Lifestyle

Be thankful for what you have; you'll end up having more. If you concentrate on what you don't have, you will never, ever have enough.

{ —OPRAH WINFREY }

Joy is the fuel of Exponential Living. Where many people mess up is by viewing joy and happiness the same way they view peace—as an effect, not a cause. They believe that if they can just get the *conditions* of life right, they will be happy. One of the most liberating discoveries you can make is that *happiness is a choice*. Each and every one of us (unless we are chemically handicapped in some way, such as by addiction or a mood disorder) has the power to make the choice to be happy on a daily, hourly, minute-by-minute basis.

I know what you're probably thinking. "Yeah, yeah, I've heard that kind of thing before." You've probably seen sayings like "Choose to Be Happy" on T-shirts or on posters in Hallmark stores. But, like most of us, you've ignored the simplistic-sounding message and chosen to remain stressed-out and miserable, waiting for the day when happiness finally arrives on your doorstep, wrapped in a bright red bow.

My goal in this chapter is to help you understand that you really, truly, honestly do hold the controls to your happiness in your own hands. You *can* be happy and joyful right now; you don't have to wait for any of the conditions in your life to change.

Happiness is the vehicle, not the destination. I know it sounds too simple, especially for us high achievers who believe complex is better. But it really is a message I can deliver with a "KISS" (keep it simple, stupid).

Why Don't We Choose to Be Happy?

I want to keep this discussion of happiness positive. But unless we look at some of the "negative" reasons we block happiness from infusing our lives, we'll continue making the same mistakes, day after day. So let's have a look.

Why *do* we humans have such trouble being happy? This is one of the most studied, discussed, and analyzed questions in history. The truth is, there is no simple answer. There are countless factors that contribute to human unhappiness, and we can't possibly get into all of them here. Depression, for example, is a complex condition—partly chemical, partly spiritual, partly psychological—that robs people not only of the ability to feel happy but also of the motivation to do the very things that would make them happier. But for our purposes, there are several critical failings that are responsible for a major chunk of the human unhappiness out there.

Those failings, as I see them, are:

1. We fail to control negative thinking.
2. We shut God out.
3. We confuse our reality with our truth.

4. We put a ceiling on our happiness.
5. We fail to accept our "new norm."
6. We compare ourselves to others.
7. We hang on to anger.
8. Work.

We've looked at the first two of these factors in previous chapters, so we won't go into them too deeply here. The first is our tendency to let the mind run away with worries and anxieties, which causes a cascade of negativity. As I've already suggested, you can deal with this issue by developing the habit of watching your thoughts, halting the negative ones before they turn into a runaway train, and focusing on empowering thoughts instead. Master this one habit and you will go a long way toward opening the door to happiness.

The second factor is our tendency to close the door on God. In my view, it is virtually impossible to maintain lasting happiness if we disregard our connection with God. You might find moments of *relative* happiness, but your spiritual loneliness will inevitably catch up with you. *Belief* in God, alone, does not cure this. Many people *mentally* believe in God, but still close off receptivity to divine grace and guidance. To be happy you must have *fellowship* with God and an open channel for Him to touch your life day by day. I've talked about this before, so I won't go into it more here.

Now let's look at the remaining factors we haven't yet explored.

We Confuse Our Reality with Our Truth

What keeps many high achievers from Exponential Living—from happiness in general—is that they confuse their reality with their truth. I use these two words in a very particular way, so let me explain.

Your *reality* is the set of life circumstances you observe with your senses, at this particular point in time—the stack of bills on the kitchen counter, the eight-year-old car in the driveway, the number on the bathroom scale that is continually creeping higher. Your truth is the bigger, deeper, and more lasting vision you have of your present and future. If you are single and desire to be married, for example, your reality may be that you live alone in an apartment, but your truth may be that you are fully deserving of love and that the love you seek is coming to you at the perfect time. Sometimes things in your life may even appear to be moving backward—that may be your reality— but your truth may be that you are transitioning to a better you and better place. My friend Patrice Washington says it best when she declares, "Sometimes we have to take *steps backward* to *leap forward*."

I recall one day having an amazing meeting with Mark Cole, CEO of all five of John Maxwell's global companies. We share a mutual respect and we discussed some high-level ideas.

After we finished lunch and walked to our cars, the difference between reality and truth really hit me. The place where we'd dined was a members-only business club, and Mark's car was parked in the "Reserved for Chairman" spot. By contrast, on this particular day, my husband, Jovan, and I had $6.04 in our bank account. I had received a notice in the mail that my life insurance policy had been canceled for nonpayment, and I had asked my mom to roll up my change so I could use the $200 in coins to pay for one week of summer camp for my youngest daughter.

That's when I understood the power of not focusing on my reality so that I could stay empowered by my truth. I committed to focusing on my truth—which was that powerful positive forces were aligning on behalf of me and my career—and being fueled by my joy.

This allowed me to stay focused on the ideas and implementation discussed with Mark during our meeting, which represented my truth as much as the six dollars represented my reality at that particular time.

Since I left my lucrative career in the music industry, there have been times when my finances have presented a scary-looking *reality*. But regardless of my financial status, my *truth* is that I am wealthy with love, hope, possibility, power, and influence. I am living my dream. My truth is much bigger than my reality.

What does this have to do with happiness? Everything. You see, most of us are in the habit of looking at our reality as an indicator of how happy we are "allowed" to feel. When our reality shows us a picture that is less than what we desire, we lower our happiness level accordingly. We truly believe we are not *entitled* to feel happy if our reality is showing us less-than-desirable results.

Our culture reinforces this error. It teaches us that happiness comes from having the right possessions and conditions around us— a nice car, an expensive house, cool vacations, a sexy partner, a loving spouse—and so we think we cannot be happy until those conditions are met. Worse, we think we would be *idiotic* to feel happy if there are poor conditions in our life such as bills we can't afford to pay, a painful health condition, or a marriage in crisis.

Most of us view our reality like a thermometer. That is, we look out at our present reality and take its "temperature." If the reading is lower than what we desire, we lower our happiness level. We are constantly adjusting our happiness level based on our temperature reading of reality.

We must remind ourselves that *we* control the thermostat. And our inner truth *is* that thermostat. When we pay attention to our inner truth instead of our outer reality, we can set our happiness temperature as high as we want. And when we do that—when we choose a high degree of happiness—interestingly enough, the "temperature" around us tends to rise to match our thermostat. Good things start to happen.

Every time you wake up in the morning, remind yourself that your job is not to adjust your happiness level to your current life conditions; your job is to set a high happiness level within, based on your empowering truth. Before you open your eyes, smile and tell yourself, "I choose to be happy and I am happy." As simple as this sounds, it's life changing.

Think about two types of investors—the successful one and the unsuccessful one. The unsuccessful investor has no vision, confidence, or faith in his investment. So every day, every hour, he worriedly checks the stock reports. If his stock portfolio goes down, he becomes fearful. If it goes up, he becomes happy. But only conditionally so. If his portfolio goes down for several days or weeks in a row, he panics and sells it off, losing his investment.

The successful investor has faith and confidence in his investment. He chooses to live by the truth that the stock market always goes up eventually. He doesn't watch the stock reports. He doesn't panic when his portfolio goes down temporarily; he knows dips are inevitable from time to time. He leaves his investment alone and, in fact, keeps putting more money in it, confident in the big picture: that his investment is growing overall and will reward him in the future. That confidence also brings joy to his present moment.

Be like the successful investor whose happiness is unaffected by the ups and downs of his reality, confident in his long-range vision.

We Put a Ceiling on Our Happiness

Another reason many of us don't allow ourselves to be happy is that we don't trust that it will last, and we fear the "crash" when it collapses. We believe it's better not to feel too happy in the first place. We tell ourselves, "I'd better not get too high, because then the low will feel even worse."

And so we put up walls—defenses—to protect us from hurt, disappointment, and loss. We set a speed limit on our happiness engine, refusing to allow ourselves to feel too much joy. What we don't realize is that the wall itself ends up being the very thing that robs us of our joy. We live life in a perpetually guarded state, and our guardedness repels happiness.

For most of my life, I believed I had to protect my heart from joy, which was the thing I desired most deeply. I feared that if I enjoyed life—if I let my guard down and laughed freely and openly—I wouldn't be braced for the inevitable punch that was surely coming my way soon.

We shut out love, trust, faith, and joy because we don't want to experience the pain of losing them. By doing so, we protect ourselves from receiving the very things we want. What could be more insane? If someone wanted to give you or your business ten thousand dollars, would you refuse it because you might lose it? Of course not. But we shut down possibilities in our emotional lives for reasons we would not employ in our professional lives.

What walls have you erected in your life? Where have you placed a speed limit on your happiness? In what areas have you stopped trying, caring, experiencing, and hoping, because you have decided, "They can't take away what I don't have in the first place"?

I urge you to let your walls down. Give love freely. Share your time and wealth. Pursue your dreams. Laugh. Dance naked in front of the mirror. Don't let fear of loss or failure choke off the very joy you're afraid of losing. Because remember: even if you do fail or lose, that can't rob you of your happiness. The only thing that can rob you of your happiness is *you*. And you are doing that right now by keeping the walls up.

We Fail to Accept Our "New Norm"

For many of us, one of the greatest barriers to choosing happiness is that our lives have changed in significant ways, but we have failed to accept our "new norm."

Eight years before my dad passed, he had a major heart attack and subsequent stroke. For six months he was hospitalized, and when he got out, he was no longer able to walk. An active man whose ideal Saturday was spent puttering with his car and working on his lawn, he was now in a wheelchair. He couldn't even change a lightbulb.

Physically, everything had changed, but mentally he was the same person as ever. For the final eight years of my dad's life, he could not accept his "new norm." He couldn't accept that he was in a wheelchair. He was depressed, short-tempered, and largely unable to enjoy the life he was still living. Though he was living independently, he was forever trapped in the pain of what he could no longer do.

During this time, I got married and had his first grandchild. The fact that he couldn't play with her like he did with me added to his depression. His mother was still alive, yet during those last eight years he never traveled back to his hometown, less than two hours away, to visit her. It wasn't his physical challenges that held him hostage; it was his inability to accept his new norm.

Life is constantly changing. How many of us are hindering our joy because we haven't accepted some new norm or other? How many of us are making decisions and choices that are not aligned with the truth of our lives today?

LaShon Allen-Spearman owns a company, TaskMasters, Inc. I've worked with her company for almost a decade. During one of our meetings, she shared with me, "I am so overwhelmed and out of sync. I feel like I am always behind in every area of my life. My biggest internal struggle is my patience with my family. Sheri, I need help with time management."

I listened intently as she described all her daily scheduling challenges, and then said, "I don't believe you have a time-management issue. Your challenge is accepting your new norm. As you describe your challenges to me, every other sentence starts with 'I used to . . .' You seem to be basing your happiness on your old norm."

In the words of LaShon herself:

My old norm was: I was a single young business owner with no kids, no husband, and not a full-time student. I was able to produce more work because I had no responsibilities except my clients and getting the job done.

My new norm is: I am a wife, mother, business owner, and full-time student. [I realized] my priorities and responsibilities had changed, but my mind hadn't. I was still trying to be who I was five years ago, but that was no longer my life.

When I was able to accept my new norm, my perspective on my situation changed, allowing me to focus on who I am today versus who I used to be. I now know my priorities and limitations, and I don't feel bad saying no. Why? Because I am living in my new norm!

My father's and LaShon's new norms were quite different, but they each had a choice to make. Would they accept their new norm or cling tenaciously to the old?

We Compare Ourselves to Others

> Let your conduct be without covetousness; be content with such things as you have. For He Himself has said, "I will never leave you nor forsake you."
>
> —HEBREWS 13:5

One of the surest ways to ensure a dissatisfied life is to fall into the habit of comparing yourself to others. While this tendency has always plagued mankind (there's a reason two of the Ten Commandments deal with "coveting" and three of the cardinal sins are greed, lust, and envy!), it has grown worse in our era of TV and social media. Technology has made it available not only in the lives of the rich and famous, via TV shows and websites, but also in those of our relatives, friends, coworkers, and college classmates, via social media sites. Thanks to social media, anyone can spend hours a day surfing through the lives of his/her peers. "Oh, look, x just got a publishing deal," or, "Hey, y's daughter just got into Harvard Medical School." If your life isn't where you want it to be—and that's probably true for 98 percent of us—then you'll end up feeling worse about yourself after each of these trolling expeditions. Others will seem to have what you don't have. You'll feel inadequate and incomplete.

The problem with social comparison is that it never stops, no matter how much success you attain. A colleague of mine shared a story about visiting an old college friend. This friend had done really well careerwise: he earned a seven-figure salary and lived in a house worth about four million dollars. But as the friend gave my colleague a tour of his gorgeous seaside property, he pointed across the bay at a nine-million-dollar home and sighed longingly. "Now, that's the house I'd like to get my hands on." It never stops.

When looking wistfully at other people's lives, we tend to forget that we're not seeing their true and complete reality. The person in the nine-million-dollar home may have lost a child or have a spouse who's paralyzed. All those carefully posed selfies and enviable vacation photos on Facebook represent only a carefully curated version of our friends' lives.

We Hold On to Anger

At the beginning of my journey of Exponential Living, my husband pointed out that I didn't enjoy what I was doing. That I was always miserable. The truth is, I loved what I was doing, but he was right— I was always miserable. At least, I came across that way. I thought my fierce demeanor was what drove me to achieve. I hear this from a lot of high achievers (especially in the world of sports); they think their anger gives them an edge in life. That may be true, in a very limited way, but it also robs them of joy along the way.

I felt I had good reasons to be angry, due to circumstances in my life—what those circumstances were is unimportant; we all have circumstances we can choose to be angry about—but holding on to anger put me in a very unhealthy place. Anger pollutes your relationships, robs you of clarity, and weighs you down like an anchor. Some people hang on to anger deliberately; others do it unconsciously, due to unresolved issues. Both unresolved anger and deliberately held anger are joy killers.

In my work on myself and with clients, I have identified several keys to dealing with and releasing the anger:

1. Accept that releasing the anger does not erase the wrong that was done to you. Many people fear that if they stop being angry, they're saying, in effect, "I'm okay with what happened to me." Not so. A wrong is still a wrong. But you have a choice as to how it's going to continue to affect you.

2. Accept that the anger is not your strength. Your strength lies in your true power, not in your emotional reactivity to past events.

3. Accept that weakness is not what allowed you to be hurt. Many people think they were hurt because they were weak. They then confuse vulnerability with weakness. They think becoming invulnerable will prevent them from being hurt again. But it's their very "invulnerability" that ends up hurting them.

4. Accept that it was not your fault but someone else's decision to hurt you. Another person's decision to inflict pain on you was 100 percent about them, 0 percent about you.

5. Accept that you can be whole and free again. You can. 'Nuff said.

6. Accept that holding on to the anger does not protect you. Rather, it eats away at you and erects walls that keep joy out.

To experience Exponential Living, you must develop a healthy relationship with anger. You don't have to deny your anger, but you also don't have to hold on to it. Anger has a valid place in our lives—it's an emotion we are all entitled to feel—but it can't be allowed in the driver's seat. A healthy relationship with anger is one that acknowledges and respects the emotion, but doesn't hurt you or the people you love by admitting more negative energy into your life than positive.

Work

And of course, one of the main ways we high achievers squash the flow of joy in our lives is through our relationship with work.

As high achievers, we want it all. We want to do what we love and make a lot of money doing it. We have a strong belief that we can accomplish anything we set our minds to. And this belief allows us to achieve many things.

But sometimes work can begin to overshadow everything else. We work hard to provide a great life for our families but then the work becomes all we focus on, and we get disconnected from them. We continue to provide material things for our families but we lose our connection with them. And we feel guilty about it. This tug-of-war robs us of joy. In all of my years of working on Exponential Living, this has been the number one issue high achievers share with me. They anguish over how to give time and attention to both the people they love and the things they love to do.

Once we achieve success, our work seems to demand even more of our attention. We tend to forget the fact that time spent *away* from our work actually makes us even better *in* our work—the books we read, the places we go, the nonwork conversations we have, the laughter we enjoy, the downtime that recharges us. All of these positive, restorative moments allow us to approach our work with renewed passion and energy.

I was once on vacation in Aruba with my husband and youngest daughter. I had bought a time-share there before we were married and for years had wanted to go there with them. And now here they were! God had blessed us with this beautiful opportunity. But I had a lot of important, time-sensitive work tasks I needed to complete that week. Those commitments were weighing heavily on me and I felt torn between getting my tasks done and being "present" with my family. I prayed about this and realized I had to let go, trust in my work team back home, and make a stand on how important my family time was to me. I set all my "important" work tasks aside.

Four years later, I remember the time I spent with my family. I remember my four-year-old going down the slide and swimming for the first time in five-foot water. I remember watching her play in the sand, facing the ocean as the sun set. I remember enjoying drinks out of a coconut. I remember driving from one end of Aruba to the other and eating at a family-owned roadside "restaurant." I remember my daughter seeing iguanas and enjoying trick or treat at the resort. I remember all of these amazing moments and more, but for the life of me I can't remember those pressing work commitments that I almost allowed to rob me of time with my family.

Your definition of success must be broadened to include joy in the here and now. That means you must become aware of the things that *bring* you authentic joy, and you must build them into the structure of your life. Don't just *hope* these things will happen once in a while. Make them as important as your work goals. If all of your focus is on what you are trying to achieve in the future, how will present joy find a way into your life? High achievers are often so inexperienced at savoring joy that even when they attain all their goals, they don't have a clue how to be happy. They've had no practice.

Happy is a choice. Joy is a lifestyle.

Amen.

Three Keys to Joy

So we've looked at some of the ways people—especially high achievers—block the flow of joy into their lives. So what are some of the things you can do to actively choose happiness every day and create a lifestyle of joy?

The most powerful practices I know of are celebration, gratitude, and forgiveness.

Celebration

As high achievers, many of us view celebration as something that happens when major goals are achieved or we acquire something we've wanted for a long time. We celebrate the awards, the promotions, the championships, the big new contracts. We celebrate the new house, the new car, the boat, the wedding, the birth of a child. We see celebration as a special event that is reserved for life's big moments. When those moments occur, we crack open a bottle of champagne and kick up our heels for a few hours; then it's back to work, work, work till the next celebration.

To invite joy into our lives we need to get in the habit of celebrating the small things. On a weekly, daily, and hourly basis. That doesn't mean having daily champagne parties (though I'm open to that suggestion!); it means nurturing a *celebratory spirit* throughout the day. Honor and recognize things like your child getting onto the school bus for the first time, the fact that you made it to the gym today, or confirming that meeting you have worked for months to set. Many, many positive things happen on a daily basis, even when your reality doesn't look rosy. A clerk gives you a compliment, your child does a drawing for you, you find a great sale on an item you want . . . It's easy to overlook those things, and to focus only on goals and problems. But when you do that, you shut the good things out. On the other hand, if you take a few moments to celebrate every little good thing that happens, positive events gain access to your mind, heart, and spirit. They feed your joy. Celebrating small things becomes a habit, and can play a huge role in making joy your lifestyle.

Celebrating yourself is critical too. I have a hard time with this one, but it's important. And it is not arrogance. It is a form of praising God, thanking and honoring Him for all He's done in your life. Celebrating yourself lifts the burden of heaviness and depression. It opens up your mind, heart, spirit, and soul to see and receive new vision and new perspective. It allows you to see opportunity instead of obstacles.

Gratitude

Gratitude is the "magic" key that vaporizes negativity. Don't believe me? Just try holding gratitude and resentment in your heart at the same time; it's impossible. Gratitude is such a powerful energy, it feels like a force of nature when we cultivate and express it.

Gratitude is as simple as registering appreciation for the people, things, and conditions that are *present* in your life rather than pining for the things that are absent. Remember, your power lies in what *is*, not what isn't; power flows from your actual accomplishments and blessings, not from the abstract goals you are striving for. Gratitude honors what is present in our lives. As such, it is the key to our power.

The real beauty of gratitude is that you can turn it on anytime you choose, and tap its power. No matter how bleak the circumstances, it is always possible to find a thousand things to be grateful for—your health, your life, your home, your children's love, your friends. And so gratitude is a resource that is always available to you.

The power of gratitude isn't just poetic; it's measurable. A recent *Forbes* article by Amy Morin called "7 Scientifically Proven Benefits of Gratitude That Will Motivate You to Give Thanks Year-round" cites a flurry of scientific studies showing that gratitude

>> Makes others more likely to seek a relationship with you.
>> Improves your physical health and makes you more likely to exercise and practice good self-care.
>> Improves mental health by reducing depression and "toxic emotions," while increasing happiness.
>> Increases empathy and decreases aggression.
>> Improves sleep.
>> Raises your self-esteem and reduces social comparison.
>> Helps you overcome trauma and develop greater resilience.

To turn on the benefits of gratitude, all you need to do is thank someone sincerely or say in your heart, "I am grateful for [fill in the blessing]."

Forgiveness

The third major joy igniter is forgiveness. To forgive is to lay down the burden of anger and blame. I say *burden* because when you fail to forgive a past injustice, it is *you* who carries the weight of that injustice, not the perpetrator. As with anger, many people hold on to blame and hurt, believing it gives them some kind of righteous edge and makes them stronger. It does not. No matter what "crime" has been committed against you or your loved ones—betrayal, insult, deceit; even rape, murder, or assault—you only continue to give power to the perpetrator by carrying the injury in your heart and letting it sap your joy.

To forgive someone does not mean to say, "Hey, you and I are bosom buddies now." Nor does it mean that you condone or minimize the act that was committed against you. What it means is that you release *your* attachment to being wounded by it. Forgiveness is not about the other person. It is not necessary that the other person be remorseful about hurting you or "worthy" of your forgiveness. The other person does not even have to accept your forgiveness. Forgiveness is an act you do for you and for your relationship with God. If the other person is also moved to a better place by it, that's a wonderful fringe benefit.

Forgiveness, like gratitude, has a very distinct spiritual energy. It happens when you say, with your full heart, mind, and spirit, "I release myself of the burden of bearing blame and anger for [fill in the blank]." If this is an honest declaration, you will feel the burden float out of your body. Immediately, you will feel lighter—physically, mentally, spiritually, and emotionally. You will feel joy rushing in to fill the spaces where your anger and blame formerly resided.

Protect Your Joy

I have been urging you to be less guarded, so that joy can find an entry point into your life. But the one thing you *must* guard is your own joy. You must hold on to it and protect it, because the world has a way of robbing it from you. Here are a few ways to do that.

Center yourself in the morning. *Before* getting caught up in the worries and franticness of your day, pray, meditate, be quiet. Don't check social media or e-mail first. Don't focus on your kids first. Get up fifteen to thirty minutes earlier if you have to, just to give yourself some peaceful, quiet time to start your day. For me, as a woman of faith, that means time to be present with God. For others it just means being present, period.

Be careful whom you invite into your dream. Sometimes we allow the words and actions of others—often of those closest to us—to rob us of our joy. We expect these people to share our vision and we are crushed when they do not.

Know this: there are many dreams that only you are able to see, and that only you have the vision to pursue. Don't get caught up seeking help and support from those who don't see your vision, even if those people are very close to you. It's easy for fans in the stands to say what the players on the field should be doing. But they don't really know the game you're playing.

While I was building and launching Exponential Living, I approached certain people to collaborate and partner with me. We had worked together for many years and I greatly respected their work ethic and business development skills. With several of them, I had supported their dreams and assisted them in many ways. Most of them were willing to assist me, but never willing to partner and collaborate with me. At first I was disappointed—okay, honestly, I was very mad and hurt; then I finally accepted that I can't expect someone else to share a vision, an anointing, that God gave only to me.

Don't allow those who are unable to align with your vision or its timing—even if they are very dear to you and their lack of support hurts you at first—to steal your joy. When you are pursuing a dream that's bigger than your reality, don't get distracted trying to convince someone to see what they are not capable of seeing. It will only drain your power and your joy. Speak in your own authority, and speak only to those who are aligned with your vision. If your friends and family can't see your vision, don't share it with them, not fully; just share the joy you get from pursuing it.

Embrace your flaws. A personality trait I have observed in many high achievers is that they have trouble accepting their flaws. As a result, they become driven to prove that they are essentially perfect. And whenever their flaws *are* revealed, they become defensive or despondent. Evidence of their flaws robs them of their joy.

News flash: we all have flaws. Often these flaws themselves—anger, jealousy, impulsiveness—can rob our joy. But *hiding and denying* these flaws robs our joy even further. When we hide our flaws, to ourselves and the world, we create walls of defense around us. And we've already seen what walls can do.

Accepting and embracing your flaws neutralizes their ability to steal your joy. When you fully accept your flaws, you can laugh about them, talk about them, plan around them. No one can hurt you or steal your joy by pointing out your flaws to you because you already know and accept them. When you are open and accepting of your flaws, you can consciously work on them, and the people around you can help you. ("Hey, Dad, you're doing that thing again!") As a result, you are able to clean up personal failings faster and increase your happiness level. You also make it "okay" for the people around you to do the same. Flaws become part of the joyful mix of life, not joy robbers.

Don't give up on YOU. High achievers are prone to giving up. What? That sounds like an absurd statement. After all, high achievers can point to all of their external victories as proof that they most certainly do *not* give up. But what high achievers give up on is *themselves*, not their ability to achieve.

When it comes to *internal* growth—when the milestones are not measured by dollars and accolades—they often throw in the towel. I work with many high achievers who are at the top of their careers and whose families are doing fine, but they feel weighed down and depressed. Joy has long since departed. They wear a bright mask for the world, but the reflected light from that mask makes it even darker on the inside for them. The only solution they know is to throw themselves into their work and numb their pain with more achievements. But the numbness always wears off, and each time they have to renumb themselves, it costs them more to dull the pain.

In other cases the externals start to fall apart. The marriage becomes shaky. The business runs into trouble. Issues at work become worse. When this happens we become completely focused on the one thing that is going wrong, rather than the hundred things that are going right. And the whole foundation of our lives feels like it's crumbling.

What needs to be solid and unshakable, in either case, is YOU! And the key to that is your joy. Turn to your gratitude and live in the parts of your life that are going beautifully. Remember that you are entitled to joy regardless of your outer circumstances. Use that joy to connect to your truth, not just your reality (remember the difference?). Stand joyfully in your truth. Be like the confident investor who believes in her own stock and knows that what goes down must come up. Quite often there isn't anything you need to fix in your outer world; you just have to commit to not giving up on YOU.

Finally, I'd like to leave you with one of my spiritual truths. It's not grammatically perfect but it's definitely my truth.

1. Happy is in the mind.
2. Joy is in the heart.
3. Grateful is in the spirit.
4. Gratitude is in the soul.

Vision, Action, Results

Exercise 1: Yesterday's Prayers

One way to ignite gratitude is to acknowledge prayers of the past that have already been answered for you. I make a habit of writing down the things I am praying for. Sometimes, when I'm feeling lost and confused, I will look at my old "prayer lists" and I'm pleasantly (and humbly) surprised to see how many of my prayers have come true. I can then see that my present life is a "printout" of my past prayers.

For this exercise, write down as many of your past prayers as you can remember. (If formal prayer has not been part of your life, write down some past goals that you have longed for deeply in your heart.) After you compile your list, read it out loud and put a check mark by each one that has "come true."

Take a long moment to feel gratitude for past prayers answered, goals achieved, and "wishes come true."

Exercise 2: Choosing a Better Perspective

Please answer the following questions:

» What are some of my biggest disappointments? What can I learn from them?
» In what areas of my life do I need to stop comparing myself to others?
» What am I robbing myself of by comparing myself to others?
» What do I need to be more appreciative of?
» What three to five things can I remind myself of every day in order to ignite my joy?

>> When has gratitude sustained me when happiness was too hard to feel? How did my gratitude affect my outcome? How did gratitude affect my mind-set during the experience?

Complete the following:

>> I am blessed because . . . (list at least three things)
>> I need to stop complaining about . . . (list at least three things)
>> I can improve my quiet time with myself by . . .
>> I am grateful for . . .

Exercise 3: Accepting My New Norm

So much of our unhappiness often flows from the fact that our lives have changed, but we have not yet accepted those changes. So we are living in the expectations of yesterday and measuring our happiness against them. Here are a few questions that have helped me to accept my new norm. Perhaps they can help you.

>> What have I accomplished that I no longer need to pursue?
>> What do I need to stop doing, forget, and move on?
>> What recent accomplishments do I need to acknowledge and begin enjoying?
>> What am I frustrated about that is no longer my truth?
>> What am I holding on to that is no longer my reality?
>> What am I still doing that is no longer serving me?
>> Who am I angry with that I need to forgive?
>> What changes do I need to make based on my current reality?

"Bonus" Exercise: The Recess Challenge

Recently I was at my daughter's school to volunteer and I noticed her class's schedule:

1. Classwork
2. Chapel
3. Classwork
4. PE
5. Lunch
6. Recess
7. Classwork

I was glad to note that my daughter's school understood the value of recess and PE. Breaking up classwork with scheduled time to burn energy, rejuvenate, and just have fun allows kids to come back to their work renewed and refreshed.

Then it hit me: Why don't adults take "recess"? What if we set aside fifteen to twenty minutes a day to go do something fun and joyful like dance, listen to music, throw a ball, play the piano, read or listen to something funny, or play a video game? Would our productivity go up or down? (Hmm, I bet I know the answer.)

I offer you this challenge: for the next fourteen days, build a recess break (or two) into your day. During recess, do something you find really fun, something that has nothing to do with work and that uses a different part of your brain than your work does. After two weeks, assess your work output and your work attitude. Has your productivity gone up or down? What other changes have you noticed?

EXPONENTIAL CONVERSATION

Joy Pervis is a talent agent who is known for discovering and developing some of the most successful and recognizable actors working in Hollywood, including Dakota Fanning and her sister, Elle, Kyle Massey, and others. Known as the "Star Maker" to many Hollywood execs, she has placed more recognizable working actors in LA than any other talent scout/agent living outside of the Los Angeles area. She now travels the country scouting kids and adults for placement with the Osbrink Agency (LA) and J Pervis Talent Agency (Atlanta).

Whenever you are in Joy's (her name is not accidental) presence, her smile and energy are a living example of someone whose happiness flows from the truth of who she is, not from the reality of her circumstances. She beams joy from her very presence.

SHERI RILEY: You have a successful business, you have an amazing family, you have this ability to smile, which means you've found something that allows you to live more than just this narrow 10 percent that some of us in the [entertainment] industry live in.

JOY PERVIS: Well, it's interesting because I think more people want to be in our industry than any other industry out there. But in our world, it can be very dark. There were times that I felt like I needed to step out of this industry. So I really struggled with that for several years, but I also realized that the only way to make a difference is to put the light in the darkness. I think that's what my main thing is.

I started with kids in the industry. I was very blessed to have an eye for talent. There's something about kids that is so innocent and magical. We get them before they're tarnished. So I've always enjoyed that aspect of it, but along the way it becomes very challenging. Our industry is one that is all about "me"—not me personally, but I'm talking about the individual you're working with. It's "What did you do for me yesterday, what are you doing for me today, what are you going to do for me tomorrow?" It's a very superficial world and we work with so many people that are very narcissistic. It's a challenge to stay at that level of peace and to stay at that level where you are as confident and encouraging and nurturing as you can be. But I love what I do, I totally love what I do, and I've been blessed to be able to discover and work with so many people that are living their dream right now.

SHERI RILEY: How did you fuel yourself to do that?

JOY PERVIS: I've always been a positive person and I have always loved life. So that's been something all my life. I just love life. I love people. Happiness is an area that I do. I've had a lot of adversity in my life. When I was twelve years old my father was killed in a tragic automobile accident, which I saw happen. Children deal with tragedy in different ways. God gives them certain techniques and vehicles to work through that. Mine was, I learned to compartmentalize very easily. I learned you take that adversity, you take that tragedy, you take whatever, and you put it over *here*, and you deal with it when you can and when you need to. But you don't let that affect how you treat people, how you *are* when you walk into a room, how you interact with people.

All of us have a backstory, all of us have certain things and situations that affect us every single day of our lives. But I don't believe that everybody around us should carry our burden.

SHERI RILEY: So, when you compartmentalize, do you just leave it there and never deal with it?

JOY PERVIS: I do deal with it.

SHERI RILEY: And how do you do that?

JOY PERVIS: Well, I think when I had that tragedy happen to me really early in life, that's how I dealt with it [compartmentalizing], and I went through the next part of my life, almost forty years, where things were wonderful. Things fell into place for me. My journey and my career were going very, very well. I didn't have anything attack me until about six years ago. And when I say I was attacked, I was *attacked*.

In the last six years I have been going through a very terrible litigation, where my integrity and my character were being attacked. And my husband and I, we literally went through hundreds of thousands of dollars in attorney fees. We lost practically everything. Every tangible asset that we have just disappeared, practically, just trying to pay the attorney fees and keep up with everything. Going through that, it can consume you. . . . I tried not to let that affect me, but you can't help it. It affects you in some way. Again, I tried to compartmentalize it when I was dealing with other people. I would try not to allow it to affect how I dealt with people, and the atmosphere of people around me. But you know, you do have to deal with those things.

SHERI RILEY: Okay, so you said six years ago, and that's around the time you and I met. I have to say—for the reader—that every time I was around you, you *were* light, you were filled with joy, you were very much in tune with my daughter and me. I understand now that you compartmentalize that, but you still had to find the strength to give that much of yourself, like you said, in a narcissistic industry. Where did you find that strength?

JOY PERVIS: I was that person who grew up in church, went to church every week. God has always been an important factor in my life. However, it wasn't until midway through that journey of that six years—through this horrible experience that I and my family were going through—that something very beautiful happened: I found my faith. For fifty years I thought I had it, but it wasn't until then that I realized I just found it.

SHERI RILEY: Oh, that sent chills.

JOY PERVIS: It was a beautiful thing. I'll never forget this. I'll tell this quick story. It was New Year's Eve, December 31, 2010, and I had already been involved in this litigation for a couple of years. It was New Year's Eve, we were outside our house, and we had a fire going and people around us and the neighbors were doing firecrackers and all this stuff. New Year's Eve is the time when you do the countdown and then "Happy New Year!" And I looked at my watch and it was ten minutes before midnight and I looked at my husband and I said, "I'm going inside. I'm going to bed. Good night."

He said, "We're ten minutes away from New Year's!"

I said, "Happy New Year, everybody. I love you all." I went into my bedroom and I got on my knees and I started praying. I prayed out 2010 and I prayed in 2011. It was that moment that I found my faith. It was the most beautiful experience ever. All that energy and that focus that I put on [the lawsuit], I completely put on Him. And do you know that's now my New Year tradition? Ten minutes before that clock strikes, I release myself, I go into my room, I get on my hands and knees, and I pray out the old year and pray in the new one.

SHERI RILEY: Now after that moment—because the realities of life are still happening, this legal issue is still happening, your company is still going, the needs of your clients are still there, you've got the family that's still pulling at you—what was different for you?

JOY PERVIS: The difference is that the energies I had been focusing on what was going on around me—I completely changed it and I literally focused on Him. And it changes your attitude! It was the light; it was the light coming out. The light that I thought I was giving before, that was just my general love for people and enjoying what I do, but after that, it was a totally different light.

SHERI RILEY: I say, "He became the fuel."

JOY PERVIS: Yes.

SHERI RILEY: You weren't pulling just from your own reservoir anymore. How do you celebrate?

JOY PERVIS: I celebrate through praise and worship.

SHERI RILEY: Is that where your gratitude comes from as well?

JOY PERVIS: Yes, every day, every morning.

SHERI RILEY: And what does that look like for you, if you don't mind sharing?

JOY PERVIS: Well, it's an everyday thing. I get up in the morning and I give Him my first. I pull out my Bible, I read it, and I do my personal conversation with Him. It's beautiful.

SHERI RILEY: I've been around you in your world and you don't come across as a Bible-toting, beat-you-over-the-head type. Everyone experiences your power, your joy, and your peace. How do you do that?

JOY PERVIS: I grew up in a very judgmental religion, and so that's not the way that people recognize the light in you. I think you just have to love. You have to love people. I think it's through that love that you show and the interaction you have with people where they go, "There's something different. What is it? I want some of that."

SHERI RILEY: How do you define success?

JOY PERVIS: I learned this through the last six years: success is not the big house, or the car you drive, or the material things you surround yourself with. That's what the world acknowledges as success, but I've found that it's all in *here*. It's all in here. If you have that peace inside of you and that peace is what gives you joy, that, to me, is success. Success, to me, is knowing that my family is together. Going through what we went through, my family should not be together. I should probably be in a mental institution right now, on the streets!

I look back at it all and I say, "Would I change anything?" Yeah, I would change it. It wasn't a fun experience to go through, and it not only affected me, but it affected my family and everybody around me. However, I wouldn't change a thing if it were the only way to get to where I am today. Inside.

SHERI RILEY: In our industry, we meet a lot of people, especially high achievers—they know how to compartmentalize, but they don't know how to go deal. And that's the power of your story. In dealing with those challenges, it strengthened you instead of tearing you down. Is that a fair assessment?

JOY PERVIS: Absolutely.

SHERI RILEY: What are you happy about? What are you grateful for? And what is your gratitude?

JOY PERVIS: I'm happy that I have good health and that I have a very close family. I'm grateful for all the incredible blessings that just continue to shower me. I am so incredibly blessed. My gratitude is to Him for that one beautiful moment in the darkest times.

I AM JOY PERVIS AND I AM EXPONENTIAL LIVING.

Key Takeaways

» When you find yourself in a world of darkness, your only real choice is to be a light in the darkness.

» Tragedy need not permanently affect who you are and the positive energy you bring into a room.

» A great way to choose happiness is to pray out the old and pray in the new.

» When you're feeling stressed, shift your attention from your worries onto God. It brings peace every time.

» Success is the peace you feel inside. Period.

PRINCIPLE 7

Build Lasting Confidence

Do not throw away your confidence; it will be richly rewarded.

{ —HEBREWS 10:35 }

Drive is a very useful trait. Drive to achieve a goal or complete a project is often what pushes us out of bed in the morning and powers us through setbacks and obstacles. Drive can take us to high levels of success in our careers.

But drive doesn't elevate us in our personal development. That's the job of confidence. High achievers have no shortage of drive. Confidence, however—that's another matter.

A tipping point occurred in my life when I learned the difference between drive and confidence. One day, a few years into my record-company career, I came to the crossroads I described earlier. I had achieved many goals, but repeatedly found myself feeling empty and unfulfilled. I kept trying to fill this void by working harder and achieving more. There'd be a brief "high"; then I would crash again, and would have to start the process over again. Finally, I just ran out of gas. I knew I needed more. In the process of doing some deep self-examination, I realized that I was very driven to achieve but had very little confidence in myself. At first, I resisted this insight because, after all, how could I have reached such levels of success without being confident?

And so I asked this question of several of my achievement-minded friends, peers, and business colleagues (and have continued to ask it of countless clients). In the vast majority of cases, I received the same answer: yes, I am driven but my confidence is nowhere near as strong as my drive. Sometimes it almost seems that the more drive people have, the less confidence they possess. Perhaps it is their fundamental *lack* of confidence, in fact, that spurs them to constantly seek approval and relief through doing more and more.

Drive is a wonderful thing, let me just say. I have no issues with drive. In fact, I rely on my drive. It's my drive that has me writing these words at three forty-five a.m. But confidence is where all the good stuff is found.

Confidence is our power to be 100 percent fulfilled even when we are doing nothing. Confidence is what fills us up when the world stops cheering our name or when tragedy happens in our family. Confidence is what sustains us when our marriage hits a bad patch, and all we can do is hope, pray, and be still. Confidence is not a surface feeling that comes and goes. Confidence is the deeply rooted ability to stand courageously in the full knowledge and acceptance of who we are and what we are about.

Drive is what pushes us to our achievements and goals; confidence is who we are when we get there. Drive is our protective strength. Confidence is our vulnerable strength.

Why do I say *vulnerable* strength? Well, because in order to develop true confidence, we don't need to pump ourselves up and shout motivational mantras into the mirror. Rather, we need to be able to *face* ourselves, to be fully present to ourselves, complete with all our ability, beauty, and strength, as well as our flaws, weaknesses, and undeveloped potential. And to do such a thing, to be emotionally naked with ourselves—exactly as we are, not as we hope and wish we were, not as we tell the world we are—requires profound vulnerability. But when we are courageous enough to do this, we begin to develop a comfort with ourselves that carries us into the world with grace and surety. Many high achievers spend literally an entire lifetime avoiding an honest encounter with themselves. They cloak themselves in drive, but they don't know how to be vulnerable enough to find their confidence.

Fake Confidence

Many high achievers use their drive and achievements to develop fake confidence. We've all met these people. They're full of smiles and handshakes and "can-do" attitudes. They brag; they show off. Sometimes they use intimidation, wealth, and power plays to prove how sure they are of themselves, as if being a bully or a conqueror were the ultimate show of confidence. Or they develop false humility. They are forever putting the needs of others above their own. This self-sacrifice, though, serves to position them as people strong enough to endure for everyone.

But fake confidence is a barrier. It distracts us from building a deep-rooted relationship with ourselves. False confidence pushes people away or allows us to be treated like a martyr. It's an arrogance (or self-deprecation) that's annoying and destructive. Confidence of the heart, on the other hand, does not push people away or allow people to mistreat us; it is a magnet that draws people to us. Truly confident people are attractive in the deepest sense of the word. Others want to be around them and soak in their energy.

Lasting confidence is something we must work for and build. It requires standing on uncharted ground—the tender and unexplored terrain of our own being. Confidence is not automatically granted to us by growing older. It is gained through spending honest, unguarded time with ourselves and coming to know our true power. (For me, spending time with God is an essential aspect of this.) There are five-year-olds who are beautifully confident and ninety-five-year-olds who are terrified to be alone with themselves for even sixty seconds.

Confidence is about who we are, not just what we do.

Hitting the Wall

In coaching high achievers, I have found that their drive eventually pushes them to levels of success that their character can't sustain. Driven corporate executives, athletes, performers, and entrepreneurs inevitably come to a place in their career where they hit a wall. The athlete suffers an injury or starts losing his/her winning edge; the executive is passed over for a promotion; the entrepreneur's hot sales start to cool off or burn out. Suddenly, rewards and achievements are no longer coming at the pace or predictability they once did, and the passion that ignites the drive is gone. Connections to people are not as impactful as they formerly were. Execution isn't rewarded the way it once was. Talent alone is no longer enough to solve a problem. Clarity about direction fades into confusion. A new skill set, a new understanding, is needed. They begin to feel themselves slipping into unfamiliar territory. Their confidence is badly shaken.

When some high achievers hit these challenge points, they begin to work harder, but increased intensity doesn't bring them the results they're looking for. They are stuck in the mud, spinning their wheels.

At this point, some people go the "betrayal" route. They choose to feel offended by the fact that what they were doing before isn't working anymore, and they blame other people or situations for this. Instead of having the confidence to push through to a new level, they become bitter.

Once this sets in, we start to give our power away. We begin to self-sabotage and spend more time thinking about the behavior of others than focusing on our truth. We start sifting every situation and conversation through the filter of resentment. This causes us to shrink in our growth and make bad decisions.

Other high achievers, when they hit this wall, recognize, on some level, that this is a learning point/turning point in their lives. This is the time when new clients often seek me out for coaching. They know something needs to change.

When a client comes to me at one of these crisis moments, the first thing I usually do is explore with them whether their success up to this point has been a result largely of drive or of confidence. The answer usually turns out to be drive. In some instances, clients never had confidence to begin with. In other cases, they started out with confidence but, over time, their confidence has slipped away as their drive has gotten stronger.

Once I get past the client's defensiveness and help him realize that he has been operating on drive alone, there is usually a tremendous sense of relief. The client admits to feeling exhausted from living a life of drive, and is eager and open to find a new way. That is when the real work begins. That is when we start to explore what it might be like to live and work from a place of confidence.

The ultimate goal—with my clients and with you—is to learn to operate from a place of confidence *and* drive, rather than just drive alone.

A Return to Confidence

When I'm working with clients to build lasting confidence, I often find that there is a three-step process. It doesn't always go in this order, but I'll share it with you:

1. **Focus on What You Are, Not What You Are Not.** Come to a recognition and acceptance of all the skills, talents, and gifts you possess. Instead of focusing on what you are *not*, take stock of all the positive traits and abilities you actually possess.

2. **Only You Can Be the Best You.** Go deeper and come to a recognition and acceptance of *who you are*, beyond what you are capable of doing. Learn to appreciate the beauty and power of your own uniqueness.

3. **The Courage to BE.** Develop the power to be present wherever you are right now. Ultimately, confidence is about the ability to be fully present in every moment of your life, not fearfully driving ahead to what's next.

Let's look at these three foundational steps more closely.

1. Focus on What You Are, Not What You Are Not

Many high achievers work constantly from a place of fear, rather than from the fullness of their creativity, innovative thinking, athletic ability, or other amazing capabilities. Their fear of not measuring up to some inner or outer standard causes them to habitually focus on what they are *not*, as opposed to what they are.

For many high achievers, there has been some injury to their self-esteem in the past, and they are driven to prove (to a parent, to a teacher, to themselves, to the world) that they are not what others have defined them to be. Maybe someone called them a loser, or said they would never amount to anything when they were a child. So they became determined to prove that person wrong. In the case of other high achievers, they simply feel inadequate or unworthy and try to compensate for those feelings by racking up achievements. Others just become so focused on *who they want to become* that they lose sight of *who they are now*. In any of these cases, the drive to achieve comes from a negative place—from what they aren't, rather than who they are.

This constant focus on what we are *not* prevents us from taking an objective inventory of our strengths. As I pointed out earlier, we can't live in our power when we're stuck on what we *haven't* accomplished yet. To regain our power (and confidence is really just acceptance and ownership of our power), we need to own the things we have actually accomplished and live in the traits, talents, and gifts that we were born with and that represent who we are.

Most high achievers, in fact, possess many excellent and admirable traits. Too often, they are the last to recognize these traits in themselves. They are too focused on beating themselves up for their perceived failings and driving themselves to become more. Often when I sit down with clients and explore with them all of their actual capabilities, they are moved to tears. It is as if they are meeting themselves for the first time.

Many high achievers, for example, have traits such as

» Vision
» Focus
» World-class talent
» Ability to motivate themselves and others

>> Drive
>> Leadership
>> Resilience
>> Organizational talent
>> Goal-setting ability
>> Giving heart

. . . just for starters. But they've developed blinders to these traits.

Again: while it is important to always try to improve ourselves, our confidence comes from living *within* our existing talents and capabilities and valuing them for what they are now.

It is time to take stock of *your* talents, skills, and abilities. (There is an exercise to help you with this later in this chapter.) Remember, it is the presence of these traits that has empowered you to accomplish whatever you have accomplished so far in life. Your accomplishments did not come from what you lacked, but from what you possessed. So make the shift. Accept and celebrate the things you do well and the talents and gifts you possess. List them on paper. Get to know them. Make a vow to stand in the fullness of these abilities, rather than in the absence of what is missing.

Above all, make a vow to live in the fullness of YOU.

2. Only You Can Be the Best You

> Be yourself; everyone else is already taken.
>
> —OSCAR WILDE

Beyond having confidence in your true abilities, you must have confidence in your*self.* This does not mean confidence in your degrees, knowledge, job titles, position, social status, or possessions. Rather, it is about having a pure and abiding confidence in the person you are. Exponential Living is a daily focus on being your best *you*. Many of us spend 90 percent of our waking lives focusing on being the best singer, athlete, lawyer, pastor, parent, doctor, corporate executive, business owner—you get the point—that we can be. But roles are just that: roles. Who is the "actor" *behind* the roles? At the end of a great performance, an actor goes home to herself and must be able to find peace, alone, on her sofa. Are you able to do that when you step out of your roles?

Who is the *you* that resides beneath all of the roles you play—parent, teacher, manager, student, salesperson? What does it mean to be you, not your parents, your friends, your coworkers? What do you value about yourself? What do you deeply care about? What inspires you? What do you love? What fills you with delight? What makes you laugh? Cry? Stand up and cheer? What are your quirks and oddities? What qualities do you exude? Can you imagine spending a week in silence with only your own company? Can you separate who you are from all the things you do?

When you learn to be the most complete *you* possible, your confidence expands beyond what you do and what you have. It becomes anchored in *who you are*. Then, when obstacles, forced changes, and other challenges come up, your sense of *who you are* is strong enough to carry you through these valleys.

Remember: nobody on planet Earth can beat you at being you. Nobody. When life is kicking your butt and things just aren't going your way, when your relationships are all jacked up, when you don't have the money to pay your bills, when your kids have lost their minds, when your boss and coworkers are stressing you out—*who you are* should remain your rock. *Who you are* is not about your financial status or your relationship status or your position in the company, but your heart, your character, your values, and the amazingly unique and *good* person you are.

For me, it all goes back to my relationship with God. I know I have value because God did not create anything that is a waste of time, space, or oxygen. I am therefore impelled to believe that I—like you—am divinely made and ordained with a path and purpose that matters profoundly. To think small of myself is to think small of my Creator, and I refuse to do that. Instead, I choose to believe that *who I am* is embedded in greatness. And to honor that, I must never apologize for who I am, back down from what I deeply believe, or make myself smaller so that others can feel larger. Being my best *me* is not just a pact I make with myself; it is one I make with God.

3. The Courage to BE

One question all we achievement-minded people must eventually ask ourselves is "Am I going to work and work until I have everything I desire—and then realize I was miserable getting there?" Or, alternatively, "Will I *fail* to achieve what I desire and then, on my deathbed, finally notice all of the things I should have enjoyed along the way?"

Neither of those outcomes works for me. And yet, most high achievers I have worked with are on one of these two tracks. They are so work focused and future focused, they lack the fundamental ability to simply *be*.

What about you? When you are doing nothing, do you feel like a fulfilled, whole, and productive human being? When you are at rest, do you feel worthy of receiving good things?

For me, writing this book wasn't hard because of the daunting challenge of putting over ninety-five thousand words on paper. The hardest part was to focus on one thing, writing for almost a year.

Everything in me wanted to be doing the work of marketing and promoting the book rather than quietly being who I am so that the power of these principles could flow through me and onto the pages. The power of this book is not about what I do. It is about who I am and the truths I've been able to receive so that others may live in the power of peace and of Exponential Living. I had to live in the confidence of my own being to even deliver this book to the world—something I would not have been able to do ten years ago.

We live in a single-use, microwavable, instant-gratification culture. But what remains true is this: works of significance are crafted in the stillness of reflection. What's created quickly goes away quickly. What's created mindfully and carefully lasts for a lifetime and longer, and leaves a legacy. The funny thing is that those who are dedicated to speeding through a life of *doing* often don't leave anything of lasting value behind. It is those who have mastered the art of *being* who give humanity its real treasures. Albert Einstein did not produce his world-changing insights by laboring sixteen hours a day in a lab, but by allowing himself ample time for his imagination to wander.

Once we learn how to comfortably *be*, without doing, we are then able to carry that *being*ness into the working world. That is what presence is. Presence is the ability to be immersed in *being*, even as we are *doing*.

The Future Is in the Present

The ability to be present is the heart of confidence. It is such a simple thing—presence—yet painfully elusive to many. Presence is the ability to give 100 percent of our attention and our being to whatever we are doing at any moment—whether that's delivering a business presentation, listening to a child's story, watching a sunset, painting a rose, or lifting weights at the gym. Most high achievers have a very difficult time with presence. Their eyes are on the prize—the future—and their minds are filled with to-do lists. They are constantly focused on what's next and what they *should* be doing. Their minds are anywhere but right here, right now. They're all about someday.

What we need to understand is that someday is now. This moment *is* the someday we yearned for in the past; it is also the someday of the future. How so? Well, the amount of presence we give to this moment shapes the future. By giving 100 percent of our presence to what we are doing now, we allow the greatest possible someday to unfold. But if we overlook the present moment—or deal with it impatiently—because our eyes are on the future, we actually ensure a lesser future. A football player who looks at the end zone and takes his eyes off the ball doesn't complete the catch. His mind is on the future of scoring a touchdown instead of on being present enough to first catch the ball. The winning athlete, however, focuses only on what he is doing *this moment*, confident that if he does this, the score—and his career—will take care of itself. Our futures unfold with similar effortlessness when we give full presence to everything we do.

I witnessed a great example of this when I worked at LaFace Records. My first assistant was an amazing woman named Tashion Macon, who is now a sister to me. Our first interaction was when she assisted me with my move from Cleveland, Ohio, to Atlanta, Georgia. From the beginning, Tashion was gracious, professional, and on top of every detail. Though she was clearly capable of greater things, she was thoroughly present to even the most "mundane" tasks. When I started at LaFace, with the unrealistic deadlines and workload I had those first six weeks on the job, it was her extensive knowledge of the company, its procedures, and its marketing strategies that allowed me to prosper in my new position. From day one, I told her she would be doing my job as the product manager, and this would allow me to accomplish even more in my role. She was more than up to the task. She tackled every challenge with presence and confidence.

Six months later, I called her into my office and advised her to close the door. "Tashion, I am going to help you find a new job," I said with a smile.

With concern etched on her face, she asked, "Are you firing me?"

"Just the opposite," I assured her. "You are too brilliant and talented to be my assistant. I'm going to help you find a job at a new company as a product manager or whatever you want to be."

And that's exactly what I did. After she left my office, I began making phone calls and arranging interviews. It wasn't long before she secured the marketing job at Dr. Dre's new label, Aftermath Entertainment. Since then, she has worked at NBC Universal, the Marketing Arm (formerly Davie Brown Entertainment), and the Pitch Agency (formerly Equity Marketing). The work she did in all of those positions led her to implement the largest promotion, to date, in T-Mobile's history. She put together a massive T-Mobile-sponsored flash mob for a season opener of *The Oprah Winfrey Show*. Oprah said this was the first time her production team had ever been able to surprise her. Tashion has since gone on to complete her PhD and accomplish many other things.

The point I want to make is that every task Tashion ever did, every little skill she had ever acquired through being present to her work, became part of creating, managing, budgeting, and implementing this huge, nationally recognized promotion. Similarly, your future is magnified by how well you attend to this moment—no matter what you are doing. When you know this, your "someday" no longer seems like a distant place or an unobtainable idea that may or may not happen. You can rest in the confidence that today *is* your tomorrow, and today *is* your success. Today *is* reaching your goals. Today *is* bringing your desires to fruition, even if you are in the lowest place of your life.

Knowing that the future will take care of itself if you are 100 percent present to this moment is the ultimate confidence builder.

Surrender and Fight—A Sweet Oxymoron

To be confident in yourself and your actions, you must stop doubting and questioning yourself in every moment. This requires the art of surrender, which we talked about in a previous chapter. But it also means, paradoxically, that you have to fight. Fight against your destructive tendencies and your doubt. Fight against what the world calls success. You must surrender to what you truly believe *and* fight for your confidence.

Surrender, again, is not quitting. It is *allowing* bigger and better things to happen on your behalf. It is the confidence that gears are turning even when you're not frantically pulling levers. I've always been very clear and focused about what I wanted to achieve in life. But there came a point where, for about two years, I didn't have a clue what direction I needed to take. I knew Exponential Living was my purpose and passion, but I didn't have a clear plan on how to birth it to the world. This was a very frustrating time for me. How could I be so clear at fifteen, yet be so lost and confused at forty-two?

I kept searching and praying, trying to find what was next. And one day, I finally surrendered. I didn't quit; I surrendered. I surrendered to the process. I realized that I was in a new place in my life. A place called "achievement." I had accomplished every goal I had set for myself! This phase of my life wasn't about where I was going next; it was about being whole and at peace with where I was. Gaining that insight was what revealed to me the true key to Exponential Living, peace, and also gave me the confidence to let the process continue to unfold day by day, without agonizing over every detail.

Surrender doesn't negate our desire for things like financial success and great relationships. But it empowers us to be content and joyful right where we are right now. It allows us to live in confidence—which, in case you haven't noticed, is really just another way of saying to live in peace and power. These concepts and ideas are all working together, interwoven.

Build Lasting Confidence

Confidence is easily eroded. That's why Principle 7 is "Build *Lasting* Confidence." Having lasting confidence is like being a boxer who has strengthened his core. When he takes a gut punch, he still feels the force of the blow, but he doesn't buckle. He's so well-conditioned, the punch doesn't throw him or bend him over. Lasting confidence comes from learning to stand in our truth, day after day. That's how we condition the soul and spirit.

There are many things that attack our confidence regularly. We've looked at some of these "enemies" in past chapters—things like fear and comparing ourselves to others. In order to withstand punches from these enemies, we need to anticipate them and prepare for them. Here are some confidence killers and how to deal with them:

Major setbacks. There are times in your life when everything crashes to a halt. You get fired or downsized; your business loses a major client or a big chunk of its profits. Or sometimes the setback is personal—people you care about walk out of your life or stop communicating. Something in your life changes dramatically, in a way that feels like failure. Your confidence wants to take a nosedive.

What to do. Recognize that setbacks are also opportunities. They are times to invest in yourself through education, learning new skills, and evolving and developing your existing capabilities. You may not have time to do these things when activity is occupying all of your attention. A setback tells you that a new journey is at hand. Preparation for a journey does not begin while you are *on* the journey; it begins *before* the journey. So use downturns in activity as opportunities to prepare. Build confidence in your abilities and your*self* rather than let your confidence erode through worry.

Abusive relationship with self. Many high achievers have what amounts to an abusive relationship with themselves. They are constantly disappointed and angry at themselves for being less than perfect. They privately question their decisions and call themselves names they would never say to others. They use this constant self-berating as a "whip" to spur themselves forward in the race. What they don't realize is that this barrage of self-flagellation comes at a dear price: it murders their confidence. So even though they may make it to the finish line, the "horse" they arrive with is bruised and beaten down.

What to do. For heaven's sake, be kind to yourself. *You* need your kindness more than anyone else does. Do little things throughout the day to nurture and care for yourself. Learn to filter your self-talk. As soon as you hear self-abuse creep in, flip it around and express gratitude for your successes and forgiveness for your failures.

Timing and order. Many of us high achievers become frustrated when things don't happen in the timing and order we want them to. Doubt creeps in, which causes a domino effect in our emotional, psychological, and spiritual life. We begin to question everything. We become weary, burned out, and short-tempered. We make snap decisions that have negative consequences.

I recall one time, for example, I was scheduled to give a talk to an audience made up entirely of multimillionaires. At the time I was struggling financially myself, so I questioned whether I should even be there. Was I a fraud because I was broke? My confidence in what I was doing was thoroughly shaken. A dear friend reminded me that I was *being* exactly who I was and that the work of my hands would soon produce the financial reward I expected. My lack of confidence, I realized, was a timing-and-order issue, not an issue with my purpose.

What to do. In order to allow the best possible results to flow to you, release your attachment to seeing things happen in the timing and order *you* choose. Remind yourself that you don't know all the facts and that if you were actually allowed to orchestrate your life, you would mess it up profoundly. God has a plan for you, God does know all the facts, and God will bring things to you at the best possible time and in the order required. Often right before a "slingshot" moment—one of those sudden and impactful moments when life takes off in a positive new direction—circumstances seem to be their bleakest and most hopeless. In these slingshot moments, it is easy to focus on how far it feels like God is pulling you back. Instead, get excited about how far you will fly when He releases you. Stop asking for God's timing to change, but ask God to change *you* in His timing. Release the need for control, and have confidence that things are happening or *not* happening for a reason.

"False failures." High achievers often have amazing life experiences—starring roles in plays or films, championship seasons, great vacations, successful product launches, amazing achievements by their children, etc.—that create awesome emotional, spiritual, and psychological highs. Then, when life returns to "normal," it feels like a crash or failure. These crashes can chip away at our confidence and cause us to spin into a dangerous funk. We may battle with depression. We often self-sabotage. We overeat, underexercise, medicate ourselves with drugs—legal or illegal—and engage in other negative behaviors. Often it's not something new that triggers these issues for high achievers, but simply a replaying of a familiar cycle of highs and "normals."

What to do. Recognize the cycle for what it is. Normal is not bad. Nothing is wrong in your life; you are just going through a recalibration process. Understand that your emotions are not your truth. Just because you are *feeling* shaky or let down, that doesn't mean your life is really on shaky ground. Allow yourself to feel the letdown without being spooked by it or medicating it away. Enjoy the positive aspects of being at the trough of the wave instead of the crest. Appreciate the special things you can do now that the pressure and attention are off you for a while. Above all, just be grateful for all the great things that are still present in your life.

Building lasting confidence is tough. It's often painful. It's lonely at times. This is all part of the process. Strength doesn't build when the current is carrying you, but when you are rowing against it. Remember, though: the pain is not the end result. We don't run five miles or work out with weights for the pain. We do it for the end result of fitness and health. Don't confuse the process with the end result. When you find yourself immersed in doubt and confusion and fighting your way through it, know that you are building lasting confidence. Confidence, not doubt, is the end result.

Confidence Spreads

One of the greatest reasons to develop lasting confidence is that our confidence helps others become more confident. Confidence is infectious. It spreads. A confident player inspires confidence in teammates. A confident manager fosters confidence in employees. Confidence is like a physical energy that is felt and absorbed by those around us. One person's true confidence can be enough to inspire the confidence of an entire company (look at Steve Jobs) or even an entire country or race of people (look at John F. Kennedy, Martin Luther King Jr.). Lack of confidence can be similarly infectious. This fact has profound implications for our business and personal lives; our fight for confidence isn't just about us—it's about the entire world of people who surround us.

Nowhere is this more important than in our families. As parents, we want our children to be confident—both now and in adulthood. We, the parents, are the ones who can instill this confidence in them (or choke it off). We do it in two ways. One way is by becoming confident in who *we* are. Parents who are comfortable in their own skin— who don't spend all their time frantically chasing goals or distracting themselves to fill the void—create households where self-acceptance is honored and honest emotions are allowed. Members of the family don't feel they must "be" a certain way in order to gain approval or acceptance. Everyone is free to be himself or herself. Another way is by giving our presence to our kids. Presence is the highest way we honor another human being. When we spend attentive time with our children, we tell them they are more important than anything else. And nothing builds confidence better than that.

I had an experience with my daughter that really brought this home. When Dominique was five years old, she was cast as the six-year-old version of the lead in the movie *Let the Church Say Amen*, directed by Regina King. Three years later, we heard the movie was finally being released. Having worked in the entertainment industry, I knew that her part could have been edited out and that she might not be in the final cut of the movie. So before telling her about the release, I contacted my friend, who was one of the producers, to confirm that she had made the final cut. He assured me several times that yes, she was in the movie. I shared this great news with Dominique and she was, of course, thrilled. She asked me several questions to confirm that she was *really* hearing what she was hearing. She was going to be in a movie that was going to air on TV! She shared this exciting news with her teachers, current and past, and her classmates and friends at school. She shared it with family and friends from church.

A week before the movie was scheduled to air on BET, I contacted my friend and asked for a copy of the movie for our archives. When I watched it, Dominique was not in the movie. I. Was. Devastated. Not because she hadn't made the final cut—that happens—but because I'd told her she had, and she'd told her friends. This disappointment was going to be a lot for an eight-year-old to take. When I contacted my friend, he felt horrible about the mix-up and was kind enough to send me a clip of her scene as well as a DVD of the version she was in.

A few nights before the movie was to air, I showed Dominique the clip of the scene with her in it and shared with her that she wasn't in the final version. She immediately fell into her pillow, face-first, and cried so hard her body shook. Through a break in her tears, she raised her head, looked me in my eyes, and said, "Mommy, I told Mrs. Rush, Mrs. McCall, Mrs. Markert, all my friends in my class . . . I've waited so long for this." I rubbed her back and let her cry. This embarrassment was going to be hard for her to handle, but I had been preparing her for a moment like this for years. What I have told her is that it doesn't matter that you cry. All that matters is what you do when you are done crying. And so I let her cry and cry and cry and cry.

Her dad then talked with her. He shared with her that she is a leader and that the way she handles the news of her not being in the movie is the way everyone else will handle it. She listened attentively, and then, with complete respect and an abundance of courage, she asked her daddy, "Can I just get it all out? I'll be okay in the morning." She had the confidence to stand in her own truth in that moment—that she needed to cry, get it all out, and that she would be okay in the morning.

Her daddy honored her request and she just lay in my arms and cried. I didn't say a word. My daughter was deep in pain, disappointment, and embarrassment, and all I could do was be there for her. My silent presence said to her, "My truth is that I can't take the punch away, but I am here and I will always be here."

The next day, Dominique went off to school with her calm confidence, and when she came home she told me everything had gone well. She simply shared the news that there'd been a mistake.

The confidence Dominique displayed was a result of years of preparing her for this moment. As parents, we must spend time giving wisdom to our children years before they need it. This means giving them our presence. Many times, at the end of a hard day, when our kids are in the backseat of our car, asking a thousand questions, we tell them to be quiet. We are exhausted from a hard day and may be rushing home to jump on another conference call or answer an e-mail. Instead of being present with our children, we choose to take the "lazy parent" route. Rather than empower them, we shut them down. By the time they are sixteen and we need them to talk with us, we've already taught them how *not* to talk with us or give us their full attention. And then it's a huge uphill battle to build their confidence.

Confidence is the backbone of Exponential Living. Drive is important too, of course, but ultimately drive only spurs us to get things done. Confidence is not just about what we do and how we do it; it's about living in full ownership of who we are. Confidence is with us as we stand at the podium in front of a crowd *and* as we sit alone in a room in quiet reflection.

Vision, Action, Results

Exercise: Drive Vs. Confidence

The following are "dictionary" definitions of *drive* and *confidence*:

Drive is the quality of striving vigorously toward a goal or objective; to work, play, or try wholeheartedly and with determination.

Confidence is authentic belief and understanding of who you are, and your purpose and passion, regardless of the external environment.

These are great definitions. To them I would add the Exponential Living definitions:

Drive is our protective strength.

Confidence is our vulnerable strength.

To help you better understand the difference between drive and confidence in your own life, please answer the following questions:

1. What are some accomplishments I have achieved by driving myself toward a goal?

2. What are some accomplishments I have achieved simply by being confident and asking for what I wanted?

3. What are some differences between those two types of experiences?

Write down some skills you use in your work and home life. These might include things like writing, speaking, teaching, parenting, cooking, singing . . .

1. For each of these, on a scale of one to ten, what is the confidence I display to the world?

2. For each of these, on a scale of one to ten, what is the confidence I really have?

3. To what do I attribute the difference between the confidence I display and the true confidence that I have?

4. Can I recall a time when my confidence was shaken? How did it affect the outcome of the situation I was in at the time? How might things have gone differently if I had remained confident?

5. Can I recall a time when my confidence inspired those around me?

6. How has a fear (an untruth I've accepted as truth) minimized my confidence and fueled my drive?

7. Do I attribute my career success to being driven or confident? Explain.

8. Complete the statement "I am confident about my . . ." (List as many qualities as you can.)

9. Complete the declaration "I will build lasting confidence by . . ."

EXPONENTIAL CONVERSATION

Alan Bracken started Bracken Paving when he was nineteen years old. He had early success in business, but it was only after meeting John Maxwell that he became aware of his shortcomings as a leader and began pursuing personal growth. The results transformed Alan's leadership style, and Bracken Paving quadrupled its revenue in just six years, landing Alan and his wife, Amanda, on the cover of *Equipment World* magazine as the 2008 contractor of the year. After twenty years of success, they decided to sell their company in order to help other businesses and organizations experience this same transformation. Today, Alan travels around the country speaking on leadership and team engagement, as well as coaching executives and consulting for organizations.

In our Exponential Conversation, Alan explains how his drive helped him achieve early success in business, but how confidence eluded him until he did some deep work on himself.

SHERI RILEY: Many successful people struggle with this thing called confidence. I like to say, "Drive is what takes us there; confidence is who we are when we arrive." Tell me about when you recognized that confidence was an area you needed to focus on.

ALAN BRACKEN: I started a construction company at the age of nineteen. I did that for twenty years and had some great success. Now, moving into what I'm doing now—which is inspiring greatness in others—is a totally different feel and requires more than drive. It requires an inner strength that only comes with confidence.

I think the drive is important because, as our friend Les Brown says, "You gotta be hungry." But that's not enough. The confidence has to be in who I am as a person, not just in what I can do, and it is different. It requires more. It's harder to get there on your own. I think for me, it's required a lot of introspective digging. It's required admitting that I don't know what I don't know, and being willing to go there. I'm not there yet, but I'm moving in that direction.

I don't know anybody who's not afraid of something. One of the things I heard again today was—I think it's an Eleanor Roosevelt quote: "Do one thing every day that scares you." Yeah. I think that helps build confidence because it keeps us out of that comfort zone. Because you can get comfortable in success. I was comfortable, good at what I did, but I knew there was more. So in 2011 when Amanda and I, after twenty years, decided to sell what we were comfortable in, I was very confident in my ability in the construction industry, but we kind of gave all of that up to impact people at a higher level, in a more meaningful way. That's kind of the journey. Now, let me go back and talk about a particular story.

SHERI RILEY: Yes.

ALAN BRACKEN: So, from first grade to twelfth grade, I hated school. I graduated in 1989, barely. In 1991 I started the paving company. In 1993 I started making money and got interested in flying airplanes. After about twenty-five hours, I was soloing and my instructor came to me and said, "Alan, you need to take the written test so that I can schedule your flight test and you can get your private pilot's license." That's the day I quit. I didn't go back.

SHERI RILEY: Something challenged your confidence.

ALAN BRACKEN: Thinking about it, I realized the reason I hated school was because I couldn't read very well at all. What that meant was every grade got harder; every test got more daunting. And my self-esteem just sunk. In school, I was embarrassed. The other kids were smarter than I was. I was thinking, "What's wrong with me? Something must be wrong with me, because I just can't get it." I kept falling behind. My biggest fear every day was "Please, please, dear God, please don't let the teacher call on me today to read out loud." Because when I would read out loud I would have to sound the word out in front of the whole class, and that was just humiliating. So, about 2000, I heard John Maxwell say, "Leaders are readers," and I thought, "We've got a problem here. I'm not a reader."

SHERI RILEY: At this point, you had your construction company for how many years?

ALAN BRACKEN: Ten years. I was doing very well. I was a leader, but I wasn't a reader. I'm thinking, "What kind of leader am I? Evidently not a very good one, according to the leadership guru." So that's when I decided to step out of my comfort zone as a leader, and start reading. My wife, Amanda, encouraged me, she helped me, and I started reading and learning. In 2006, I was in my basement and I ran across my old flight logbook. I got that thing out, and in a few months I had my license. Since 2007, I've owned four helicopters, flown a helicopter from the coast of California to the coast of South Carolina. All the way across the United States. Phenomenal experience. And here's what I've realized: I would have never had the rare and amazing experiences that I've had flying had I stayed stuck, had I not stepped out of my comfort zone. It's like what Jack Canfield says, "Everything you want is on the other side of fear." If I had allowed fear to continue to paralyze me, I wouldn't have experienced all of the things I have been able to experience. And my kids wouldn't know what it's like to go down to the local drive-through and get a milk shake with their dad in a helicopter.

SHERI RILEY: When you were at the height of the construction company success, did you ever feel the angst of lack of confidence, but you "medicated" it with drive?

ALAN BRACKEN: I think my lack of confidence showed up only *outside* of my area of strength. Anything I didn't think I would be good at, I just didn't even try!

SHERI RILEY: I say, as high achievers, we have to stop spending 100 percent of our time on 10 percent of who we are, that our success traps us in this 10 percent. You got to that point where you said, "Hey, I want to do more."

ALAN BRACKEN: If I had not been on a growth journey, I would have stayed right there. Why wouldn't I? I'm making good money, I know what I'm doing, I'm good at what I do. But because I was growing, it wasn't enough anymore. Going out and making *x* amount of dollars just wasn't enough anymore. I realized that if I want more out of life, then I've got to be uncomfortable and gain that confidence in the uncomfortable.

SHERI RILEY: What did you have to say yes to, to get to that place of building your confidence?

ALAN BRACKEN: I had to say yes to what I know is my God-given purpose, which is inspiring greatness in others and speaking. I had to say yes to giving up what was secure, what was safe, what was comfortable, what I knew and was good at. But here's part of the growth: several years ago I decided I want to live in my "strength and passion" zone. When I made that commitment, I was still good at paving, still good at the construction. That's a strength, but it wasn't a passion anymore. So I had to go back to "Well, who put the passion in me to help others?" God. So I had to say yes to that, step out in faith, and believe in something I couldn't see yet. But faith and action get results. I think that's a key to confidence. Faith, what you can't see, along with action, what you *can* do, builds confidence. Just sitting around, having faith without any action, doesn't lead to confidence. But when we have some faith and we mix it with some action and we get some results, that leads to more confidence. That's kind of been the progression. As I learn to speak better, people say, "Well, you're getting better." That builds more confidence for me to keep going in that direction and keep doing the things necessary to continue. But I had to say yes to God's purpose for me: inspiring greatness. Encouraging people to reach their potential. And it starts at home with my wife and kids and the people I'm working with. I've had to say yes to all of that.

SHERI RILEY: How do you define peace? And how important is peace to you?

ALAN BRACKEN: Peace, to me, is when I can really, with confidence, trust that I've done my part in the direction of my purpose. So there's a lot of things I can't control, but the things I can control—when I've done those, I have peace. When I haven't, I don't have peace. So personally, when I know I haven't connected and encouraged my wife, there's not as much peace. Peace comes from relationships for me. If the relationships aren't going well with the people that matter, I don't have peace or happiness.

SHERI RILEY: How do you get to the place of peace when you're not "doing"?

ALAN BRACKEN: Yeah, that seems to be more challenging for me. So, last week was a tough week, so I probably wasn't having a lot of peace, until I reflected and asked the question "All right, did I live out my purpose to the best of my ability?" And I said yes. Well, just knowing that, there was a sense of "Oh, okay. Don't worry about the rest." So just knowing I did what I could do. It has to come from the inside. If we're waiting on the external to give us peace, we're in trouble.

SHERI RILEY: When I say "Exponential Living," what comes to mind for you?

ALAN BRACKEN: Above average. Exponential is above normal. The best possible life. That's what it would mean to me. And that would have to be based on your wiring, an individual reaching their potential. I don't think you can have exponential anything until you really reach your potential as an individual. So it's kinda like a compounding thing. Probably for me it would be a journey in the direction of knowing that there's always more that I can do, more people that I can positively affect. *[He reflects a bit and amends his previous statement.]* If I base Exponential

Living on reaching our potential, then—since we never *reach* our potential—it's just a constant journey of being the best we can possibly be.

SHERI RILEY: I love it! Is there anything that relates to confidence or building confidence that we haven't touched on that you would like to share about your journey?

ALAN BRACKEN: The power of taking time to reflect and ask the people closest to you where your insecurities are and trying to identify some of those insecurities. Working on those insecurities. I think that can help drive confidence as well. I think that it can be scary, and I think few have the courage to really do that consistently. I know I struggle with that. One of the questions I ask Amanda is "How am I coming across? What's it like living outside of me?" So we go back and forth with that. It brings up issues that need to be worked on, character issues. For me personally, as I've worked on my character weaknesses, that's helped shore up some insecurities and has led to greater confidence. I think first that it has to be an admission, the taking responsibility. I think that's where it starts. Being willing and vulnerable to admit—a lot of high achievers have a problem admitting they are bad at something. You've got to take responsibility first for yourself and then move forward. I think that's the key, being willing to be wrong so you can be better. Being right . . . I don't think that's what leads to Exponential Living. So it's sacrificing and being willing to give up the right to be right. I can remember early in our marriage, I was convinced that I was right and Amanda was wrong—let me tell you how that didn't work out. And it didn't get better until I was willing to sacrifice being right. What I found out was I wasn't really right; I just *thought* I was right. So I think that's a big key, admitting that you don't know, and getting help.

I AM ALAN BRACKEN AND I AM EXPONENTIAL LIVING.

Key Takeaways

» Confidence is inner strength, not outer achievement.
» Pushing out of your comfort zone on a regular basis gives you confidence to handle whatever new challenges come your way.
» Faith and action produce results. Results build confidence.
» Be willing to admit to being wrong so that you can be better.

The Courage to Be Faithful

You've got to get to the stage in life where going for
it is more important than winning or losing.

—ARTHUR ASHE

This Principle is called "the *Courage* to be Faithful." There's a good reason for that. Courage is essential at this stage of the game.

Throughout the book we have talked about the importance of creating your own definition of success, one that includes not only career achievements, but also things like thriving relationships, inner peace, clarity, service, and a sense of purpose. Well, it's one thing to *talk* about a new definition of success; it's another to actually live it. That takes an incredible amount of courage—the courage to be faithful to who you are, even in the face of doubt, adversity, ridicule, your own insecurities, and, sometimes, lack of support from people important to you. That's what I mean when I use the word *faithful* in this Principle. I mean to be faithful to *yourself*. To your true self. Your 100-percent self.

To have that kind of faith, you must be courageous enough to commit to the process of change. You must be courageous enough to deal with the inner "demons" that are hindering your personal growth and professional elevation. You must be courageous enough to leap into the unknown by making choices not everyone will understand, including, at times, yourself.

This kind of courage is precious.

For a top Realtor to believe that spending time with his spouse is going to be more rewarding than winning another Agent of the Year award takes courage. He might know, in his mind and heart, that this is the right thing to do, but all of his habits and life experiences, and the value he assigns them, have been attached to achieving high sales quotas. To make a change in his life, he will need to adopt a new paradigm and make it stick. That's a hard battle to fight. Selling fifty houses in a year, for him, is a relatively easy battle, because the world recognizes this as a legitimate accomplishment and pats him on the back for it. His ego gets supported and rewarded. Spending time with his spouse doesn't necessarily feed his ego at all. It may make him feel good, but here's the thing: he's not *driven* by feeling good. Feeling good is not in his definition of success. So his ego gets no immediate reward from spending engaged time with his spouse. He will need courage to broaden his definition of success and to fight for it.

Many people do not have that kind of courage. In fact, Principle 8 is the stage where I "lose" many of my clients. Not everyone makes it through this principle—not all of my clients, not everyone who reads this book. Principle 8 is truly the bridge to Exponential Living. Make it through this one and you're home! But it won't be easy and it will take all the courage you have.

Healing Is the Key

Here's something you need to know: you're not going to fully experience Exponential Living from where you are right now. You can't use your present mind-set to usher a new paradigm into your life. As Albert Einstein put it, "No problem can be solved from the same level of consciousness that created it." A 10-percent mind-set cannot understand or implement Exponential Living.

You must become more whole, more complete, more of who you really are. You must elevate to a new level. You must step into your greatness. And that means *healing* from those life experiences that created wounds, defensive strongholds, limiting beliefs, false mental paradigms, or challenges to your self-esteem and confidence.

Ultimately, the courage to be faithful, to be your true self, rests on your willingness and ability to heal.

What Does Healing Have to Do with It?

What does healing have to do with courage?

We are all "walking wounded," carrying our past traumas and our personal baggage with us through our lives, hindered by deep unresolved issues that we lug around with us because it seems easier than actually unpacking them. Words spoken to us as children, experiences of shame or abuse or neglect, have become embedded in us as self-limiting beliefs. Very few of us are operating from the fullest, highest version of ourselves as a result. We all have walls, blocks, injuries, false beliefs, burdens, and blind spots that hold us back from Exponential Living. Fear is bound up in these walls and encumbrances. We tell ourselves that the walls protect us, but in truth, they hold us back. And even when we try to release ourselves, fear often keeps us locked inside.

When I am doing speeches and workshops, I often ask the participants to join me in making this three-part declaration:

I will dive into my deepest fear . . .

To elevate to my highest faith . . .

To accomplish my greatest achievements.

High achievers are energized by this declaration because it focuses on achieving something great. But they also feel a flutter of terror when they say the words, because they intuitively understand that they're not going to get to the truest form of success unless they face their deepest fears. That's really what healing is about. It's about facing the fears that keep us stuck in self-limiting thoughts and behaviors and in the comfort zone of our 10 percent. Healing is about accepting, loving, and welcoming the part of us that lies beyond the fears and allowing ourselves to be lifted up by it instead of weighed down.

Healing Scares Us, but It Shouldn't

What things do you need to heal from? They are different for everyone, of course. A book can't possibly root out the specific issues and blockages that are holding you back personally. These issues often go back as far as childhood and may take real effort to identify and dissect.

Sometimes we have wounds that come from childhood trauma. One of my clients, for example, suffered sexual molestation as a child, as too many others have as well. These individuals often struggle with embarrassment, anger, low self-esteem, depression, intimacy issues, and feelings of victimization, at least until they are able to deal head-on with the abuse, release themselves from blame, and allow themselves to heal. Another client of mine lost her mom at the age of nine when her mother died an untimely death. From that time onward, she held her mom up on a pedestal—which is understandable—but was unable to admit to herself that she was angry at her mom for leaving her so early, and with God for taking her. As she wrestled with this issue in one of our sessions, it came to light that she believed *love itself* had died when her mom did. So part of her had given up on the idea of being loved and lovable. She had to heal that part of herself in order to embrace Exponential Living.

Peace, the foundation of Exponential Living, can be attained only when healing has taken place.

Healing isn't always from wounds or trauma; sometimes it's from unnecessary limitations. A parent, grandparent, teacher, coach, or someone else we respect may have said something that established a mind-set in us that is now holding us back in some way. For example, another client of mine recalled a time in childhood when she was visiting her grandfather, who lived on a farm. One day she was out working with him in the field, grudgingly, and he said to her, "Do you like to eat?" She replied yes, of course, and her grandpa said, "Well, then, if you like to eat, you better learn to like working hard." That idea burrowed into her young mind and carried into adulthood. When I started working with her, she was a very driven and very successful businessperson, but she was always working. Deep inside, she believed that if she wasn't working, working, working, she wouldn't have the rewards she sought from life. It was tremendously liberating for her to release that old belief, mind-set, and paradigm and to realize that she could thrive in her life without working 24-7.

I had a similar experience in my own life. My grandmother once said to me, "You talk too much." She probably didn't even remember having said it, but it struck me and stayed with me. I was just a child and I *believed* that remark and took it to heart. For forty years I struggled with it. You can imagine the limitations it brought up for someone destined to have a career as an empowerment speaker and life strategist to be told that she talks too much.

Where are the walls in your life? What are they made of?

I can't tell you. Everyone carries their own deeply personal reasons for blocking themselves off. But my guess is, you already know. You see, what I have discovered is that most of us—especially those who are self-aware and growth oriented enough to be reading books on self-development—*know* where our big life issues lie. We may say "I don't know" when someone asks us, but that's not really true. (Remember, I never allow "I don't know" as an answer.) The fact is, we *do* know.

We *do* know those things that are holding us back. We do.

After a certain amount of living, we've hit the same walls enough times. We've gotten stuck in the same places. We've had the same kind of "bad luck" and problems repeat themselves over and over. For some of us, it happens in the area of relationships—we just can't find a kind and trustworthy mate. For others it might revolve around money or body weight or an emptiness we can't fill—maybe we constantly charge too much on credit cards, keeping ourselves forever in debt, or carry around an extra thirty pounds that we continually lose and regain. We keep making the same choices that we know are detrimental to our lives. There's at least one area (often more than one) where our old wounds and/or false beliefs about ourselves are keeping us locked in behaviors that aren't serving us. It's as if we have a line of bad code in our software that's causing our whole life program to run poorly.

We even have a sense of where the root causes of these issues lie. We may not know *exactly* what's causing our issue(s), but we have a pretty good idea where to look.

But still, we don't want to. Why? We are afraid. Afraid of the truth, in the same way we are afraid of knowing who we truly are. We think that dealing with the big blocks in our lives might cause us some kind of harm or trauma, or will at least get us off track or waste our time. We think that if we mess around with that deep-down issue that's been making our lives shaky, it will be like pulling a beam out of the foundation of a house. The whole structure of our life will come tumbling down.

Quite the opposite is true. That one "beam"—the one we're so afraid to touch—is exactly the thing that's been causing our life to rest on shaky ground. By pulling out that one piece, looking at it with open eyes, straightening it, sanding and polishing it, and putting it back in place more solidly, we actually give our whole structure more stability. We can then build the "house" of our lives much stronger and straighter. Or sometimes by replacing this piece with an entirely new piece of wood, we can cut out the "cancer" that's eating away at our peace, our clarity, and our ability to experience Exponential Living.

My friend Lisa Cambridge-Mitchell, who is the former senior VP of marketing at RCA Records, has always been successful and career oriented. A few years ago, she went through a crisis in which she lost a job that was very meaningful to her and struggled with identity issues. Because of her business savvy and a solid employment contract, she was making more money than she ever had, and she tortured herself about it. She was embarrassed and angry, and had to face her deep-rooted fears. In order to get to the other side of it, she told me, "I had to give up the person who I thought I was." It struck me that this is one of the biggest fears human beings have: letting go of our attachment to who we *thought* we were, in order to embrace a wider definition of ourselves. Most great novels and movies revolve around this theme. Letting go of the self-*concept* in favor of the *self* seems like such a daunting and intimidating thing to do, and yet we are always, always, always liberated when we shed such illusions and embrace our truth.

Here's what you really need to understand: everyone who faces down their "big fears" ends up growing because of it. That's where faith in the process comes in. I have never met one client (or friend or colleague) who has done the hard work of rooting out their limiting fears and has regretted it. That client of mine whose mom died when she was nine? There was once a time when whenever she and I saw each other, she would start to cry. Now whenever she sees me, she bursts out laughing and has another victory to share with me. Her eyes sparkle as she tells me about all the wonderful changes that have been happening in her life. By contrast, when I see some other clients—those who have been unwilling to face down the sources of their anger, their sorrow, their mistrust—they are still just as angry and depressed as ever, and are living with the consequences of that.

Again, I can't tell you exactly what issues are keeping you from experiencing Exponential Living—only you know what those are or are able to uncover them. All I can do is encourage you, with all my heart and soul, to summon the courage to face them. This is the kind of work I do with clients, so you might consider working with a life strategist or therapist—there is great courage in the act of reaching out for help from others. (If you have suffered serious trauma, you should consider seeing a trained and qualified psychotherapist.) But whether you work alone or with a helper, doing this work *will not break you,* I assure you. The pain you are afraid of facing is not nearly as bad as you think it will be, and you *do* have the strength to get past it and heal. I promise. You have within you the Courage to Be Faithful—to YOU!

Why We Avoid the Challenge

Why do people willingly endure a lifetime of emptiness, "stuckness," and limitation instead of facing some short-term pain and effort that will lead toward a better life all around? There are many reasons and tactics we employ to keep ourselves from change, but here are a couple of the big ones.

Denial

In the Oscar-winning movie *American Beauty*, one of the main characters says, "Never underestimate the power of denial." Denial is that remarkable human ability to shut out whatever we don't want to see. If something makes us uncomfortable, we just pretend it doesn't exist. After all, if we refuse to see it, we don't have to own it or work through the pain resulting from it. I have counseled many clients who've been stopped in their tracks by denial. They are able to progress for a while—up to the point where they need to face their really deep issues. Then they go into denial. They refuse to see the obvious. Many people spend their entire lives bumping their heads against a ceiling created by their denial.

Blame

Another great way to avoid confronting the truth is to blame someone else for our pain. As long as we focus on why our problems are someone else's fault, we don't have to deal with our own role in holding the pain. We can stay locked in anger. People with persistent anger issues must get past blame to get to true healing. Spouses who have cheated and been cheated on, for example, must, at some point, get past the blame, anger, ego, and guilt in order to look honestly at the ways they themselves may have contributed to flaws in the relationship.

Rationalization

A favorite technique of many busy high achievers is to rationalize our misery. We acknowledge that we are stressed-out, unhappy, and unfulfilled, but we tell ourselves this comes with the territory of being successful; it's the price we have to pay. "If you can't stand the heat, stay out of the kitchen" is our motto. For example, we might convince ourselves that sixty-five-hour weeks and strained family relationships are normal for our high-stress, high-achieving profession, because we see our colleagues working long hours and having family issues.

Distraction

Another favorite device of high achievers is distraction. We keep our minds and lives so full of to-do lists that we don't take time to think about the deep-level stuff. We work almost nonstop, and then, in the little time off we take, we fill our hours with noisy, flashy, consumable entertainment.

Self-Sabotage

Self-sabotage happens when we deeply desire a change in our lives, but are so afraid of it not happening that we engineer our own failure. We fear that if we give it our best effort and the change we desire doesn't happen, we will be unable to handle the additional pain or the blow to our self-image. So we deliberately do things that impede our success. That way, when it doesn't happen, we can have a "valid" reason why it didn't work—not that we failed. I have seen single clients, for example, post unappealing, halfhearted, or even hostile-sounding profiles on matchmaking websites, then tell themselves they "tried" to meet someone but failed because "all the good ones are taken" or "no one wants to date people with kids."

Minimization or Deferral

Some of us acknowledge that we have issues we need to deal with, and pay lip service to those who encourage us to work on them, but we tell ourselves the inner work isn't really that important, or that it's something we can put off till later in our lives, when we "have the time." Some pro athletes, for example, live like irresponsible teenagers year after year, telling themselves they'll work on their maturity when they get out of the game.

Fear of Destruction

Finally, many people really do believe—unconsciously, perhaps—that they will be annihilated if they face their issue head-on. The issue they're avoiding has taken on such size and power that it seems like a sharp-toothed monster capable of eating them alive. In these cases, the issue often first entered their lives when they were only young children.

Many types of pain, in fact, *are* too much for children to bear—abuse, neglect, deep shame, the death of a parent or sibling. Children have not yet developed the inner resources or maturity to process these things, so they "wall off" the hurt in some way, much the same way the body forms a cyst to "wall off" infection. The issue then becomes like a boogeyman in the closet, all the scarier because you can't see it, but you know it's there. As we get older, we may think, intellectually, that we are able to face the monster, but on an emotional level we continue to hold back. The monster still feels huge, powerful, and threatening to us. What we do not realize is that, as adults, we now have the wisdom, power, and strength to defeat the monster; it is not as big and scary as it seems. Instead we continue to avoid it and feed it with our fear.

When we resist facing our fears, what we're really afraid of is our own emotions. Big emotions scare us. But remember: emotions are just energy patterns. They can't kill us or even hurt us. When strong emotions come up, instead of dodging them in fear, we can simply welcome them, *have* them, and *be* with them. Allow them to express themselves within us. When we learn to do this, we discover that the emotion just "has its say," and then fades away, instead of controlling us like a puppet. I'll give you an exercise to help with this in "Vision, Action, Results."

These are just a sampling of the many inventive ways we humans avoid facing the things that keep us stuck. What is your favorite tactic? Unless you are honest about the ways you avoid the truth, you'll never be able to get unstuck.

It's Like Surgery

Spiritual/psychological "ailments" are like bodily ailments in many ways. It hurts a little to root them out, but healing is the reward. We all know people who suffer from debilitating pain or physical limitations—such as chronic back pain—but are afraid to seek treatment. They fear the pain of surgery and recovery.

Healing *is* uncomfortable, yes. But it's a price well worth paying. Like going through surgery, it has several distinct stages:

The Injury or Illness. Healing often starts with an initial blow or collapse. Something goes painfully wrong. This gets your attention and makes you aware that something is "off" in your life and situation. Without the crisis you would be unaware that you need "treatment."

Diagnosis. You seek some help, perhaps from someone with more training and expertise than you have or from a book like this one. You learn what steps are needed to treat the problem.

Surgery. During surgery, the doctor doesn't need your input, help, or insight. She puts you to sleep for a reason. It is because you need to trust the process. You need to go through certain prescribed steps and perhaps engage a professional to help you. For those of faith, here's where you must believe that God has a plan for your life and is working things for your benefit.

Recovery. In the recovery phase, you "awaken" from surgery, aware of what you've been through but not at full strength. The transition process has knocked you off your feet and caused you some pain. Familiar people may have left your life, old habits may have been abandoned, new conditions may be in play. The change has been painful, no doubt, but now you are on the road to recovery.

Rehab. Here is where you focus in on the things you must do to fully receive and employ the benefits of the transition. The real work begins now. You get stronger and more empowered and come to understand that you're in a new chapter of your life and you are not going to slip back into old habits and ways of thinking.

New Growth. Finally, when you have reached full strength within the context of this new chapter of your life, you discover that you are able to do things you could not do before. Thanks to removing walls, blockages, and dysfunctions, your "ceiling" of capability has now been raised. You are free to grow in ways you could not before the surgery. Exponential Living is yours for the seizing.

All it took was courage: the courage to face the entire healing process. Courage comes in four forms:

Mental Courage: the ability and willingness to confront limited thinking, flawed logic, outmoded beliefs, and/or anxiety/discomfort of the mind.

Physical Courage: the ability and willingness to confront pain, hardship, tiredness, and suffering of the body.

Emotional Courage: the ability and willingness to confront, experience, and release strong and/or scary-seeming emotions.

Spiritual Courage: the ability and willingness to undergo the process of personal transformation in accordance with spiritual ideals and spiritual guidance.

When we summon these different forms of courage within us to heal our minds, bodies, hearts, and souls, there is nothing that we can't overcome.

Transition

Healing, I hope you now agree, is the basis of the Courage to Be Faithful. Healing brings about the wholeness needed in order to make Exponential Living a reality in our lives. If we are not willing to heal old wounds, fix broken beliefs, and shift our mind-sets and paradigms, our power will continue to leak out through those gaps, and our true self will be blocked from emerging.

Beyond healing *ourselves*, though, we must also "heal" our reality. We must go from lifestyle A, where we are living only in our 10 percent, to lifestyle B, where we are living in the fullness of our 100 percent. We must intentionally make a shift in our perspective, our thinking, our speech, and our behavioral habits. To do this, we must commit to the process of transition. We must change the way we live.

This is where the rubber meets the road, because it doesn't matter how well you understand the principles of Exponential Living if you don't implement actual changes. You may *say* you want a more passionate marriage or a closer relationship with your kids, but unless you take steps to create those conditions and interactions—steps like committing to being home four evenings a week, setting aside two or three hours every evening as family time, or going to bed with your spouse every night instead of staying up till one a.m. writing e-mails— they won't happen.

Here is where the courage to be faithful to the process comes in. When faced with making changes, humans fight tooth and nail. A battle rages within us. Part of us wants to make the change; part of us doesn't. The part that wants to make the change is our 90-percent self, which seeks greater expression; the part that doesn't want to make the change is our 10-percent self, which seeks familiarity, even if that familiarity means continuing to be miserable.

Transition brings up a great deal of fear. Fear of the full power within us. Fear of failure. Fear of the unknown. Fear of loss. This last one is particularly daunting. That is because we can *see, taste, and feel* the things we stand to lose—those things are part of our current reality—whereas the things we stand to *gain* are only abstract ideas.

I've talked to clients who *want* to be in a relationship, but are afraid to lose their freedom; clients who *want* to start their own business, but are afraid to lose their steady paycheck; clients who *want* to start a family, but are afraid to lose their "me" time; clients who *want* to change careers, but are afraid to lose their prestigious job title. There is always something real and tangible we must give up for the sake of something we cannot yet see and touch. We must believe that this better life we imagine exists and is possible in our reality if we have the courage to be faithful to ourselves.

Many of us want guarantees. Before we make a big change, we want assurances that the move will bring achievement, that we'll end up happier and more successful than we were before. Unfortunately, such guarantees are not to be found. That is why I say this step requires courage. There is no getting around it. Those who make change in their lives must leave behind what is familiar and step into the great unknown. They must rely on faith to carry them to a destination that is uncertain. This requires immense courage. But such courage is always rewarded in the long run. That doesn't mean everyone who makes courageous change is immediately successful, or finds success in the way they imagined it. Sometimes the journey takes much longer than we hope and sometimes the journey leads somewhere unexpected. But it *always* leads, ultimately, to expressing and living more of who we truly are, and that is *always* rewarding.

There are a few things we can do, though, to make transitions more successful. . . .

Be Ready, Willing, and Committed

You must have the right mind-set in order to begin this transition. For me to agree to work with a client, they must be ready, willing, and committed. Because what I know for sure is what my friend and mentor Paul Martinelli, president of the John Maxwell Team, says: "The only thing I am convinced of is that I can't convince you of anything." Personal development is a daily choice from within. I, as a coach and strategist, can serve as a guide on the journey, but no one can do the work for you or make *your* inner commitment to change.

Ready. You must understand why the change needs to be made. You feel mentally, emotionally, physically, and spiritually prepared for change. You must be tired of living in the limitations of your old habits and mind-sets.

Willing. You must make the change of your own volition, not just because someone told you to do it. You must accept the fact that you will need to give up some things that are familiar and comfortable to you. You must welcome the idea of adopting some new mind-sets and behaviors.

Committed. You must be "in it to win it." You must be prepared for setbacks and challenges.

Focus Your Vision on the Destination

My mentor John Maxwell says, "Don't leave a place; go to something else." Another way of saying that is "Don't focus on what you are moving *from*; focus on what you are moving *to*," or as I like to say,

"When it feels like God is pulling you back in a slingshot, don't stress about how far backward you seem to be going; stay focused on how far forward you are going to fly when God releases you." In my coaching work, the clients who are successful with transitions are those who keep their vision trained on where they want to be, not on their current reality.

Your current reality is a reflection of the mind-set that created it. It is full of your old doubts, compromises, and limitations. You must lock your eyes on a powerful new reality that reflects your new and emerging mind-set.

Mourn in a Healthy Way

When we are transitioning to a new place, it is important to mourn the loss of the things we leave behind. Even when we leave behind a situation or a version of ourselves that we don't want anymore, there is still a loss to be acknowledged. High achievers tend to avoid mourning. They believe that acknowledging loss is equivalent to losing momentum. But mourning is not hanging on to the past; it is *letting go* of the past. Mourning is a way of saying good-bye to the old so that we can say hello to the new. It is a vital rite of passage.

Mourning is not only for the death of someone we loved. Mourning is for the death or loss of anything important to us. This can be the death of a great idea, a company, a business partnership, a mind-set, or a relationship. When we mourn these losses, feeling the honest grief that comes up, we are able to gently release our attachment to things that were dear to us at a past place in our journey. By honoring who we *were*, we are better able to honor who we are becoming. Conversely, when we fail to allow the grieving process to run its course, we can become hardened in our hearts and enter a place of denial.

Act as if You're Already There

Finally, a great strategy during transitions is to act as if you're already in the place to which you're transitioning. For example, if you want to be married, start hanging out with married people. You are not the third wheel; you are in training. Want to lose some weight? Start doing the things you'd do if the weight was already gone. Buy clothes in your goal size. Want to change careers? Start actually doing your new job; don't wait till someone hires you.

Have Faith in the Process

I recently had a chance to talk with James Lopez, head of motion pictures at Will Packer Productions. He told me how he made the transition from the music business, where he was senior vice president of marketing and brand partnerships for Atlantic Records, to the film business.

> *I knew the first step was leaving New York and going to LA. . . . What I did was, I took a look at what I had access to at Atlantic Records, and I said, "Okay, what do I deal with on a daily basis that's going to get me closer to the film industry?" Sound tracks. So I started to get more involved with sound tracks. I started running around town, talking to agencies, managers, about music-related film projects—so we could do the sound tracks.*
>
> *Now, the chairman [of Atlantic] was very interested in getting involved in film projects as a producer. So I kind of took that and*

ran with that. I went around town saying, "Hey, we'll help finance smaller films that are music based." And I started getting inundated with scripts. I started reading material at home and on weekends, in my spare time.

. . . I also looked at what else I had at my disposal that would get me closer to film production. Video production.

At the time, we were having our video commissioners fly from New York to LA to handle production of videos. I talked to our head of video production and said, "I'm out here. Why don't you just let me be the person who's on set?" He said fine. So I started producing music videos.

Then I had a conversation with music artist T.I., and we were talking about the first video of his Paper Trail *album. We got into a little debate and I was, like, "We need to push the envelope." He was, like, "You're such a harsh critic—why don't you write one?" So I came up with a simple idea for a video, and he goes, "Why don't you direct it?" So I found a great codirector, and we went and found a great DP, and we codirected a video. And that video went on to be nominated for a VMA award. It was "No Matter What." I did another video called "Hi Hater" from Maino and then I did a B.o.B. video.*

Through T.I., I ended up meeting Clint Culpepper, president of Screen Gems, who gave me my first job in film. We struck up a friendship and started communicating about scripts and projects and urban culture.

Like I said, I had been reading tons of material for two or three years prior to meeting him. I remember my wife asking me, "Why are you reading all this stuff that's not what you do?" And I said to her, "I'm preparing for the day when I do this for a living."

. . . The day I walked through those gates at Sony Pictures and sat down at that desk, I was, like, "All these years I was preparing

myself for this moment." So although I had no actual film experi-ence, I took to it like a fish to water.

What advice does James have for those who want to make their own career transitions?

I tell people, "Try to do the job you aspire to now when you're not being paid to do it." So, if you're in accounting and you want to be a marketing exec, look at the product you want to market—whether it's a film, an album release, a shoe—and build a marketing plan. Research what marketing plans look like, read a few of them, and try to put a marketing plan together for something you have a pas-sion for. People may look at you and say, "That's a waste of time!" but you're exercising muscles you haven't been able to exercise before. And the more you do that, the more you are preparing yourself for when you do get that opportunity. Imagine sitting down with some-one for a job interview and you slide a document over to them and say, "This is the marketing plan I've put together for your product." You come in having done the job that you're interviewing to do.

The courage to be faithful to the process of uncovering more of your true self is the hardest part of this journey, but it is necessary and worth the effort. It heals and seals the gateway for Exponential Living.

Vision, Action, Results

Here are some exercises aimed at helping you heal and make coura-geous change in your life.

Exercise 1: Finding the Blocks

Below, write down some major goals you would like to be accomplishing in your 100-percent life. These might be things like finding a love relationship, developing one of your talents, living a lifestyle true to your authentic self, or living in a community that feeds and excites your spirit.

For each of these 100-percent goals, complete the following statement:

I would *be living this goal now BUT* . . .

Now list the BUT or BUTS—the obstacles and barriers—that come up for you.

For each BUT, answer the following:

» How long have I had this BUT in my life?
» When do I first remember encountering this BUT?
» What is the source of this BUT? (Remember, "I don't know" is not an acceptable answer.)
» How real is this BUT (and how much is it just a false obstacle)?
» What would I have to do to get past this BUT?

Now, for each goal you listed above, complete this sentence:

» I commit to living this goal by . . .

Exercise 2: Faithful to Me

In order for you to experience Exponential Living, healing must take place. Healing isn't limited to hurtful or traumatic events only; it also includes recovering from choices we have made regarding health, careers, and relationships, as well as from ways of thinking we've adopted.

Answer the following for each of the goals you listed above, in Exercise 1:

>> What aspects of my life and environment are hindering my progress in this area?
>> What triggers are currently leading me to self-sabotaging behaviors?
>> Why do these triggers hinder me?
>> Which triggers do I need to change? How can/will I do so?
>> Which of the four types of courage will I need in order to pursue this goal in earnest? (It may be more than one.)
>> What can I do to summon, support, and encourage more of this form of courage in my life?
>> Complete the following statement: *I have the courage to . . .*
>> Complete the following statement: *I commit to new behaviors and thoughts about . . .*
>> Who can hold me accountable for the new choices I've committed to?

Exercise 3: Processing Emotion

Many of us get in the habit of avoiding certain emotions. These might include anger, shame, vulnerability, love, sadness, and fear, among others. We begin to develop a belief that the emotion is dangerous or can hurt us. Here is a simple but powerful process you can use to honor your emotions and incorporate them into your life. After using this process for only a short while, you may find that you're able to deal with the big emotions that are holding your blockages in place.

≫ The moment you feel an emotion that is making you uncomfortable, stop whatever you are doing. Close your eyes and pay attention to the feeling. Don't *act* on it, don't try to make it go away, don't tell yourself you shouldn't be feeling it.

≫ Allow the feeling to sit in your body. Welcome it without judgment. Don't label it good or bad, desirable or undesirable. Don't even try to categorize it as one particular emotion or another—anger, sadness, fear. Just feel it as energy in your body. Allow the energy to just *be* there. Notice that, if you don't attach judgments or labels to an emotion, it is neither painful nor pleasant. It just *is*.

≫ Now allow the truth of the emotion to emerge—the hurt, disappointment, frustration, anger, sadness, emptiness. Feeling its full impact, stay there without adding anything else to the emotion. Just let the truth of it exist. Yes, it hurts; cry. Yes, you've been let down; it's okay. Yes, your life was changed; you're still here. Brace yourself and recognize you are not this emotion. The only power this emotion has is what you are experiencing right now. It is only a feeling, with only the power you give it now; it is not who you are. You are stronger than this experience. Now that you fully feel this emotion, you own it; it does not own you. You are the victor, not the victim, not controlled by this emotion. You will now release this emotion and its grip from your spirit and soul. Now say out loud, with authority, "I am more than a conqueror and I am free." You may have to do this a few times—that's fine. With each time, your spirit and soul are set free.

» When the time feels right, express gratitude for the emotion. This emotion has taught you many lessons. You've developed strength and courage from dealing with this emotion. There are positives in your life because you dealt with this emotion and chose to live, survive, and thrive. Be thankful that you found your way to this day; many have not.

» Now that the emotion has moved on, replace that negative grip with positive energy and love for yourself and for God.

» Get in the habit of using this process and you will never fear another emotion.

EXPONENTIAL CONVERSATION

For this chapter I spoke with Junior Bridgeman, the well-known retired NBA player. Junior spent most of his career with the Milwaukee Bucks, where, as their famous "sixth man," he played more games (711) than anyone in the history of that team and had his jersey retired in 1988. Junior also served as president of the NBA Players Association. He is now a phenomenally successful businessman through his private company, Bridgeman Foods, which owns 195 stores, including Wendy's, Chili's, Fannie May Chocolates, and other franchises, and employs over nine thousand people.

Junior talks a lot about faith. He is also a "man of faith" in a spiritual sense. As you read his remarks, keep in mind that what he and I are mainly talking about is the kind of faith I describe in this chapter: faith in the process of standing tall in your own truth. Junior, as you'll see, had one of those hurtful childhood memories we discuss in this chapter, which motivated him to excel in sports. Having healed from that hurt, he now stands in a fuller, more "exponential" version of himself.

SHERI RILEY: What is your definition of courage?

JUNIOR BRIDGEMAN: I think courage is responding even when there is fear. It's not the absence of fear, and it's not doing anything irrational. I think it's just doing something, responding, taking a step, even when something inside of you is afraid of what the outcome will be. But you go ahead and take that step, make that leap anyway.

SHERI RILEY: Tell me about a time that you had to stand in your own truth. When you had to stand in that place of courage.

JUNIOR BRIDGEMAN: When I was playing in the league [NBA] we started something we called chapel service, and players would meet before the game. It was only fifteen to twenty minutes, and we'd have somebody come in and talk to them. This was at a time, the seventies and eighties, when players were trying to find something. Through all of their "success," there was still something a lot of players thought was missing. So we started the chapel service—that's what we called it—and yet there were coaches who thought that was not needed and it was not the right place to hold it. I remember one coach telling a center on our team that he didn't buy into any of that, because if you had to do that, seek spiritual encouragement, it meant you were weak. The player said, "Well, Coach, if you know anything about the Bible, you know the people of faith in the Bible were anything but weak." The next week he was traded. So a lot of that went on.

SHERI RILEY: What have been your limiting beliefs and how have you overcome them?

JUNIOR BRIDGEMAN: You know, the thing that playing professional sports does—I'm sure this is true with entertainers and anyone who is in the limelight—is it really enhances your pride in yourself. It gets you to think that everything happens because of you. When you play in the league, even though you're in a team game, it's still reinforcing that attitude that it's about me. When you're onstage, and everybody's cheering and applauding because you sang or whatever you did, that just reinforces that idea that it's me, I'm doing this. I'm more important. I'm better, I'm bigger, whatever adjectives you want to use. That's why when players leave the game, they have a hard time adjusting. So somewhere along the line, I just went back to that foundation that it wasn't about me. I was put in this position, I realized, but it was really by the grace of God. So you just really have to come to that understanding, that revelation.

SHERI RILEY: Was there something that happened that kind of brought that back to the forefront for you? Or did you meet anyone who changed your life in that way?

JUNIOR BRIDGEMAN: Yeah, I think it was when Lorenzo Romar, who is now the head coach at [the University of] Washington—when he came to the [Milwaukee] Bucks. He was a good player, not a great player, but he was the type of player that seemed to be able to interact with everybody. He could sit down and strike up a conversation. So, he'd sit down with guys on the team and they'd be talking and he'd say, "Well, let me ask you something: Are you a Christian?" So your initial response is "Well, yeah." But then you think about "What does that mean when you say that? Are you living your life like that?" It caught a lot of people off guard. Some guys would say, "Well, that's not important," or, "I like where I am now," or, "That's personal to me." He wouldn't say anything else—he'd just kind of let them go on— but you'd know by his asking the question that it was something that was going to roll around in everybody's head, which is what it did. But through that, we started a Bible study with the team. Went through the whole year. So that was a big turnaround for me. Just to show you how things work, there were five of us that started that and four of us were gone after that year.

SHERI RILEY: There's that courage thing again. Is there something that you've healed from that has allowed you to walk in your place of peace?

JUNIOR BRIDGEMAN: Tough question. When I was trying to play sports, I wasn't really very good until probably tenth grade. I just remember a statement made by my father. I had come home from football practice with a scratch on my face. I wasn't really playing during the games, but I'd had a great day in practice and I was all pumped up. And we were sitting down at the table, and he looks at me and goes, "Well, how'd you get hurt? Because you don't play anyway." So it just—boom! When I think about it after all these years, that's what drove me to be a better athlete.

SHERI RILEY: Often it's those little remarks in childhood that get under our skin and affect us for life, for better or worse. Or for better *and* worse.

JUNIOR BRIDGEMAN: When you were talking about Exponential Living and finding peace, the thing that came to mind is Solomon. He said that he tried everything and through it all it was chasing after the wind. He had to find that inner peace that didn't come from money, didn't come from anything else.

I think I've just been fortunate enough to meet and experience a lot of people in this world from all different walks of life who have achieved all different kinds of things. I spent a day and a half with the man who, at that time, was the second-wealthiest person in the world. That was Sam Walton. You read the stories of him driving a red pickup truck; that was all true. We went to his house. There were no guards—you just drove right up—and it was a one-level ranch. It was a nice house, but the most extravagant thing was a Japanese garden he had built in the back for his wife. Here's a guy that was worth eight billion dollars or whatever it was. And then there's all these people who don't have nearly the money he had, but their whole core is about keeping what they have.

SHERI RILEY: What has been one of your biggest mistakes? And what did you learn from it?

JUNIOR BRIDGEMAN: I would say the biggest mistake most people make is not having enough faith. With faith comes confidence. There was an individual in Milwaukee, and on his ninetieth birthday everybody gathered around him and they asked him, "So, what would you do differently?" He thought about it, and most expected him to say, "I wish I had spent more time with my family, grandkids, all of that." And he said, "I wish I had taken more risks." So I thought about all the times you look back and say, "Why didn't I do that?" or, "Why didn't I say that?" or, "Why didn't I share my faith?" or, "Why didn't I go in this direction business-wise?" It's because of that fear, which is lack of courage, and not acting on faith.

SHERI RILEY: How do you define success?

JUNIOR BRIDGEMAN: It's not about money, it's not about power, it's not about position, and it's not about influence. Success can be defined all different kinds of ways, and I think it gets down to the individual. To the person who works the line at Ford every day and you came home and you raised your kids and you provided for your family, that is success. To the schoolteacher who teaches for thirty years and has an influence on making children into avid learners or better people, that's success. To the entertainer who touches somebody when they perform, that's success. Through it all, I think it's having an impact on somebody else. It's not [just] becoming the president of who knows what. It's when you look back on your life—did you have a positive effect? Did you make somebody else's life better? Did you do that in a positive way? We've got a big sign up in the training room that I think sums it up: "Success is never final." I think that's also true.

SHERI RILEY: How important is inner peace to you?

JUNIOR BRIDGEMAN: Oh, it's the most important thing. Without that, you might be able to do some things, but you'll never accomplish what you need to accomplish. You may think you need to have certain things—this house, these cars, all those kinds of things—but when you have inner peace, the most important things become the most important things.

SHERI RILEY: When I say "Exponential Living," what comes to mind for you?

JUNIOR BRIDGEMAN: Multiplying, by touching and influencing and having an impact on one another. The effect I may have on this person now adds on to two more people, and they affect two more people and it just kind of goes from there.

I AM JUNIOR BRIDGEMAN
AND I AM EXPONENTIAL LIVING.

Key Takeaways

» Courage means taking a step even when something inside you is afraid of what the outcome might be.

» Faith is what allows us to take risks. Risks are what allow us to grow.

» "Success is never final," because there is always more truth about ourselves to be revealed.

» When you have inner peace, the most important things become the most important things.

Exponential Living

Be brave enough to live creatively. The creative is the place where no one else has ever been. You have to leave the city of your comfort and go into the wilderness of your intuition. You can't get there by bus, only by hard work, risking, and by not quite knowing what you're doing. What you'll discover will be wonderful: yourself.

—ALAN ALDA

You might be wondering how and why Exponential Living can itself be a principle of Exponential Living. That's kind of like making "bake a chocolate cake" the final step in a recipe for chocolate cake, right? Aren't the other eight principles supposed to *add up* to Exponential Living? No, not quite. Exponential Living is a principle of its own for a good reason. That is, Exponential Living is not a *result*. It is not a destination you arrive at after mastering the other eight principles. You go through eight principles to *empower you to choose* Exponential Living, but you must still choose it. Moment by moment.

Unfortunately, life doesn't stop handing out challenges simply because you have done some inner work on yourself. You don't get to kick back and say, "I've arrived. I've mastered Exponential Living." What Exponential Living does is give you a new framework with which to deal with challenges, a framework based on honoring the truth of who you are. But it is still something you have to fight for and pursue. It is not a place; it is a lifestyle, a process you choose to engage in.

Or not.

The power to choose Exponential Living can only come from within, not without. That's because so many aspects of modern culture are set up to reward a 10-percent life. We are bombarded with messages, day in and day out, that tell us possessions, prizes, privileges, and prestige will make us happy. We are taught to strive for and place value on external accolades and goals. We are discouraged from asking deep questions. We are valued based on what we do, not who we are. The world is content to keep us in *doing* mode, 24-7-365, from cradle to grave. And we have a choice: we can either buy into this group hypnosis that keeps us going, going, going like demented Energizer Bunnies or we can choose a "handmade life" based on *our* values, tastes, needs, gifts, and truths, and rooted in peace, clarity, and courage. But if we choose the latter, we're pretty much on our own. That's when the world stops giving us road maps and we must find our own way. There are no preworn paths to Exponential Living; the path unfolds beneath our feet as we take each bold step forward. And the path is different for everyone.

Who you are is individual and unique, but it's easy to forget that when outside forces are constantly pressuring you to make predefined, socially approved choices. You can passively drift along in the current of where the world wants to take you and how the world wants to define you. This is the easy choice to make, and the one that most people make for their entire lives. But to experience Exponential Living is to become an active swimmer who creates his or her own current. Being a swimmer, not a passive drifter, is a daily and hourly decision, not a "one and done" proposition. But once you realize you have a life vest supporting you—and you do: it's God and the power

He has placed within you—you can confidently "swim" in your own direction with a feeling of deep peace and security.

Who you are is never finished expressing itself. You are a dynamic, unfolding story. So what Exponential Living means to you now is one thing; what it will mean to you in a year, or five years, or ten years, will be something entirely different. By then your true self will have opened up to reveal facets of itself that you can't even see yet from where you are standing right now.

So don't fall into the trap of thinking that Exponential Living is a *state*. It's not. It is a lifestyle, it is a mind-set, it is a paradigm shift, it is a celebration, it is an adventure, it is a bursting forth, it is an expanding, it is a deepening, it is a joyful *becoming*, but it is not a condition.

It is a verb, not a noun.

In this chapter, I'd like to offer some final thoughts on how you can kindle Exponential Living in your own life. Because, when all is said and done, to *choose* Exponential Living is the most important principle of all.

Being Overwhelmed CAN Be a Good Thing

An issue that often comes up in my work with high-achieving clients is the feeling of being overwhelmed. High achievers, in general, have a tendency to take on a lot of responsibilities, and so they are no strangers to feeling overwhelmed. But as they embrace Exponential Living and begin to give space to their previously hidden 90-percent lives, they often feel *more* overwhelmed, not less. That's because they become keenly aware of people and situations that require their attention on the relationship front, on the health front, on the family front, on the self-development front . . . They can begin to feel bombarded from all sides and can start to think, "I should have just kept my head down and kept working."

But being overwhelmed can be a good thing. I often coach clients who are feeling overwhelmed to reframe the feeling as a positive one instead of a negative one. After all, one definition of *overwhelmed* is "receiving too much of a thing." When we truly desire to live a life that is fulfilled in all areas, we are destined to sometimes have more on our plates than we have the time, energy, ability, or help to "handle." We may find ourselves, for example, facing a week where we're put in charge of a new project at work, our spouse wants to spend some time away with us, we have friends in town for a visit, an important political campaign needs our help, and our daughter's birthday is coming up. This is actually a blessing and the manifestation of what we have worked and prayed so hard to accomplish.

My favorite book says that we have so much power and strength that "our cup will run over." It also says that we will receive "blessings that we will not have enough room to receive." When a cup is overflowing, that means it has been filled and more is being given than can be held. You have everything you *need* and are now overflowing with things you *want*. We get frustrated and anxious when we're overwhelmed, but it is wise to step back and note that we are, in fact, receiving the very blessings we've worked so hard to obtain.

The fact that many people and things require your attention is evidence that you are meaningfully engaged with the world. You are important to others. Your input makes a difference to them. People need you. This is the greatest gift anyone can really ask for—to be needed and wanted and have an impact. To matter to another person.

And what about those times when you are overwhelmed with financial struggles, health issues, and other concerns that don't seem to have a positive side at all? The answer is as simple as it is complex. God's plan for our life is perfect, and the struggles we face are never there to defeat us but to make us stronger and help us understand our power even more deeply. When a problem that feels bigger than your ability to handle shows up, the challenge is to find a place within you where you can face this huge new problem and still be at peace. It always comes back to peace. When more and bigger problems arrive, you are being shown that your capacity for peace is infinite.

A client of mine who is a fitness trainer recently told me that she may be unable to pay the rent on her fitness studio on time. Remarkably, though, she felt completely at peace about it, and knew the situation would work itself out. This was an incredible change for her and I pointed out, "Nine months ago, when you and I started working together, you would have *lost your mind* if you had been unable to pay your rent. That situation would have broken you. Now look at you. You are at peace and moving in your power." And from this decision to choose peace, she was very clear about implementing her next best steps, which are some exciting new opportunities that are expanding her business. She's also executing these new ideas, which are stretching her out of her comfort zone and firing her up with courage that has ignited her confidence and renewed her fight to keep moving. This is Exponential Living.

There is a big difference between being overwhelmed when committed to the Exponential Living Principles and being overwhelmed when *not* committed to them. When we are not engaged consistently in the Principles of Exponential Living, we are overwhelmed by the pressure of trying to live in our 10 percent. We are not living in peace, and are empty, depleted, and trying to drink from a dry cup. When we are overwhelmed from living in our 100 percent, and fully engaged in the power of peace, things can get a little crazy, but our lives are overflowing with blessings, clarity, joy, service, healthy relationships, and the fulfillment of maximizing our opportunities.

As a woman of faith, I have this attitude: I open myself up to receive the blessings when things are good, and I "grow" through the negative events when things are challenging, because I believe the passage in Jeremiah 29:11 that says, "'For I know the plans I have for you,' declares the Lord, 'plans to prosper you and not to harm you, plans to give you hope and a future.'" Once we surrender to God's plan for our lives, we find peace living in the overflow, and joy in the abundance of being overwhelmed. And I love this quote: "God never gives you a dream that matches your budget. He's not checking your bank account; he's checking your faith."

Yes, There Really Is a Plan for You

The greatest gift you can give yourself as you embrace Exponential Living is to accept that you are not running the show. You are not COO of the universe. As grand as your plans for yourself are, there is an even greater plan for you. And that plan unfolds in its correct time and season. It really does. To know this is to lay down a heavy burden.

My good friend Peerless Price is a great example of this truth. If you're a football fan, you know that name. Peerless was a wide receiver in the National Football League. He played his college ball at the University of Tennessee, where he had a key role in the team winning both the SEC and national championships, and was then drafted by the Buffalo Bills. He spent nine years playing in the NFL, where he played for the Cowboys and the Falcons before returning to the Bills.

Here's the story he told me about having faith in God's plan:

I grew up in the church, and I think as you grow up and go to college and have life experiences, you can lose sight of your faith and what God has done for you. When I was in college, my sophomore year I was planning to leave—I was going pro. I was making plays, I was playing with Peyton Manning, we were the number one team in the nation. I really started feeling myself. You couldn't tell me anything. I was the big man on campus, starting wide receiver as a sophomore at the University of Tennessee. I had been told just two years earlier that I was stupid for going there, because they had signed four of the best receivers in the country the previous year. People were, like, "You'll never play." I was, like, "I'm gonna prove these jokers wrong." [And I did.] So, I'm all SEC. I'm this and that. I'm out of here. I'm going pro. This is my last year.

We go to our Orange and White Game—that's our annual spring game—and the place is sold out. There's one hundred thousand fans there. I've got two catches, two touchdowns, one hundred fifty yards. The third catch I took it about eighty, so I have three catches for about two hundred forty yards! As I'm running into the end zone, I'm high-stepping. Then, when I get to the end zone, I do a little dance, and the guy I beat is mad as heck. So, I'm dancing, and as I'm tossing the ball to the ref, the guy's trying to slap it out of my hand. So, as he slaps it out of my hand, he falls, loses his balance, and lands on my leg. He snapped my ankle. Broke my fibula, tore all the ligaments in my ankle. So, a plate and eight screws later, they tell me I'll be out twelve to eighteen months.

In that situation, you realize God has a plan for you. You can plan it, but it's still gonna be His way. He still gives you decisions to make, but in the end He still is the reason I am here. He has a plan for us. My plan was to leave college early, but God's plan was for me to stay till I was a senior, because we ended up winning the national championship [my senior year]. I got MVP of the SEC championship, MVP of the national championship game. So, if I had left, if that injury didn't happen, none of that would have happened. That moment when I broke my ankle, I was "Why me?" That's where faith comes in.

The thing is, life is a marathon, not a sprint. I can reflect back to standing on the podium, national championship game, underdogs, supposed to lose to Florida State. We win, and I'm just, like, "I was supposed to be here. God had predestined for me to be here." So, my bigheaded self with my own plan was "I'm leaving as a junior because Peyton's leaving and we lost four other guys in the first round of the draft. We're gonna be terrible my senior year. I gotta get outta here." But God has a plan. He has this thing figured out; we just have to trust Him.

When you allow the plan for your life to unfold, it happens in the best and most efficient way possible for you. Second-guessing that plan or thinking that you know better only makes it take longer and creates more pain and difficulty. The best thing you can do is just keep making efforts to grow, keep praying, and allow what happens to happen.

God does answer prayers, but we need to have the faith to allow those answers to play out according to God's plan, not ours. There was a time when after many years of disappointment, my faith was wavering and I was struggling to believe. I would hear the minister preach about God's love and abundance and I'd say "Amen" and "Hallelujah" with my mouth, but in my heart I was saying, "Yeah, whatever. God isn't doing any of that for me." Finally, I was able to flip the switch to gratitude. I began to appreciate what God *had* done for me. My marriage, my daughters, my health, my wisdom . . . I realized God *was* answering my prayers, but not on the schedule my "bigheaded self" (to quote Peerless) thought was correct.

I now feel a tremendous sense of lightness from knowing that it's not all on me to make my life work out. Thank God for that. In fact, it's when you surrender control that all the pieces come together— provided that surrender is rooted in faith, faith that there's a purpose for our life that we can't fully see with our rational minds. Whether you practice a spiritual belief or not, faith, coupled with consistent execution, is the only way to allow for the true plan for your life to emerge. Even the hardest-working high achiever can attest to having many things happen in their life that their hard work didn't directly bring about.

Money Is a Symbol

No book on high achievement would be complete without talking about the topic of money. Money, after all, is the thing that many high achievers spend a lifetime chasing and acquiring. However, much in the same way that people chase lists of goals in order to find peace rather than pursue peace directly, many people pursue money instead of the things that money represents.

A good friend of mine recently called me for some mentoring and advice. In the previous few years, she had gone through several major life transitions that had really rocked her world. She'd gotten married, become a new mom of two young children, lost some loved ones, and begun a career that hadn't advanced at the pace she would have preferred. She called me because she was considering a career and life change. The reason? She wasn't making enough money. She insisted that money was the only issue in her life, and that she simply wasn't making enough of it.

But as our conversation went deeper, it became clear that all of the major losses and transitions in her recent life had affected her deeply, and what she was really seeking was security. Money wasn't her issue; security was. And like most of us, she equated money with security. She felt that if she made more money, she would have more of the security she desired. But the truth was that neither money, nor love, nor career would give her that security. Feeling peace and security was a choice she had to make directly, as we all must.

In her case, I told her that she might start by being kind to herself, giving herself some grace, and recognizing all of the transition she had been through. It might mean giving herself time to grieve the loss of loved ones and the loss of the life she had before marriage and children. It might mean celebrating the amazing life she now had with her husband and children. Doing these things might make her begin to feel more secure and peaceful in the new life she had. Seeking money as a solution was putting the cart before the horse.

Many of us do this with money. We identify (either consciously or unconsciously) the big thing we feel our life is missing, and then we convince ourselves that money is the means of getting it. Of course, money is useful and having enough to live comfortably is a great relief, but to many it becomes more than just a means to an end. Some of us may crave approval, and so we tell ourselves that earning a lot of money, and the status that comes along with it, will bring us approval. Some of us may want to escape an impoverished background and mind-set, so we go after money to get a taste of abundance. Others may crave romantic love, so we pursue money to make us more attractive.

But the money never brings us what we think it will. Money is just a symbol. That's all it is, and that's all it ever will be. Money can buy us things and experiences, but it can't fill the gaps in our souls, buy us peace, or give us clarity.

A big step in Exponential Living is to dethrone money and stop making it more important than it really is. In order to do this, I recommend you do the same thing I tell my clients to do. Find out what the money *represents* to you. Use the Socratic method—that is, keep asking yourself questions until you get deeper answers. For example:

I want money so I can afford a nice house and a nice car.
—Why?
So that I can appear successful.
—Why?
Because women like successful men, and I want to be attractive to women.
—Why?
Because I want to be loved by a good woman.

So, what you really want is love. If that's the case, own that. Examine the reasons you don't believe you are lovable as you are now. Ask yourself what lifestyle choices you can make to open yourself up to love and create more opportunities to meet others. Perhaps by *giving* more love, you will receive more love?

Most people stop here with the last *why* above. And answering it honestly will lead to a happier life. But in order for you to experience Exponential Living, I encourage you to ask yourself yet another *why*.

—Why do you want the love of a good woman?
Because the time in my life when I felt most at peace was when I was a little boy and had the powerful love of my mother.

So, what you are truly seeking is peace. And none of the things we chase in life can provide us peace. We must pursue peace first, and all of these other things—such as security and validity—will be added to our life and will feel more fulfilling.

Exponential Living is about pursuing real peace instead of *symbols* that we believe will bring us peace. Symbols, such as titles, awards, and money, always come up short. When I meet high achievers who have "everything"—meaning earthly possessions, as well as clarity, vision, peace, and self-love—this inevitably comes from their relationship with God and themselves. When I meet high achievers whose lives feel empty, it is usually because they are chasing money as a primary goal, measuring their self-worth by their bank account balance. Money is a wonderful thing and it can hugely enrich your life—when it's an *extension* of your peace and clarity, not a substitute. This is Exponential Living.

Look at Your Feet, Not at the Finish Line

Not long ago, my husband, Jovan, and I were running the longest run we had ever tried, with a hill at the end. We'd *walked* this path many times, so I knew where the end—the "finish line"—was, but I had never run this distance before. It was a stretch for me physically. When we got near the hill, I looked up at it as I ran. Looking at the finish line caused me to be become anxious and question my strength to complete the uphill journey. It stopped me from being present to myself in that moment, which limited my confidence and strength.

When I realized I'd mentally taken myself out of the game, I stopped looking at the finish line and just looked at the ground instead. I put one foot in front of the other. Again and again. Before long, of course, I had made it to the top of the hill. With energy to spare.

In Exponential Living we must know what our "finish line"—our vision of success—is, and we must hold that vision confidently within us. But we don't have to anxiously check our progress every five minutes; our job is just to focus on each step, show up in every moment in excellence, allow for the grace of God, and be thankful before, while, and after reaching each of our goals. Oprah Winfrey says her number one spiritual practice is trying to live in the present moment . . . to resist projecting into the future or lamenting past mistakes . . . to feel the real power of now. That is the secret to an inspired life. And that is a major component of Exponential Living.

And please remember this: sometimes it's not about finishing first—it's just about finishing. Don't worry about how many others are beating you to the finish line. They may be running a different race entirely. The only race you can run is yours.

To Everything There Is a Season

Things happen in their proper season. A good NFL coach knows that winning the Super Bowl is not only about what happens in the big game; it's about mindfully committing to a year-round process. It starts with signing contracts and drafting and trading for the right players. It proceeds with off-season conditioning programs, and then training camp to focus on fundamentals, then preseason games, and then putting together a winning regular season, game by game, opponent by opponent. Each step is as vital to ultimate victory as making a big play in the Super Bowl is. Champions are the ones who treat the whole process that way.

From time to time you may need to remind yourself, "I am in training camp now, but that doesn't last the whole season. I must not let the pain, hard work, focus, and spiritual, physical, mental, and emotional stretching distract me from why I am in training camp. I am here to win the championship. In fact, I am winning the championship right now, through my focus and dedication; I just haven't seen the final result yet."

Vision, Action, Results

Exercise 1: Exponential Vision Statement

Write your Exponential Living Vision Statement. This should capture your vision for a life in which Exponential Living has become your new paradigm. (This can be done in bullet points, journal-style writing, a corporate-style mission statement, pictures . . . however you choose to express your Exponential Living.)

Close your eyes for ten minutes and imagine how your life will *feel* as you allow your vision of Exponential Living to take root in your life.

Exercise 2: My Exponential Life

Please answer the following:

1. What have I become aware of that I wasn't aware of before reading this book?
2. After reading this whole book, what are some parts of my "90-percent life" that have not been getting enough attention from me?

3. After reading this whole book, what are some elements I would like to add to my definition of success?

4. Over the next thirty days, what will I focus on to experience Exponential Living?

5. Over the next ninety days, what will I focus on to experience Exponential Living?

6. Over the next year, what will I focus on to experience Exponential Living?

7. Over the next five years, what will I focus on to experience Exponential Living?

8. What do I need to forgive myself for in order to move forward with Exponential Living?

9. What distractions do I need to remove in order to enhance my focus?

10. What physical and mental steps do I need to take to commit to the process of Exponential Living?

11. Who are one to three people I will share my journey of Exponential Living with, who I know will support me, hold me accountable, and celebrate my victories with me?

12. What are some things I can and will do every day to celebrate Exponential Living?

EXPONENTIAL CONVERSATION

For our final Exponential Conversation, I wanted to chat with someone I knew could talk about every aspect of Exponential Living with confidence and wisdom. That's Mark Cole.

Mark is leadership "guru" John Maxwell's lieutenant general. As you know by now, I have worked closely with John Maxwell, who has been a mentor to me as I have claimed my place in the world of self-development leaders. Mark Cole serves as the CEO of all five Maxwell organizations: the John Maxwell Company, EQUIP, the John Maxwell Team, the John Maxwell Leadership Foundation, and Maxwell Motivation. With a passion for leadership development and organizational growth, Mark is committed to adding value to individual leaders and leadership teams. He and his amazing wife, Stephanie, have two daughters, Tori and Maci, and a grandson, Ryder.

Mark and I have had many interactions over the past five years, and I have always found him to be a glowing example of Exponential Living.

SHERI RILEY: When we *pursue peace*, we stay calm and we stay in a place of power. When we *choose clarity*, we have vision, we have direction, and we're able to make solid choices and decisions. And when we *live courageously*, we're able to stand in integrity, in our authentic ownership of who we are. From the very first interaction I had with you, those three things came through you.

MARK COLE: In all of us is a desire to be settled in who we are, to be comfortable in our skin, and be confident we're on the track that we're designed for, that we're called to do. There is something peaceful when you know you're in your sweet spot. And I love the idea of living courageously. My challenge, though—and I believe it's something all leaders want—is clarity. Being a type A, driven leader who's trying to lead five organizations, my biggest challenge is not pursuing peace—got it, want it, and I love that sweet-spot feeling. My challenge is not being courageous. It's when those two meet. How do I live courageously *and* feel peaceful? Those two are at odds at times, and I think when you get clarity, that's the bridge. Clarity is the link to match peace and courage. Because courage, most of the time, is intense. There's very little peace in it sometimes because you're thinking, "Why isn't anybody else getting this?" But clarity bridges that gap.

SHERI RILEY: That's it. That's exactly why you represent Exponential Living. It really is a combination of the three. Most of the time we have one or two, but not the three.

MARK COLE: That's exactly right.

SHERI RILEY: The first principle of Exponential Living is "Live in Your P.O.W.E.R." How do you know when an opportunity is a distraction?

MARK COLE: If you want to live in power, if you want to understand how to be exponential in your results, in your living, in your influencing others, you're going to have to be comfortable in the things only you can do. As I've watched John, and as I've learned to adapt and apply this lesson to my life, there are some things I can do very well, and there are some things I can't do very well. . . . I've learned I don't have to be good at everything. Find the three, four—maybe five on a good day—things I can be good at and be satisfied at that. Living in power is being able to be comfortable in your own skin [and not having to be good at everything]. The second thing I would say about living in power is this concept of no rearview mirrors. You're not as good as you thought you were yesterday, you're not as bad as you thought you were yesterday. Don't get caught up in what people say about your past, good or bad, and let that define you in where you are today and what you're doing tomorrow. The fact that I made some mistakes yesterday does not inhibit my ability to be effective today. A lot of times it *enhances* my ability to be successful.

SHERI RILEY: For high achievers, that's so important. "Healthy living is more than a diet" is one of my Principles. It's about relationships. I know you travel a lot. How many days of the year do you travel?

MARK COLE: It's significant. March of this year I was in the office for three days, and in April of this year I was at home for five days. Not every month is like that, but it's been like that a little bit.

SHERI RILEY: How do you manage the guilt of when you're away from your family and you have that pressure of what you do professionally? That's one of the most consistent challenges high achievers have.

MARK COLE: I love that you used the word *manage*. A lot of times when I'm asked that question, it's "How do you *eliminate* [the guilt]?" I love the fact that you say *manage*, because it's a daily challenge. I'm going to trade my man card here for a moment: I can't tell you the number of trips I take to the airport with tears running down my face because I'm leaving my family. I could literally talk our entire time on this, on how I manage, because it's a daily thing—I don't eliminate it. But let me try to give you one or two practical things. The first is that my family is involved in everything I do. For us, here's what that means: before I leave the house for a trip, whether it's a twenty-five-day trip to seven nations like I just did or an overnight trip down to West Palm Beach—no matter what the trip is—I sit down with Maci, my nine-year-old, and Stephanie, my wife, the night before and I say, "Guys, this is what I'm accomplishing. Here's my schedule. This is when the most critical part of this day will be happening. Will you guys put a little note on your calendar and be praying for me during that time?"

So here's what happens: when I come home, Maci says, "Hey, Dad, at nine o'clock today you had that meeting with Paul.

How did that go?" So she's engaged with me and she's on the journey with me.

The second thing I try to do, I try to be present wherever I am. So right now I want to be present with you, Sheri. When I'm home, I work hard to be present and be fully engaged with my family so that we can create memories. Recently, I was going to have three days at home and I didn't want to go anywhere—"I'm tired of *going*. Let's be at home"—but my family's ready to go somewhere. So we did a rock, paper, scissors contest for who got to choose the agenda for each of the days in that weekend. I won one day, Maci won one, and then Stephanie. The day that was ours, we got to pick where we ate, how late we slept in, what we did. Maci, to this day, still says, "Dad, when's the next time we can do rock, paper, scissors to own days?" It's building those memories.

The third thing I would add is I don't prioritize relationships. Most type A, driven people like myself put work first, then maybe their relationship with God, and then maybe their relationship with their family. I grew up with a philosophy that said, "God first"—I grew up in a preacher's home—"ministry (work) second, and family gets whatever's left over." At age thirty I had this epiphany that [my relationships are] not in competition with one another; they're all together. I have advisers—specifically my wife as chief adviser—around me that keep me in check to make sure that one is not out of kilter. I don't say "out of balance," because there's no such thing as balance. There's *tension*, and tension keeps us giving sometimes more at work, sometimes more at home, sometimes more in other pursuits of our life, but we have to live in that tension. I see them all as one priority. It's holistically who I am. I love my wife, I love my daughter, I love my relationship with the Lord, I love what I get to do here [in my office]. I'm not going to allow myself to be in priority competition with myself. It feels too conflicting.

SHERI RILEY: Ah, that's Exponential Living. When you and I were in Guatemala together, that was a very, very big endeavor. John shared with us how it was one of the biggest things at that point he'd done in his life in terms of the press and stress on him. You had the same disposition then that you have now. What do you attribute that to? How do you maintain that attitude?

MARK COLE: Peace, I believe, is a choice. It's a muscle. We've got to be reconciled in who we are, what we're supposed to do, the things we can control, the things we can't control. And we've got to constantly be exercising our muscle of peace, even in circumstances that are beyond our control.

The second thing, there is a responsibility to choose how you allow others into your internal struggles. I don't believe people pay for chaos. I don't believe people follow struggle and challenge. I believe people follow vision, they follow consistency, they follow hope, they follow peace. I think people follow that. Therefore, I have responsibility, as a leader, to make sure people sense and feel peace around me. It's not a facade—don't get it confused—but it is a responsibility to demonstrate peace to people around me. Work on inner peace, don't be fake, but always learn how to demonstrate and model peace to those who are following you.

SHERI RILEY: How do you serve your family?

MARK COLE: Knowing what's important to them, what's their language. What communicates love and connection. For my wife, it's a back rub. So no matter how tired I am, I really work hard to serve her like that—when I am mindful of that. Maci's is time and playing Disney Infinity. I am not a computer gamer, but understanding that these things are significant to them, it's the way that I will serve them. It should never be said by others that we're generous and by our families that we're selfish.

SHERI RILEY: How do you define working and maximizing?

MARK COLE: I always start with the end in mind. John says, "I can't be 100 percent all day. So I find the areas in my day where I

have to be at 100 percent and I make sure I'm 100 percent then."
Those are the times you're trying to maximize. Other times, be
there, be present, but you don't have to be 100 percent.

The final thing I would say is, understand there are seasons
of sowing and reaping. There are seasons of maximizing. There
are seasons of spreading seed and pursuing opportunity, and
then there are seasons of farming that opportunity. A lot of
times we forget that we need to close the door that we have
opened. As leaders, as visionaries, sometimes we become our
own enemy when we think we're supposed to maximize all
the time, and we're not.

SHERI RILEY: Do you have a sense of gratitude? Not just from what
you're accomplishing, but from the depth of the 100 percent
that you're living.

MARK COLE: I love to celebrate other people. I love to take time in a
meeting and see how many people's names I can call out as
being a contributor to the success of our company. I love doing
that. I love to celebrate others . . . but I'm extremely uncomfortable celebrating me. I'll give you a couple of examples. I have
no joy in opening presents at Christmas. I have no joy of a surprise birthday party. In fact, it's embarrassing.

SHERI RILEY: I'm so glad you're giving the authentic truth. So, do
you feel like celebrating yourself keeps you off the goal of gratitude and joy?

MARK COLE: I do. [But] I believe that slowing down and recognizing
accomplishments *is* good. I want to say this: I do that. I do that
internally. It's when it becomes external that I get really uncomfortable. I journaled this weekend about the things my leadership
has accomplished. I found myself incredibly fulfilled, energized,
and grateful in that. But to go public with that . . .

SHERI RILEY: But you do celebrate yourself, in private. Because so
many don't.

MARK COLE: I agree with that. And I think you do miss the significance
of the journey and you miss getting something to encourage you

in the next journey if you don't slow down and do that. But for me it's always a personal kind of reflection. The only time you'll hear me talk publicly about what I'm thankful for having accomplished is when I have an ulterior motive of encouraging people or building hope for the next, bigger challenge that we're up against. So it's to instill hope, not to engage in [self-]celebration. I do it internally and personally, but I don't do it very well publicly.

SHERI RILEY: I ask a lot of my coaching clients, "Are you confident or are you driven?" You can be both, but for the sake of the question, are you confident or are you driven?

MARK COLE: Two things have happened with age. The first is exposure to John, and he is more confident than he is driven. He is very confident and comfortable in his skin. His mentoring has really helped me to realize that confidence will take you longer and farther than drive. . . . The second thing we realize through maturation is that what we spend our time on needs to be the things we're good at. So we spend time on the things that give us a greater return. When you're spending time on things that for years have brought you return, there is a confidence that comes with that; that replaces the drive or complements the drive.

SHERI RILEY: Is there something in your journey that you know has been a hindrance that you had to overcome? Not necessarily a negative experience, but something you had to heal from?

MARK COLE: I'm a relational guy. I love building relationships. I believe relationships are the linchpin to any- and everything you want. I used to feel that relationships just happened, so for thirty years of my life I felt like I could just show up and relationships would be good. Because I'm naturally good at them. I can walk into a room, I can connect with people, and magic happens. We learn things about each other and then we're able to do things together. I can read people, I'm intuitive in relationships, I understand when somebody's struggling, even sometimes before they do.

What that did was make me undisciplined and perhaps a bit lazy in relationships. So at thirty years of age, I went through a divorce. Divorce, as I was brought up, that's the end of the world. There's no life after that. That failure, in the area that I was best at, relationships, was the very wake-up call that has helped me to realize that in every relationship I need to be intentional. So even with you, Sheri, I am incredibly aware that we need to be intentional in our interaction. What do we want to do? What are we trying to accomplish? We're still trying to get our daughters together. I want to do that for many reasons, and I can list those reasons to you, but I would not have even known I needed such a list for the first thirty years of my life because I just let relationships happen. Now through that epic failure, through that incredible, life-altering time in my life, I realized that just because I'm good at something does not negate my responsibility to be intentional. So relationships would be one of the examples of where I am natural, but I was not intentional, and now I can be intentional—and I don't eradicate the natural—but the outcome is exponential.

I AM MARK COLE AND I AM EXPONENTIAL LIVING.

Key Takeaways

- » Don't try to do everything. Every day, focus on the two or three things you are really good at.
- » Live without rearview mirrors. You're not as good as you thought you were yesterday and you're not as bad as you thought you were yesterday.
- » You can't be at 100 percent all day, so be 100 percent only for those things that require your fullest attention. The rest of the time, just be fully present.
- » Prioritizing and balancing relationships doesn't work. *All* of your relationships are important and should work together in a tapestry.
- » Be intentional in everything you do and with everyone you interact with.

Parting Thoughts

This book is my heart and my life. I have lived the 9 Principles for well over a decade. I have been coaching clients for over five years, using these Principles, and have seen their lives transformed. Even people who have worked with me indirectly—transcribing calls, reviewing the curriculum, editing the text—have shared with me how their lives have shifted by being exposed to these Principles. These Principles work. Everything in this book is based on real-life experience. As I have shared in the book, I am my first and most important client.

And that's the transformational power of this book. This book is not theory. It is more of a journaling of Exponential Living. Over the years, I've seen how pastors, leaders, and others who have the power to change people's lives often fall short because they can be so committed to helping others that they don't take the time to implement in their own lives what they are sharing or guiding others to do. They teach a great message, and unfortunately they don't live it. And so their message loses its power.

I've committed to not having that happen. Every word in this book, every word I speak from the podium about Exponential Living, I work every day to live. At the end of one of my coaching sessions with a client, she said to me, "Wow, Sheri, you are living these truths. You understand because you are going through this same life experience and doing the same work." That was the highest compliment I could ever receive. I never want to get so full of myself that I believe it's me creating the Principles, or that it's my words that are transforming lives. I am simply the messenger. We are on this journey together. I may be the representative, but I am definitely not the creator.

I sometimes fall short in the pursuit of these Principles, and so will you. It's not my perfection of the Principles that allows me to live in peace, clarity, and courage. It's my commitment to *pursuing* peace, *choosing* clarity, and *living* courageously—to working at it every day—that brings me peace.

My prayer for everyone who reads this book is transformation. I don't want your experience to be just a transaction—you purchase the book or someone gives it to you. You read it, enjoy it, and it goes on a shelf to gather dust. My prayer for a decade before this book went on sale was that every word would bring transformation. That you would be inspired to move into action, achieve great results, and experience a shift in your mind-set and paradigm. That you would write in the margins, post quotes around your house, and share your testimony of how this book transformed your life. That you would be stretched permanently beyond your 10 percent. That you would be forever committed to Exponential Living and the power of peace.

I hope those prayers find a way from me to you through this book. The words in this book have saved my life, literally. And I've been blessed that my journey has been an inspiration for others to know the power of peace.

Together, let's change some paradigms. Let's help those around us to understand that their power lies in who they are, not just what they are able to do; that being kind is not a weakness and does not minimize your influence; that being courageous is not about how many people you step on to step up; that peace of mind, service to others, a sense of purpose, and vibrant relationships are what wealth is all about. Let's protect our thoughts with peace and positivity and refuse to entertain ideas that eat away at the core of our beliefs. And let's hold on to the most powerful life jacket ever created. And that is our faith. The beauty of our tomorrow is held in the power of our faith today.

You CAN do this.

You MUST do this.

You WILL do this.

Peace is possible. Peace is our power. Peace is the new success.

"All things are possible to him who believes" (Mark 9:23).

Amen.